AMERICAN POLITICAL, ECONOMIC AND SECURITY ISSUES

JUDGE MERRICK GARLAND

JUDICIAL OPINIONS AND POTENTIAL IMPLICATIONS FOR THE SUPREME COURT

American Political, Economic and Security Issues

Additional books in this series can be found on Nova's website under the Series tab.

Additional e-books in this series can be found on Nova's website under the eBooks tab.

AMERICAN POLITICAL, ECONOMIC AND SECURITY ISSUES

JUDGE MERRICK GARLAND

JUDICIAL OPINIONS AND POTENTIAL IMPLICATIONS FOR THE SUPREME COURT

COLLIN WEBER
EDITOR

nova publishers
New York

Library of Congress Cataloging-in-Publication Data

ISBN: 978-1-63485-991-2

Published by Nova Science Publishers, Inc. † New York

CONTENTS

PREFACE

On March 16, 2016, President Obama nominated Judge Merrick Garland of the U.S. Court of Appeals for the District of Columbia Circuit (D.C. Circuit) to fill the vacancy on the Supreme Court created by the unexpected death of Justice Antonin Scalia in February. Judge Garland was appointed to the D.C. Circuit by President Clinton in 1997, and is currently its chief judge, an administrative position that rotates among the active judges on the circuit. Prior to his appointment to the bench, Judge Garland served in the Criminal Division of the U.S. Department of Justice, where he notably oversaw the prosecution of the 1995 Oklahoma City bombing case, as well as other cases. It remains to be seen whether or how the Senate might proceed in considering Judge Garland's nomination; however, the nomination remains effective until it is withdrawn or this term of Congress ends, whichever occurs first. This book provides an overview of Judge Garland's jurisprudence and discusses what the impact on the Court might be if he, or a judge of a similar judicial approach, were to be confirmed to succeed Justice Scalia.

In: Judge Merrick Garland
Editor: Collin Weber
ISBN: 978-1-63485-991-2

Chapter 1

JUDGE MERRICK GARLAND: HIS JURISPRUDENCE AND POTENTIAL IMPACT ON THE SUPREME COURT*

Andrew Nolan, Kate M. Manuel and Brandon J. Murrill

SUMMARY

On March 16, 2016, President Obama nominated Judge Merrick Garland of the U.S. Court of Appeals for the District of Columbia Circuit (D.C. Circuit) to fill the vacancy on the Supreme Court created by the unexpected death of Justice Antonin Scalia in February. Judge Garland was appointed to the D.C. Circuit by President Clinton in 1997, and is currently its chief judge, an administrative position that rotates among the active judges on the circuit. Prior to his appointment to the bench, Judge Garland served in the Criminal Division of the U.S. Department of Justice, where he notably oversaw the prosecution of the 1995 Oklahoma City bombing case, as well as other cases. It remains to be seen whether or how the Senate might proceed in considering Judge Garland's nomination; however, the nomination remains effective until it is withdrawn or this term of Congress ends, whichever occurs first.

This report provides an overview of Judge Garland's jurisprudence and discusses what the impact on the Court might be if he, or a judge of a similar judicial approach, were to be confirmed to succeed Justice Scalia.

---

* This is an edited, reformatted and augmented version of a Congressional Research Service, Publication No. R44479, dated April 27, 2016.

In particular, the report focuses upon those areas of law where Justice Scalia can be seen to have influenced the High Court's approach to certain issues, or served as a fifth and deciding vote on the Court, with a view toward how Judge Garland might approach those same issues if he were to be confirmed. The report begins with his views on two overarching issues—the role of the judiciary and statutory interpretation. It then addresses 14 separate areas of law, which are arranged in alphabetical order from "administrative law" to "takings." The report includes one table which notes the cases where the Supreme Court has reviewed majority opinions written or joined by Judge Garland. Another table, in the appendix to the report, identifies Judge Garland's colleagues on the D.C. Circuit and lists notable cases involving Judge Garland and that colleague. A separate report will list all opinions authored by Judge Garland during his tenure on the D.C. Circuit.

On March 16, 2016, President Obama nominated Judge Merrick Garland of the U.S. Court of Appeals for the District of Columbia Circuit (D.C. Circuit) to fill the vacancy on the Supreme Court created by the unexpected death of Justice Antonin Scalia in February.[1] Judge Garland was appointed to the D.C. Circuit by President Clinton in 1997,[2] and is currently its chief judge,[3] an administrative position that rotates among the active judges on the circuit.[4] Prior to his appointment to the bench, Judge Garland served in the Criminal Division of the U.S. Department of Justice (DOJ), where he notably oversaw the prosecution of the 1995 Oklahoma City bombing case,[5] as well as other cases.[6] It remains to be seen whether or how the Senate might proceed in considering Judge Garland's nomination;[7] however, his nomination remains effective until it is withdrawn or this term of Congress ends, whichever occurs first.[8]

This report provides an overview of Judge Garland's jurisprudence and discusses what the impact on the Supreme Court might be if he, or a judge of a similar judicial philosophy, were to be confirmed to succeed Justice Scalia. In attempting to ascertain how the Court's jurisprudence could be affected if Judge Garland were to fill the vacancy created by Justice Scalia's death, however, it is important to note at the outset that it is difficult to predict accurately an individual's service on the Court based on his prior experience for various reasons. Accordingly, a section of this report entitled "Predicting Nominees' Future Decisions on the Court" provides a broad context and framework for evaluating how determinative a lower court judge's prior record may be in predicting future votes on the Supreme Court.

The report focuses on those areas of law where Justice Scalia can be seen to have influenced the High Court's approach to particular issues, or served as a fifth and deciding vote on the Court,[9] with a view toward how Judge Garland might approach that same issue if he were to be confirmed. The report begins with his views on two cross-cutting issues—the role of the judiciary and statutory interpretation. It then addresses 14 separate areas of law, which are arranged in alphabetical order from "administrative law" to "takings." Within each of these sections, the report reviews whether and how Judge Garland has addressed particular issues in opinions he authored or joined, or in other votes in which he participated (e.g., votes regarding whether the D.C. Circuit should grant en banc review to decisions of three-judge circuit panels). The report analyzes majority, concurring, and dissenting opinions, as well as opinions of three-judge *district* court panels in which Judge Garland participated.[10] Where relevant, the report also notes Judge Garland's writings prior to joining the D.C. Circuit, which often centered upon issues of administrative or antitrust law.[11]

The report discusses numerous cases and votes involving Judge Garland. However, it focuses particularly on cases in which Judge Garland participated that divided the D.C. Circuit, as these cases arguably best showcase how he might approach a legal controversy whose resolution is a matter of dispute and is not predetermined by prior case law.[12] In addition, the report highlights areas where Judge Garland demonstrated views on the law that contrasted with the views of some of his colleagues. Moreover, to the extent that Judge Garland's votes in particular cases may reflect broader trends and tendencies in his decisionmaking that could be manifested if he were to be confirmed to the Court, the report highlights such trends. Nonetheless, this report does not attempt to catalog every matter in which Judge Garland participated during his 19 years of service on the D.C. Circuit.

PREDICTING NOMINEES' FUTURE DECISIONS ON THE COURT

It is important to note at the outset of this report that, at least as a historical matter, attempting to predict how particular Supreme Court nominees may approach their work on the High Court based on their previous experience is a task fraught with uncertainty.[13] For example, Justice Felix Frankfurter, who had a reputation as a "progressive" legal scholar prior to his appointment to the Court in 1939,[14] disappointed[15] some as he became a voice for judicial restraint and caution when the Court reviewed laws that restricted civil liberties and civil rights during World War II[16] and the early Cold War era.[17] Similarly, Justice Harry Blackmun, who had served on the U.S. Court of Appeals for the Eighth Circuit for a little over a decade prior to his appointment to the Court in 1970,[18] was originally considered by President Richard Nixon to be a "strict constructionist," in the sense that he viewed the judge's role as interpreting the law, rather than making new law.[19] In the years that followed, however, Justice Blackmun authored the majority opinion constitutionalizing the right to terminate a pregnancy in *Roe v. Wade*,[20] and was generally considered one of the more liberal voices on the Court by the time of his retirement in 1994.[21]

The difficulty in attempting to predict future Supreme Court votes remains even when the nominee has had as lengthy a federal judicial career prior to nomination as Judge Garland.[22] Federal appellate judges are bound by Supreme Court and circuit precedent[23] and, therefore, are not normally in a position to espouse freely their views on particular legal issues in the context of their judicial opinions.[24] Moreover, unlike the Supreme Court, which enjoys "almost complete discretion" in selecting its cases, the federal courts of appeals are required to hear many cases as a matter of law and, as a result, tend to hear "many routine cases in which the legal rules are uncontroverted."[25] Perhaps indicative of the nature of federal appellate work, the vast majority of cases decided by three-judge panels of federal courts of appeals are decided without dissent.[26] Unanimity is particularly frequent on the D.C. Circuit where Judge Garland serves.[27] Accordingly, while Judge Garland's work on the D.C. Circuit may provide some insight into his general approach toward particular legal issues,[28] the bulk of the opinions that Judge Garland has authored or joined may not be particularly insightful with regard to his views on specific areas of law or how he would approach these issues if he were a Supreme Court Justice.

Even in closely contested cases where concurring or dissenting opinions are lodged,[29] it still may be difficult to determine the preferences of the nominated judge if the nominee did not actually write an opinion in the case. The act of joining an opinion authored by another judge may not necessarily reflect full agreement with the underlying opinion.[30] For example, some judges, in an effort to promote consensus on a court, will refuse to dissent unless the underlying issue invokes particularly strong disagreement.[31] As one commentator notes, "[T]he fact that a judge joins in a majority opinion may not be taken as indicating complete agreement. Rather, silent acquiescence may be understood to mean something more like 'I accept the outcome in this case, and I accept that the reasoning in the majority opinion reflects what a majority of my colleagues has agreed on.'"[32]

The caution with which one interprets a judge's vote isolated from a written opinion may be particularly important in the context of a judge's votes with respect to procedural matters. A judge's vote to grant an extension of time for a party to submit a filing, for example, generally does not signal any sort of agreement with the substantive legal position proffered by that party.[33] Thus, while votes by Judge Garland in favor of having certain cases—which had been ruled on by three-judge panels—reconsidered by the D.C. Circuit sitting en banc have garnered considerable attention from some examining his judicial record,[34] those votes should be interpreted with some degree of caution. On the one hand, a vote to rehear a case en banc could signal disagreement with the legal reasoning of the panel decision and may suggest that a judge wants the entire court to have an opportunity to correct a perceived error by the panel.[35] On the other hand, as one federal appellate judge noted in dissenting from a decision to deny a petition for rehearing en banc,

> Most of us vote against most such petitions and suggestions even when we think the panel decision is mistaken. We do so because federal courts of appeals decide cases in three judge panels. En banc review is extraordinary, and is generally reserved for conflicting precedent within the circuit which makes application of the law by district courts unduly difficult, and egregious errors in important cases.[36]

As a consequence, a vote for or against rehearing a case, or on other procedural matters does not necessarily equate to an endorsement or repudiation of a particular legal position.[37]

Finally, it should be noted that, despite having served on the federal appellate bench for nearly two decades, Judge Garland has said very little about some areas of law because of the nature of the D.C. Circuit's docket, and as a consequence, it may be difficult to predict how he might rule on certain issues if he were elevated to the Supreme Court. Because of its location in the nation's capital and because of various jurisdictional statutes,[38] the D.C. Circuit hears a significant number of cases on administrative[39] and environmental law matters.[40] In contrast, cases at the D.C. Circuit rarely, if ever, involve "hot-button" social issues such as abortion, affirmative action, or the death penalty.[41] As a result, this report focuses primarily on areas of law where Judge Garland has written extensively, and notes only in passing those areas where little can arguably be gleaned from his judicial record on account of Judge Garland having participated in few, if any, decisions directly addressing those particular areas of law.

ROLE OF THE JUDICIARY

In contrast to Justice Scalia, who was a well-known proponent of originalism and textualism both within and outside the Court,[42] regularly arguing his views on the lecture circuit[43] and dissenting from opinions that, in his view, failed to construe legal texts in accordance with their ordinary meaning at the time of drafting,[44] Judge Garland's approach to the craft of judging is less immediately apparent. In a questionnaire submitted to the Senate Judiciary Committee in conjunction with his nomination to the D.C. Circuit in 1995,[45] Judge Garland wrote of the limited role that judges have under the Constitution, noting that "federal judges do not have roving commissions to solve societal problems," and the "role of the court is to apply the law ... not to legislate, not to arrogate to itself the executive power, not to hand down advisory opinions on the issues of the day."[46] Judge Garland echoed these sentiments in the statement he issued upon his nomination to the Supreme Court.[47] During the hearing on his 1995 nomination, Judge Garland also told Senators that among the Supreme Court Justices he most deeply admired were Chief Justice John Marshall, the author of *Marbury v. Madison*;[48] Justice Oliver Wendell Holmes, Jr., the great dissenter of the early 20th century; and Justice William Brennan, the judge for whom Judge Garland clerked.[49]

Beyond these general statements, though, Judge Garland has not articulated any overarching legal philosophy in a manner akin to Justice Scalia. In his public appearances outside the court, Judge Garland has tended to participate in conferences on discrete issues, such as prosecutorial misconduct,[50] indigent criminal defense,[51] or changing the rules of civil procedure,[52] rather than broadly discussing or defending particular interpretative methodologies. In his judicial opinions, Judge Garland has, at times, utilized originalism as a method of constitutional interpretation, including in a jointly issued 2000 opinion[53] that relied on the Constitution's text and structure,[54] as well as materials from the 1787 Constitutional Convention[55] and subsequent ratifying conventions,[56] in rejecting a lawsuit brought by a group of DC voters seeking the right to elect representatives to

Congress.[57] On the other hand, in neither that opinion[58] nor in other opinions has Judge Garland purported to rely on originalism or textualism as the sole or primary method of interpreting the law.[59]

Nonetheless, even without more comprehensive explanations from Judge Garland outlining his specific judicial philosophy, the nominee's writings provide some insights into his approach to judging. First and foremost, Judge Garland has been widely viewed as a meticulous and cautious jurist, writing with precision and an eye toward ensuring that the court does not overreach in any particular case.[60] *Trudeau v. Federal Trade Commission (FTC)*, the opinion of Judge Garland that has been most widely cited by other judges,[61] may be seen as illustrative of this approach.[62] There, Judge Garland, on behalf of a unanimous three-judge panel, affirmed the dismissal of a complaint lodged by Kevin Trudeau, an author and producer of television and radio infomercials, which had alleged that an FTC press release about him was "false and misleading," exceeded the agency's statutory authority, and violated his First Amendment rights.[63] The case raised several difficult issues of federal jurisdiction and administrative law that had split the circuit courts of appeals in previous cases.[64] However, in his opinion, Judge Garland succinctly clarified two complex jurisdictional questions;[65] avoided resolving a weighty administrative law question as to whether an agency's press release could amount to "final agency action" under the Administrative Procedure Act (APA),[66] a question raising serious issues about the propriety of older D.C. Circuit precedent;[67] and rested the decision on the less controversial grounds that the substance of Trudeau's complaint was simply legally insufficient.[68] As one commentator noted, the *Trudeau* case "stands out" among Judge Garland's cases as exemplifying his ability to examine a complicated area of law, while at the same time limiting the court's ruling to the matters necessary to resolve the case.[69]

Trudeau exemplifies the relatively circumspect nature of Judge Garland's judicial work, something that is arguably reflected more generally throughout the nominee's judicial career. This caution is seen especially in the numerous concurring and dissenting opinions where Judge Garland has taken issue with majority opinions that have, in his view, reached issues that were unnecessary to the ultimate holding of the court.[70] Perhaps the best indication of Judge Garland's minimalist approach to judging is provided by looking at how the Supreme Court has evaluated his work, a topic further detailed in **Table 1**. Perhaps surprisingly for a jurist who has served on an important federal appellate court for nearly two decades,[71] none of Judge Garland's written opinions have even been reviewed in a formal opinion[72] by the Supreme

Court. This suggests that Judge Garland's opinions tend to be crafted to avoid unnecessary controversy that might prompt review by the High Court.[73] Moreover, only nine opinions that Judge Garland joined have been the subject of a subsequent opinion by the Supreme Court. Of these nine opinions, five were ultimately affirmed or otherwise supported in part by the High Court.[74] This is a notably high affirmance rate—given that the Court in recent years has, on average, reversed the lower court in over 70% of all cases it heard[75]—and perhaps indicates the cautious nature of Judge Garland's jurisprudence.[76]

Table 1. Judge Garland and the Supreme Court Majority Opinions of the Supreme Court Reviewing Cases in Which Judge Garland Wrote or Joined an Opinion

D.C. Cir. Case	Relevant D.C. Cir. Holding	Garland's Role	S. Ct. Decision	S. Ct. Vote
Menominee Indian Tribe of Wis. v. United States, 764 F.3d 51 (D.C. Cir. 2014)	Indian tribe was not entitled to equitable tolling of a statute of limitations period to allow for the continuation of a cause of action for breach of a selfdetermination contract.	Joined majority opinion	Affirmed, Menominee Indian Tribe of Wis. v. United States, --- U.S. ---, 136 S. Ct. 750 (2016)	9-0
Pinson v. Samuels, 761 F.3d 1 (D.C. Cir. 2014)	Monthly installment payments required under the Prison Litigation Reform Act of 1995 must be assessed on a "percase" basis, as opposed to a "per-prisoner" approach.	Joined majority opinion	Affirmed, Bruce v. Samuels, --- U.S. ---, 136 S. Ct. 627 (2016)	9-0
White Stallion Energy Ctr., LLC v. Envtl. Prot. Agency (EPA), 748 F.3d 1222 (D.C. Cir. 2014)	The Environmental Protection Agency's interpretation of the phrase "appropriate and necessary" in Section 112(n)(1)(A) of the Clean Air Act is a reasonable construction of the statute.	Joined majority per curiam opinion	Reversed, Michigan v. EPA, --- U.S. ---, 135 S. Ct. 2699 (2015)	5-4

D.C. Cir. Case	Relevant D.C. Cir. Holding	Garland's Role	S. Ct. Decision	S. Ct. Vote
Mohamad v. Rajoub, 634 F.3d 604 (D.C. Cir. 2011)	Only a natural person is amenable to suit under the Torture Victim Protection Act.	Joined majority opinion	Affirmed, Mohamad v. Palestinian Auth., --- U.S. ---, 132 S. Ct. 1702 (2012)	9-0
Me. Pub. Utils. Comm'n v. Fed. Energy Reg. Comm'n, 520 F.3d 464 (D.C. Cir. 2008)	The Federal Power Act's public interest standard did not apply to challenges to contract rates brought by noncontracting third parties.	Joined majority per curiam opinion	Reversed, NRG Power Mktg., LLC v. Me. Pub. Utils. Comm'n, 558 U.S. 165 (2010)	8-1
Al Odah v. United States, 321 F.3d 1134 (D.C. Cir. 2003)	U.S. courts lack jurisdiction to consider challenges to the legality of the detention of foreign nationals captured abroad in connection with hostilities and held at the U.S. Naval Station at Guantanamo Bay, Cuba.	Joined majority opinion	Reversed, Rasul v. Bush, 542 U.S. 466 (2004)	6-3
Amfac Resorts, L.L.C. v. Dep't of the Interior (DOI), 282 F.3d 818 (D.C. Cir. 2002)	Regulations of the National Park Service governing concession contracts in the National Park System are valid. * The D.C. Circuit ruling reached the merits of the case; the Supreme Court asked for supplemental briefing on the question of ripeness and reversed on ripeness grounds.	Joined majority opinion	Reversed, Nat'l Park Hosp. Ass'n v. DOI, 538 U.S. 803 (2003)	7-2

Table 1. (Continued)

D.C. Cir. Case	Relevant D.C. Cir. Holding	Garland's Role	S. Ct. Decision	S. Ct. Vote
NextWave Pers. Commc'ns, Inc. v. Fed. Commc'ns Comm'n (FCC), 254 F.3d 130 (D.C. Cir. 2001)	Section 525 of the Bankruptcy Code prohibits the Federal Communications Commission (FCC) from revoking licenses held by a debtor in bankruptcy upon the debtor's failure to make timely payments owed to the FCC for the purchase of licenses.	Joined majority opinion	Affirmed, FCC v. NextWave Pers. Commc'ns, 537 U.S. 293 (2003)	8-1
Kolstad v. Am. Dental Ass'n, 139 F.3d 958 (D.C. Cir. 1998) (en banc)	Punitive damages can only be imposed in a Title VII action upon a showing of egregious or outrageous conduct.	Joined dissenting opinion	Vacated and remanded, Kolstad v. Am. Dental Ass'n, 527 U.S. 526 (1999)	5-4

Source: Congressional Research Service, based on various sources cited in Table 1.

Note: The purpose of this table is to show the cases in which Judge Garland's opinions have been substantively reviewed by the Supreme Court. As a result, the table includes any panel or en banc rulings written or joined by Judge Garland that were, at least in part, reviewed in a written opinion by the Supreme Court. It does not include (1) any short order by the Supreme Court, such as a grant or denial of a writ of certiorari or an order summarily and simultaneously granting certiorari, vacating the ruling, and remanding the case for further proceedings; (2) any temporary order of the Court, such as a stay of an order of the D.C. Circuit; (3) any summary affirmance of an opinion authored or joined by Judge Garland; or (4) any of Judge Garland's votes on petitions for rehearing en banc. As a result, Judge Garland's votes in support of opinions dissenting from the denial of rehearing en banc in *Parker v. District of Columbia* and *American Trucking Associations v. EPA* are not included in this list. See below "Right to Bear Arms" and "Environmental Law," respectively.

Another notable aspect of Judge Garland's opinions is that they appear, at times, to be motivated by pragmatic concerns about how particular rulings may affect the democratic branches of government. For example, in *Wagner v. Federal Election Commission (FEC)*,[77] Judge Garland, writing on behalf of a unanimous en banc court, upheld against a First Amendment challenge a law that generally banned individuals who contract to perform services for federal agencies from contributing to federal campaigns while they are negotiating or performing the contract.[78] Notably, approximately one-fourth of Judge Garland's opinion[79] for the court in *Wagner* was devoted to the "long historical experience"[80] of corruption involving federal contractors, which he viewed as evidencing that "the concerns that spurred [congressional action] remain as important today as when the statute was enacted,"[81] a considerable portion of a legal opinion to be devoted to a historical record.

Nor is *Wagner* the only case in which Judge Garland expressed concerns about how a court's ruling could affect the work of the political branches. In the criminal law context, Judge Garland dissented from the D.C. Circuit's en banc ruling in *Valdes v. United States*.[82] In *Valdes*, a majority of the court, motivated in part by concerns about whether the underlying statute provided the criminal defendant sufficient notice of the criminality of his conduct,[83] held that a police officer who took money from an undercover federal agent, in exchange for looking up license plate numbers and outstanding warrants in a police database, could not be prosecuted under the federal antigratuity statute.[84] Judge Garland dissented out of a concern that the majority opinion had interpreted the statute too narrowly to avoid "absurdities" not at issue in the case and, in so doing, "denied the government an important weapon in fighting official corruption."[85] In this sense, as one commentator has noted, Judge Garland may be "more likely" to favor "pragmatic arguments that certain" interests (like criminal defendants' right to receive notice that their acts are against the law) should be interpreted "flexibly, with an eye toward the practical consequences of given rules."[86] Such an approach toward judging arguably echoes Judge Garland's writings prior to his appointment to the D.C. Circuit, when he wrote, in the context of antitrust law, that the judiciary should generally "not interfere ... with a state's political decision...."[87] Thus, a general skepticism of judicial interference with the work of the political branches for reasons of pragmatism appears to underlie Judge Garland's often relatively functional approach to judging and could contrast with Justice Scalia's formalism if Judge Garland were confirmed to the High Court.[88]

Finally, commentators have suggested that Judge Garland's approach to judging tends to embrace compromise, consensus-building, and collegiality in particularly difficult or high profile matters where plausible arguments could be made by either side.[89] In this vein, perhaps the sharpest contrast between Judge Garland and the Justice he could succeed may lie in their respective personalities and temperaments, especially with respect to how each approaches the role of writing a judicial opinion that garners the majority of jurists on a court. While the subject of Justice Scalia's personality in the abstract has been a topic of general debate among legal scholars,[90] it is important to note that, relative to the tone of Judge Garland's opinions, Justice Scalia's writing could be quite pointed and acerbic in style.[91] More importantly, Justice Scalia's often-strict adherence to his originalist judicial philosophy at times resulted in him writing fairly broad opinions that did not garner the votes of the majority of the Court, as his colleagues were unwilling to embrace wholly Justice Scalia's take on the law.[92] In contrast, Judge Garland may be less pointed in his approach to judging, particularly with respect to his writing style. Following Judge Garland's recent nomination to the Supreme Court, his D.C. Circuit colleague, Judge Brett Kavanaugh, widely viewed as a one of the more conservative members of that court,[93] spoke highly of the new nominee, describing Judge Garland as "a brilliant jurist," "a great Chief Judge," "thoughtful," "collegial," "considerate," and someone "who works well with others."[94] Such sentiments are echoed by lawyers who have practiced in front of Judge Garland. Anonymous evaluations in the *Almanac of the Federal Judiciary* uniformly describe him with regard to his legal ability in positive terms, including having an "excellent temperament" and being "courteous" and "cerebral."[95]

Such comments appear not to be merely abstract descriptions of Judge Garland's personality; instead Judge Garland's judicial writings could be seen to reflect a tendency toward consensus-building. For example, for having such a lengthy career on the D.C. Circuit, Judge Garland has dissented relatively infrequently—on average, less than once per year[96]—something that suggests he may value collegiality above adhering to a particular legal orthodoxy in his legal writings.[97] Moreover, when Judge Garland has written the majority opinion for a court, his opinions have tended to garner few separate opinions relative to many of his colleagues on the D.C. Circuit,[98] which may indicate that the nominee places a high value on reaching a consensus in the opinions he writes.[99] Judge Garland's supporters suggest that, because of his tendency to consensus-building, he may be able to find agreement among colleagues with disparate views on the law in especially contentious cases if he were to be elevated to the Supreme Court.[100] While it is impossible to firmly predict how Judge Garland's past work might impact any future service on the High Court,[101] his work on the D.C. Circuit on a number of high profile matters could be said to support such claims.[102] For example, in 2003, Judge Garland authored a unanimous opinion, joined by a Reagan-era Supreme Court nominee, Judge Douglas Ginsburg, and Judge Harry T. Edwards, an appointee of President Jimmy Carter, which rejected a challenge alleging that, in the circumstances of the case, Congress had exceeded its powers under the Commerce Clause when enacting the Endangered Species Act.[103] Subsequently, in 2008, in *Parhat v. Gates*,[104] Judge Garland wrote for the court in invalidating a determination by a Guantanamo Bay combatant status review tribunal that the petitioner was an enemy combatant,[105] a conclusion joined by Judges David Sentelle and Thomas Griffith—sometimes viewed as two of the court's more judicially conservative members[106]—who sit on a court that often takes a skeptical view of the rights of detainees vis-a-vis the rights of the government.[107] Similarly, Judge Garland's 2015 opinion on behalf of a unanimous en banc court in *Wagner* on the ever-contentious issue of the constitutionality of campaign finance regulations may speak to the nominee's tendency to be able to garner the support of disparate colleagues in potentially difficult cases.[108] Judge Garland's ability to garner unanimous opinions in such cases resolving legal issues that have tended to sharply divide the High Court in recent years[109] may demonstrate his willingness to prioritize collaboration above ideological rigidity in his work.[110]

Statutory Interpretation

Unlike Justice Scalia, who publicly advocated for textualism and a canons-based approach to statutory interpretation,[111] Judge Garland does not appear to have articulated an overarching approach to or philosophy of statutory interpretation. However, his practices when construing statutes in his published opinions could be said to resemble those of many other judges,[112] with a couple of exceptions noted below, in that he generally bases his conclusions about a statute's meaning upon consideration of multiple factors including the text, structure, context, and history of specific statutory provisions.[113] For example, in his dissenting opinion in *United States* ex rel. *Totten v. Bombardier Corp.*, Judge Garland relied, in part, upon the "plain text" of the False Claims Act (FCA) in rejecting the majority's view that presentment of a false or fraudulent claim to the federal government was effectively required for liability under an FCA provision that had "no express requirement of presentment to an officer or employee of the United States Government."[114] He also pointed to other provisions of the FCA and, in particular, its definition of "claim," which he noted did not require presentment of a false or fraudulent claim to the federal government.[115] In addition, he drew support for his proposed interpretation from the legislative history of the FCA,[116] as well as prior interpretations of the act by the D.C. Circuit.[117]

Judge Garland's approach to construing statutory text can also be seen as fairly mainstream—and even to resemble that of Justice Scalia[118]—in that Judge Garland often highlights how people would normally understand specific statutory terms. For example, in his opinion for the court in *Southeast Alabama Medical Center v. Sebelius*, Judge Garland found that the Department of Health and Human Services (HHS) had properly included fringe benefits when calculating hospitals' "wage and wage-related costs" because, if fringe benefits were not to be seen as wages, they "fit comfortably within the broad meaning of the term 'wage-related.'"[119] Similarly, in his opinion for the court in *Public Citizen, Inc. v. HHS*, Judge Garland noted how people would normally understand the term "disposition" when rejecting HHS's argument that Medicare peer-review organizations (PROs) had met their obligation to disclose the "final disposition of [patients'] complaint[s]" by sending a form letter that noted that the PRO had reviewed the complaint and would take appropriate action, but did not specify what action was to be taken.[120] According to Judge Garland, most people would not see these form letters as disclosing the final disposition of the complaint, because the words "final disposition" are "far more persuasive[ly] read[]" to mean informing persons of the "substantive result or conclusion" of a matter, not merely that the matter has been completed.[121] Notably, Judge Garland has sometimes referenced dictionary definitions of statutory terms in such discussions,[122] a practice that often factors in textualist approaches[123] (although Judge Garland does not appear to have displayed any particular concern with ensuring that these definitions are contemporaneous with the statute's enactment, as Justice Scalia did).[124] However, Judge Garland very seldom expressly invokes the phrase "original meaning,"[125] which was a key component of Justice Scalia's approach to textualism,[126] and can serve as an indicator of a similar interpretative approach.[127]

In addition, Judge Garland's approach to statutory interpretation can be seen to resemble other judges' approaches in that he often refers to commonly accepted "canons"—or general principles—of statutory interpretation.[128] Judge Garland has invoked many different interpretative canons in the opinions he has authored while on the D.C. Circuit, including, but not limited to, canons providing that (1) similar language in the same or related statutes is to be construed similarly;[129] (2) when Congress uses particular language in one section of a statute, but omits this language in another section of that same statute, it is presumed to have acted "intentionally and purposely in the ...

exclusion";[130] (3) courts are to give effect to every clause and word of a statute, if possible;[131] (4) words used in the singular are presumed to include the plural;[132] (5) specific terms in a statute usually prevail over general ones;[133] (6) repeals by implication are disfavored and are not to be presumed to have occurred;[134] (7) titles or headings in statutory text provide only limited interpretative aid and are not meant to take the place of detailed provisions of the text;[135] (8) Congress is presumed to know how courts have construed particular statutory language when it enacts other statutes using that same language;[136] (9) the inclusion of some things in a list means the exclusion of other things not listed;[137] and (10) the word "or" is disjunctive, meaning that only one item in a list need be satisfied.[138] However, Judge Garland's resort to these and other canons of statutory interpretation appears to be driven by the specific statutory text in question and, in particular, whether one or more canons may be seen as helpful in construing the statutory text. It does not appear to be driven by a desire for standards or rules, per se, as means to cabin judicial discretion, as was the case with Justice Scalia.[139]

Two aspects of Judge Garland's practice in construing statutory text can be seen as more distinctive. One is the frequency with which he finds that statutory language is ambiguous, a finding which means that courts must generally defer to the agency's interpretation of the statutory language.[140] Specifically, Judge Garland seems to have not infrequently taken the view that particular statutory terms which are not defined, or whose meaning is not expressly prescribed by Congress, are ambiguous.[141] His dissenting opinion in *Financial Planning Association v. Securities and Exchange Commission (SEC)* can be seen to illustrate this practice.[142] The case centered upon provisions of the Investment Advisers Act that, in relevant part, exempt from regulation under the act:

> [1] any broker or dealer ... whose performance of [investment advice] services is solely incidental to the conduct of his business as a broker or dealer and ... who receives no special compensation therefore; ... or
>
> [2] such other persons not within the intent of this paragraph, as the Commission may designate by rules and regulations or order.[143]

The majority took the view that this statutory language unambiguously precluded the SEC from exempting broker-dealers who received "special compensation" from regulation under the act on the grounds that the first of these exemptions is "all inclusive" of broker-dealers because it uses the word "any."[144] Thus, in the majority's view, broker-dealers who receive "special compensation" are excluded from the phrase "other persons not within the intent of this paragraph," and the SEC cannot rely upon this language to exempt broker-dealers who receive "special compensation" from regulation under the act.[145] Judge Garland disagreed, viewing the phrases "such other persons" and "within the intent of this paragraph" as inherently ambiguous.[146] In so doing, he noted the lack of any language in the statute that purported to bar the SEC from exempting under the second provision broker-dealers who are not covered by the first provision,[147] as well as the absence of a definition of "other persons" in the act.[148]

Judge Garland's assessment of when or whether statutory text is ambiguous is significant because statutory text must be found to be *ambiguous* for a court to defer to an administrative agency's interpretation of that text under the precedent of *Chevron U.S.A., Inc. v. Natural Resources Defense Council*; if the text is seen as *unambiguous*, "that is the end of the matter; for the court, as well as the agency, must give effect to the unambiguously expressed intent of Congress."[149] Indeed, Judge Garland's penchant for finding ambiguity in statutory texts would seem to underlie the observation of one D.C. Circuit judge, who dissented from another opinion authored by Judge Garland, that "some will find ambiguity even in a 'No Smoking' sign,"[150] although this tendency could be seen to reflect a more generalized desire by Judge Garland to avoid having the courts constrain the options of the political branches.[151]

The other notable aspect of Judge Garland's approach to statutory interpretation involves his willingness to consider legislative history materials in construing statutory text.[152] Indeed, his resort to legislative history materials when construing statutes can be seen as interrelated with his willingness to find ambiguity in statutory text, as he has characterized the consideration of legislative history materials as "appropriate" when statutory text is ambiguous.[153] For example, in the *Totten* case mentioned earlier, the majority opinion by then-Judge John Roberts criticized Judge Garland's dissenting opinion, which the majority characterized as having excessively relied upon legislative history materials to construe the FCA. According to then-Judge Roberts, "[t]he dissent literally begins and ends with legislative history.... We [in the majority] will end as we began, too, but with the statutory language."[154] However, the disagreement among the *Totten* panel could be characterized as something less than a dispute between judges with radically different philosophies of statutory interpretation. Judge Garland's opinion in *Totten* characterizes the "existing statutory text" as the "starting point in discerning congressional intent,"[155] and the *Totten* majority also made use of legislative history materials.[156]

Judge Garland's use of legislative history materials in other cases can also be seen as relatively restrained in that (1) he generally treats legislative history as only one factor among many when construing text, rather than as the sole basis for his interpretation;[157] (2) he repeatedly notes that the statutory text, and not legislative history materials, is paramount in statutory interpretation;[158] and (3) he has, in several cases, recognized the limitations of legislative history materials to interpret a statute.[159] More generally, Judge Garland does not appear to have ever adopted an interpretation based on congressional purpose—as ascertained solely from legislative history materials—that was contrary to what he viewed as unambiguous statutory text to the contrary.[160]

In both his penchant for finding statutory text ambiguous and his resort to legislative history materials in construing statutory text, Judge Garland's practices can be seen to diverge from those of former Justice Scalia. While Justice Scalia was a vocal supporter of the approach adopted by the Court in *Chevron*,[161] he frequently found that statutory text was unambiguous and, thus, there was no need to consider the agency's interpretation of the text.[162] Justice Scalia also opposed the consideration of legislative history materials, including their use to confirm text-based interpretations of statutory text.[163] In this sense, Judge Garland would, if he were elevated to the Supreme Court, appear to approach matters of statutory interpretation somewhat differently from the man he would be succeeding, which could result in changes in the Court's rulings on close cases of statutory interpretation.

ADMINISTRATIVE LAW

A significant portion of the D.C. Circuit's docket consists of administrative law cases, in part, because Congress has vested the court with exclusive jurisdiction to hear challenges to a wide variety of government actions.[164] Broadly speaking, at least two key legal doctrines might be said to inform administrative law cases. The first is whether a challenged agency action is suitable for judicial review in the first place, including whether a plaintiff has standing to sue to obtain judicial relief as a result of unauthorized agency conduct. The second is whether an agency's action comports with the law.[165] An analysis of Judge Garland's opinions in administrative law cases that divided the D.C. Circuit reveals several trends that could provide insight into how he might approach these matters if he were confirmed to the Supreme Court.[166]

Before considering the merits of a legal challenge to administrative action, a federal court often must assess whether judicial review is available and appropriate in the first place—an assessment that may be informed by constitutional,[167] prudential,[168] and statutory considerations affecting a petitioner's access to the courts.[169] A court may be called upon to determine, for example, whether a petitioner has standing or is the appropriate party to bring a lawsuit challenging agency action;[170] whether the petitioner has exhausted administrative remedies prior to seeking judicial review;[171] whether the challenge concerns matters that are ripe for judicial consideration;[172] or whether legal or factual developments have rendered the legal challenge moot.[173]

While a judge's assessment of these issues often depends upon the particular facts of the case before the court, there are arguably some trends that can be identified in Judge Garland's jurisprudence. As an initial matter, Judge Garland has often sided with the majority on issues of judicial access that were litigated before the D.C. Circuit. In most decisions in which the appropriateness of judicial review of agency action was seriously contested, Judge Garland either wrote or joined the majority opinion of the court,[174] or authored or joined a separate opinion that did not dispute the majority's ultimate conclusion regarding whether judicial access was available.[175] Opinions authored by Judge Garland concerning petitioners' ability to seek review of administrative action tended to be written on behalf of unanimous circuit panels.[176] In the majority of these cases, Judge Garland concluded that the challenge was nonjusticiable because the petitioner lacked standing; the asserted legal claim was unripe or moot; or some other issue made judicial review inappropriate.[177]

On the other hand, in several cases, Judge Garland joined majority opinions where the court split on the question of whether a challenge to agency action was properly before it, and in those cases, he tended to be more permissive on matters of judicial access than his dissenting colleagues. In such instances, the judges who did not join the controlling opinion typically characterized the majority as having inappropriately allowed judicial recourse to a plaintiff who failed to satisfy the requirements necessary for judicial review of their claims.[178]

To the extent that Judge Garland's rulings on the D.C. Circuit can be seen as taking a permissive approach on issues of justiciability, including whether a party has standing to challenge administrative action, it could signal a difference in approach from that taken by Justice Scalia, who authored a number of Court opinions that served to restrict access to the courts for persons seeking to challenge or compel administrative action.[179] Because many recent Supreme Court rulings concerning standing and related matters have been closely divided cases,[180] Judge Garland's confirmation to the High Court could play a role in relaxing justiciability requirements that are often the first hurdle to challenging agency action.

In considering Judge Garland's approach to whether agency actions comport with the law—a matter on which he wrote prior to becoming a federal judge[181]—two important standards of review generally govern challenges to federal agency action under the APA and, thus, merit particular examination: statutory review, and arbitrary and capricious review.

Under the APA, a reviewing court must set aside agency action that is "not in accordance with law" or that is "in excess of statutory jurisdiction, authority, or limitations, or short of statutory right."[182] When reviewing challenges to an agency's interpretation of a statute that it administers, courts grant deference to the agency's interpretation if Congress delegated to the agency authority to "speak with the force of law," and the relevant interpretation was "promulgated in the exercise of that authority."[183] Pursuant to the framework established by the Supreme Court in *Chevron, U.S.A., Inc. v. Natural Resources Defense Council, Inc. (Chevron)*,[184] a court evaluating a challenge to an agency's interpretation must, as a first step, determine whether the legislature "has directly spoken to the precise question at issue."[185] If so, a court is required to give effect to Congress's intent, notwithstanding a contrary agency interpretation.[186] However, if a statute is silent or ambiguous on the matter, the second step in the *Chevron* analysis requires a court to defer to a reasonable agency interpretation.[187] Thus, a judicial finding of ambiguity is significant because it means that agencies are not foreclosed from altering their interpretations in the future in response to changed circumstances, whereas a finding that Congress clearly spoke to the issue "displaces a conflicting agency construction."[188]

With regard to Judge Garland's approach toward review of an agency's interpretation of law under *Chevron*, in cases that divided the D.C. Circuit,[189] Judge Garland often finds ambiguity in the underlying statute, leading him to evaluate an agency's regulation or rule through the more deferential lens of step two of the *Chevron* analysis.[190] Judge Garland's dissenting opinion in *Financial Planning Association v. SEC* is indicative of his approach in such cases.[191] At issue in that case was the Investment Advisers Act, which regulates the activity of "investment advisers," subject to six exceptions.[192]

One exception applies to "any broker or dealer whose performance of such services is solely incidental to the conduct of his business ... and who receives no special compensation therefor."[193] Another exempts "such other persons not within the intent of this paragraph[], as the Commission may designate by rules and regulations or order."[194] The SEC promulgated a rule under this second provision exempting broker-dealers who receive "special compensation therefor."[195] The panel majority ruled that the SEC lacked authority to exempt broker-dealers beyond the scope of the first exemption, reasoning that because broker-dealers were addressed in the first exemption, they did not qualify as "other persons" for the purposes of the second exemption.[196] Writing in dissent, Judge Garland argued that the terms of the second exemption were ambiguous and concluded that the agency interpretation was reasonable and entitled to *Chevron* deference.[197] He argued that the majority's reasoning in finding the statute unambiguous apparently relied on the statutory canon of *expressio unius*—the concept that the mention of one thing excludes another—but that canon is, in Judge Garland's view, inappropriate in an administrative context where Congress has left an agency with discretion to interpret its statutory authority.[198] And, for Judge Garland, the canon is particularly inapt where Congress expressly delegates authority to the agency to promulgate additional exceptions to a statute.[199] Determining that the underlying statute in *Financial Planning Association* was ambiguous, Judge Garland would have moved to step two of the *Chevron* analysis and found that the agency's interpretation was reasonable, in part, because the agency's interpretation was intended to serve the purposes of the statute for a group that did not exist when the statute was enacted in 1940.[200]

In divided cases where Judge Garland has ruled *against* an agency's interpretation of a federal statute, he has appeared to favor outcomes that could leave room for the agency to adopt more formal interpretations in the future that, if enacted, would allow the agency's legal position to eventually prevail. In other words, when voting against an agency's interpretation of the law, Judge Garland has often found that the *Chevron* doctrine did not apply because the agency has not spoken with the force of law.[201] Because a finding that a statute is unambiguous effectively eliminates an agency's discretion to adopt a contrary interpretation in the future,[202] his conclusion that *Chevron* was inapplicable in a particular case left open the possibility that the agency could later reinterpret the statute through a different procedure that could qualify for *Chevron* deference.[203] For example, in *Sottera, Inc. v. Food & Drug Administration* (FDA),[204] Judge Garland rejected the majority's view that Supreme Court precedent foreclosed the FDA from regulating e-cigarettes under the Federal Food, Drug and Cosmetic Act (FFDCA), and instead concurred in the court's judgment on the basis that the FDA had merely failed to put forth "an authoritative agency interpretation" of the FFDCA warranting *Chevron* deference.[205] In so doing, Judge Garland argued that the agency could in the future submit a formal regulation interpreting its authority to regulate e-cigarettes under the FFDCA, which would warrant more deference from the judiciary.[206] In this vein, even in cases where Judge Garland has rejected an agency's interpretation of a statute, the rationale for his vote typically has not wholly foreclosed agency discretion on the underlying legal issue.[207]

In addition to statutory review cases, the other major basis for challenges to agency actions under the APA is Section 706(2)(A) of the act, which authorizes reviewing courts to "hold unlawful and set aside agency actions, findings, and conclusions found to be arbitrary, capricious, [or] an abuse of discretion...."[208] The Supreme Court has viewed this provision as requiring agencies to "examine the relevant data and articulate a satisfactory explanation for [their] action including a 'rational connection between the facts found and the choice made.'"[209] "In reviewing that explanation, [the court] must consider whether the decision was based on a consideration of the relevant factors and whether there has been a clear error of judgment."[210] Generally, arbitrary and capricious review is "highly deferential" to the agency,[211] as "a court is not to substitute its judgment for that of the agency."[212]

Judge Garland's record in applying the APA's arbitrary and capricious standard of review appears more mixed relative to his jurisprudence in statutory review cases.[213] The arbitrary-and-capricious-review cases where Judge Garland has deferred to an agency's decisionmaking under the standard set forth in Section 706(2)(A) of the APA have tended to involve challenges to agency action on highly technical matters, particularly in environmental law.[214] Judge Garland's views in such cases may have been motivated by a reluctance for courts to second-guess the expert views of agencies that have been charged by Congress with administering a statute. For example, in *Americans for Safe Access v. Drug Enforcement Administration (DEA)*, he voted with the majority to uphold the DEA's decision not to initiate procedures to reclassify marijuana to a less restrictive schedule under the Controlled Substances Act.[215] The plaintiffs in that case challenged the DEA's conclusion that marijuana lacked a "currently accepted medical use," in part because there were not "adequate and well-controlled studies" proving marijuana's medical efficacy.[216] In oral arguments in that case, with regard to the agency's conclusion that such studies did not exist, Judge Garland asked: "Don't we have to defer to the agency ... we're not scientists, they are."[217]

These comments perhaps demonstrate a view that administrative agencies are better equipped to make such decisions than the courts. Likewise, in an analogous but distinct context from arbitrary and capricious review, in the case of In re *Aiken County*, Judge Garland dissented from the panel majority's decision issuing a writ of mandamus ordering the Nuclear Regulatory Commission (NRC) to resume the processing of a Department of Energy (DOE) application for a license to store nuclear waste at Yucca Mountain in Nevada.[218] Judge Garland's dissent argued that the majority opinion functionally ordered an agency to "do a useless thing,"[219] as the NRC had stopped the application proceeding because it did not have sufficient appropriated funds to complete the project, and Congress had, at the agency's request, appropriated only enough money to shut down the agency's licensing activity.[220] For Judge Garland, the agency simply lacked the funds to complete the application process, and the court was inappropriately questioning the agency's view that it simply could not "make any meaningful progress" with the funds it currently possessed.[221]

In other cases, however, Judge Garland has voted to invalidate agency actions or remand cases to the agency for a more developed explanation of its policy choice.[222] For instance, in *Alpharma, Inc. v. Leavitt*, Judge Garland wrote for the majority in remanding a matter to the FDA so that the agency could provide a fuller explanation of its reasoning in making the decision to approve a new animal drug application.[223] In particular, Judge Garland's majority opinion found that the agency's response to a previous remand order by the D.C. Circuit raised new concerns, as the FDA made, in the majority's view, contradictory assertions that prevented the court from concluding that the agency's decision was reasonable.[224] Nonetheless, while *Alpharma* demonstrates that Judge Garland has at times exhibited skepticism in reviewing agency action in the context of arbitrary and capricious review, no discernible trend appears in such cases akin to how he approaches the review of agency interpretations of statutes.

To the extent that Judge Garland's approach to administrative law would afford agencies flexibility in interpreting statutes that are found to be ambiguous,[225] his approach arguably contrasts with that of Justice Scalia, who readily acknowledged that his textualist approach to statutory interpretation made it less likely that the "triggering requirement for *Chevron* deference" would be found.[226] In this sense, Judge Garland's confirmation to the Supreme Court could result in significant changes to the Court's approach to the jurisprudence on administrative law.

Capital Punishment

Judge Garland's views on capital punishment may be particularly important insofar as he would, if confirmed, be replacing Justice Scalia, who believed the death penalty was fully consistent with the Eighth Amendment,[227] and two Justices currently on the Court openly have argued that the practice is unconstitutional.[228] However, Judge Garland does not appear to have had occasion to address directly the subject of capital punishment during his tenure on the D.C. Circuit since the District of Columbia does not provide for the imposition of the death penalty,[229] and federal death penalty cases are not confined to the D.C. Circuit,[230] as certain administrative law and environmental law cases are.[231] Prior to his appointment to the D.C. Circuit, Judge Garland was a prosecutor and handled cases wherein the government sought the death penalty, most notably against Oklahoma City bomber Timothy McVeigh.[232] In addition, Judge Garland also stated, in response to questioning at the 1995 hearing on his original nomination to the D.C. Circuit, that "as a personal matter," he viewed capital punishment as "settled law now. The Court has held that capital punishment is constitutional and lower courts are to follow that rule."[233] Based on only these isolated statements, with no judicial record interpreting the Eighth Amendment generally or the death penalty specifically, it is difficult to make any firm predictions about how Judge Garland might vote were he appointed to the High Court.

Civil Liability

One major area where Judge Garland could be quite influential, if he were to be confirmed to the Supreme Court, involves the limits that federal law imposes procedurally and substantively on civil defendants' exposure to monetary liability, particularly in the context of lawsuits resulting from allegedly faulty products, discriminatory practices, or fraudulent activities.[234] This is because Justice Scalia, whom Judge Garland could succeed on the Supreme Court, cast critical votes in several closely contested cases that read federal law relatively expansively to restrict plaintiffs' ability both to use (1) procedural vehicles, such as class action litigation, to facilitate civil recoveries,[235] and (2) substantive state law, including common law tort actions, to sue businesses that may have harmed them.[236] In other cases, Justice Scalia cast important votes more *narrowly* interpreting the scope of federal law to limit corporate defendants' potential civil liability.[237] Given Justice Scalia's decisions, commentators have debated how Judge Garland might affect the Roberts Court's perceived "warmth" toward businesses on civil liability matters if he were to be confirmed to the Court.[238] Some have suggested that the nominee's tendency to defer to executive agencies could make him less apt to use judicial power to interfere with marketplace externalities,[239] while others contend that Judge Garland's record, particularly on labor law matters,[240] would make him more hostile toward business interests and more likely to side with the plaintiffs' bar in interpreting federal law.[241]

While certain predictions could perhaps be made with regard to how Judge Garland might rule on civil liability matters based on his votes in other areas of law, like labor law, the docket of the D.C. Circuit—which tends to have a considerable number of administrative law disputes and relatively "few explicit business cases"[242]—makes it difficult to predict confidently how he might rule if he were to be elevated to the High Court. Indeed, there are very few cases in which he has ruled directly on matters of civil liability akin to those matters on which Justice Scalia was so influential. Moreover, many of the rulings that Judge Garland has made on civil liability matters have been unanimous ones, joined by judges of differing philosophies and backgrounds,[243] which presumably signals that precedent was seen to have largely dictated the result in such cases.[244] For example, Judge Garland joined majority decisions twice in 2013 that took the relatively unusual step of vacating class action certifications on interlocutory appeal, "command[ing]," in one case, a lower court to take a "hard look at the soundness of [the] statistical models" that formed the basis for class certification.[245] Nonetheless, a year later, Judge Garland joined a majority decision written by Judge Douglas Ginsburg that denied a petition to vacate a class certification order despite the existence of "unsettled questions of law relating to class actions at issue in this case."[246] As a consequence, on many civil liability matters, like the scope of the rules governing class action certifications, Judge Garland has arguably not exhibited any clear tendencies or preferences.[247]

Nonetheless, at least a few of Judge Garland's cases stand out with regard to general civil liability matters, and may provide some insight into how he might rule on such issues. With respect to the interpretation of federal law in displacing state causes of action, such as tort law—an issue of considerable dispute on the High Court in recent years[248]—Judge Garland notably dissented in *Saleh v. Titan Corp.*[249] The *Saleh* case arose from the abuse of detainees who were imprisoned at the Abu Ghraib detention facility during Operation

Iraqi Freedom.[250] The plaintiffs, Iraqi nationals, sued the military contractors that had provided interrogation and translation services at the prison,[251] claiming that the defendant contractors were liable for assault, battery, wrongful death, and intentional infliction of emotional distress.[252] In response, the defendants argued[253] that these common law tort claims were preempted by the Federal Tort Claims Act (FTCA),[254] a law that has a limited waiver of sovereign immunity, but exempts from that waiver the discretionary functions of federal officials and the combatant activities of the military.[255] Because federal contractors are expressly excluded from coverage under the FTCA,[256] the defendants in *Saleh* based their preemption argument on an extension of the Supreme Court's 1988 decision in *Boyle v. United Technologies Corp.*, which established a potential defense for federal contractors facing liability under state tort law if a state tort claim raises a "significant conflict" with the requirements of a federal government contract.[257]

In *Saleh*, Judge Garland and the majority disagreed on whether a sufficiently "significant conflict" existed given the facts before them.[258] Looking to the FTCA's preservation of sovereign immunity with respect to "[a]ny claim arising out of the combatant activities of the military,"[259] the majority held that the purpose of this exception is the "elimination of tort from the battlefield" in order to "free military commanders from the doubts and uncertainty" that accompany potential civil liability.[260] Judge Garland, in contrast, found that the duties imposed by tort law and the contract in the case were "congruent rather than incompatible,"[261] largely because the allegedly unlawful conduct of the defendants had not been "directed or authorized" by military personnel.[262] Judge Garland also argued that what he viewed as the "extraordinarily broad" preemption under the majority's interpretation was incompatible with the presumption that state causes of action should be left intact absent a "clear and manifest" congressional purpose to displace state law,[263] a rule of construction that Justice Scalia repeatedly criticized.[264] In this regard, although *Saleh* addressed preemption within the narrow context of suits against federal contractors, it may exemplify the general approach that Judge Garland could employ when analyzing whether and to what degree federal and state law conflict, as well as illustrate how Judge Garland might approach such matters differently from Justice Scalia. Because the conflict required in *Saleh*—which dealt with "uniquely federal interests"—is less than that which would be required in ordinary preemption cases, it would be reasonable to presume that Judge Garland would similarly disfavor broad displacement of state claims "when Congress legislates in a field which the States have traditionally occupied."[265] More broadly, Judge Garland's views on preemption, as discussed in *Saleh*, may be part and parcel of his writings prior to joining the D.C. Circuit, where he expressed deep skepticism with respect to federal courts broadly invalidating state laws under preemption principles in the context of federal antitrust law.[266]

In a related but distinct context, Judge Garland has tended, particularly in nonunanimous opinions, to read federal laws that *impose* civil liability more expansively than some of his colleagues on the D.C. Circuit. For example, in a decision ultimately reversed by the Supreme Court, a majority of the en banc D.C. Circuit held in *Kolstad v. American Dental Association* that Congress's authorization of punitive damages for sex discrimination claims brought under Title VII of the Civil Rights Act of 1964[267] should be interpreted in the context of the common law.[268] Because punitive damages at common law require that the defendant's conduct be "egregious," the majority held that the same standard should apply under Title VII, even though the text of the statute appeared to require only malice or reckless indifference.[269] Judge Garland, however, joined the dissent in *Kolstad*, which argued that the plain language of the statute should control, and that adding the common law requirement of "egregious" conduct was inappropriate.[270] Moreover, in interpreting the False Claims Act, a law that imposes certain penalties upon any person who "knowingly presents, or causes to be presented, to an officer or employee of the United States Government ... a false or fraudulent claim for payment or approval," Judge Garland wrote two opinions that tend to favor plaintiffs that prompted disagreement with some of his colleagues on the D.C. Circuit. First, in *United States* ex rel. *Yesudian v. Howard University,*[271] Judge Garland, over the dissent of Judge Karen Henderson,[272] wrote a majority opinion reversing the dismissal of claims that a university employee was discharged in retaliation for whistleblowing activity under the FCA. In so doing, the majority held that to prove retaliation for purposes of the FCA, a plaintiff need not demonstrate that the defendant knows or is advised that the underlying fraud of which the whistleblower complains would necessarily violate the act.[273] Six years later, in *United States* ex rel. *Totten v. Bombardier Corp.*, Judge Garland dissented from a majority opinion by then Judge John Roberts in another FCA matter. There, the majority held that a manufacturer could not, under the version of the FCA then in effect, be held liable for false claims allegedly submitted to a *private* entity even though the claims were paid for largely with *federal* funds.[274] However, in dissent, Judge Garland argued that the majority decision unnecessarily "immunizes those who defraud" government-funded private organizations from FCA liability, leaving "vast sums of federal monies" unprotected by the act.[275] Nonetheless, while these cases provide some insight into how Judge Garland might vote in future cases where the Court addresses the scope of liability for civil defendants, the small number of D.C. Circuit cases on business law and general civil liability issues make it difficult to predict confidently how Judge Garland would rule on such matters if confirmed to the High Court.

CIVIL RIGHTS

Civil rights are another prominent legal issue frequently raised in cases before the Court. Justice Scalia's views regarding the scope of constitutional and statutory civil rights protections were established in a number of judicial opinions, and he participated in several cases—including on gay rights and affirmative action—that were closely divided.[276] His eventual replacement could affect how the Court addresses such issues. However, unlike Justice Scalia, Judge Garland's views on *constitutional* civil rights questions are generally unknown because he has not had occasion to address such questions directly in the cases before the D.C. Circuit. Rather, most of the civil rights decisions in which Judge Garland has participated during his tenure on the appellate court appear to have centered on statutory civil rights claims and, in particular, statutory employment discrimination claims.

The most notable of Judge Garland's statutory civil rights cases is arguably *Kolstad v. American Dental Association*,[277] an en banc decision that eventually made its way to the Supreme Court. In *Kolstad*, a majority of the en banc D.C. Circuit upheld the dismissal of a claim for punitive damages filed under Title VII of the Civil Rights Act of 1964, on the grounds that such damages are available only when an employer engages in egregious misconduct, which the court viewed as lacking in this case.[278] Judge Garland, however, joined the dissenting opinion, authored by Judge David Tatel, which argued that punitive damages should be available in intentional discrimination cases if the plaintiff can show reckless indifference by an employer.[279] The Supreme Court subsequently adopted a view closer to that of the dissent than the majority on this question, concluding that while the statute imposes a separate, higher standard for awarding punitive relief in cases of intentional discrimination, there need not be a certain level of egregiousness for awarding such relief.[280] Instead, the Court held that under the Title VII, "an employer must at least discriminate in the face of a perceived risk that its actions will violate federal law to be liable in punitive damages."[281] Some commentators have noted that Judge Garland's vote in in *Kolstad*, as well as his opinions or votes in certain other statutory civil rights cases, have frequently, though not always, tended to result in outcomes that favor employees, rather than employers.[282] However, the outcomes in these cases may reflect Judge Garland's general approach to questions of statutory interpretation or administrative law, rather than "pro-employee" sentiments per se. Moreover, even if Judge Garland's *statutory* civil rights jurisprudence were seen to favor plaintiffs generally, it remains unclear how he might rule on *constitutional* civil rights questions, given his lack of votes in cases involving such questions while on the D.C. Circuit.

CRIMINAL LAW AND PROCEDURE

Judge Garland's opinions in the field of criminal law and procedure constitute another noteworthy segment of his overall jurisprudence, especially given that he would, if confirmed, replace Justice Scalia, who can be seen to have been generally,[283] although not universally,[284] solicitous of the rights of criminal defendants when construing the Constitution and criminal statutes.[285] Criminal law and procedure is an area of law with which Judge Garland was well familiar by the time of his appointment to the federal judiciary in 1997; in the years immediately preceding his appointment to the D.C. Circuit, he served as a federal prosecutor for the DOJ,[286] overseeing the investigation of several prominent cases, including those involving the Unabomber, the 1995 Oklahoma City bombing, and the 1996 Atlanta Olympics attack.[287] Perhaps because of his background prosecuting major criminal cases on behalf of the federal government, several commentators have suggested that Judge Garland would, if elevated to the Supreme Court, tend to side with the government's interests in criminal cases.[288] Such suggestions have been supported by examinations of Judge Garland's votes in criminal law matters while on the D.C. Circuit, which show that the nominee tends to vote in favor of the government.[289] Putting to the side questions about the value of such bottom-line assessments of Judge Garland's entire jurisprudence on criminal law[290]—an area of law where the federal appellate judiciary, as a whole, sides with the government a substantial percentage of the time[291]—an examination of how he resolved issues in a host of criminal law cases, particularly cases that divided the court,[292] may provide a more nuanced and perhaps more insightful approach to predicting how the Supreme Court's criminal jurisprudence may change if Judge Garland succeeds Justice Scalia.

With respect to constitutionally based criminal procedure rules, Judge Garland, when siding with the government's position, has tended to afford deference to law enforcement officers' reactions in the field, with an eye toward protecting officers' safety. For example, over the dissent of Judge Judith Rogers,[293] he ruled for the government in *United States v. Brown*, a fact-intensive case that evaluated whether a police officer, investigating reports of a shooting outside an apartment building, violated the Fourth Amendment[294] when he opened the door of a car in a parking lot outside of the apartment and subsequently searched the car's trunk.[295] Applying the totality of the circumstances approach set forth by the Supreme Court in *Terry v. Ohio*,[296] Judge Garland concluded that the officer's belief that the occupants posed a danger to his safety was justified, given that (1) the search occurred in a high crime area and was conducted at night; (2) one of the vehicle's occupants exited the car prior to the search and appeared to be "eyeing" the police; and (3) another of the vehicle's occupants jumped into the front seat when the officer approached.[297] Unlike Judge Rogers,[298] Judge Garland emphasized that an objective assessment of reasonable suspicion, as opposed to a subjective inquiry into a law enforcement officer's particularized motive for a search, must govern *Terry* inquiries,[299] a view he based on a 1996 opinion by Justice Scalia[300] that some commentators have suggested affords law enforcement considerable discretion.[301] Similarly, in *United States v. Christian*, Judge Garland, in holding that a police officer's search of a defendant's car that was near the defendant at the time of his arrest was permissible as part of a weapons search under *Terry* and its progeny, rejected the argument that the police officer did not *truly* fear for his safety because he searched the defendant's car *before* frisking the defendant's body.[302] In so doing, Judge Garland, echoing themes from *Brown*, noted that "appellant judges do not second-guess a street officer's assessment about the order in which he should secure potential threats,"[303] but rather evaluate the officer's "conduct objectively, not subjectively."[304]

At the same time, Judge Garland's constitutionally based criminal procedure rulings, perhaps in keeping with his broader judicial tendencies,[305] have tended to be narrow in their scope and limited to the specific facts of the case at hand. For example, in *United States v. Powell*,[306] Judge Garland sided with the majority in an en banc ruling upholding a search incident to arrest—a recognized exception to the Fourth Amendment warrant requirement[307]—that occurred *before* the suspect was formally or constructively placed under arrest.[308] The dissent in *Powell* disagreed, arguing that the mere *possibility* of arrest is insufficient to justify a warrantless search incident to arrest,[309] given a

1998 Supreme Court ruling that held that the search incident to arrest doctrine is inapplicable when the suspect is merely given a citation.[310] However, the majority concluded otherwise, finding that the search fell within the confines of earlier case law allowing an officer to conduct a warrantless search if the "formal arrest follow[s] quickly on the heels of the challenged search."[311] Judge Garland's vote with the majority in *Powell* could be seen to indicate a hesitancy to read later-in-time precedent broadly to overturn implicitly controlling case law.[312]

In another en banc ruling, *United States v. Askew*, Judge Garland similarly showcased his penchant for relatively narrow rulings on constitutional criminal matters.[313] In *Askew*, the D.C. Circuit divided on the question of whether the police may—without a warrant—unzip a suspect's outer jacket to facilitate a witness's identification during a *Terry* stop, with five judges concluding that, as a matter of law, the police could not do so,[314] and four judges concluding that they could.[315] Two judges in *Askew* prevented either legal conclusion from gaining a majority of the 11-person en banc court needed to create circuit precedent; however, Judge Garland, along with Judge Douglas Ginsburg, joined only a narrow section of the eventual majority opinion that avoided the broader legal question, instead holding that based on the facts in the record, the police had no reasonable basis for believing that viewing the "generic blue sweatshirt" worn by the defendant underneath his jacket would establish or negate his connection with the underlying crime.[316] In this sense, as noted by the dissent in *Askew*, Judge Garland's vote was the "narrowest ground necessary for reversing" the underlying conviction,[317] suggesting the nominee's hesitancy regarding broader rulings in constitutional criminal law matters.

Beyond the context of the Fourth Amendment, Judge Garland has often ruled on narrow grounds when filling gaps left open by the Supreme Court's or D.C. Circuit's case law.[318] For example, when authoring an opinion involving an issue of first impression in the D.C. Circuit concerning the "actual innocence" standard in federal habeas corpus cases, Judge Garland, after reviewing Supreme Court precedent, cautioned that "we should hesitate before adding a condition [of proof] not included in the express language of the Supreme Court's opinion."[319] Similarly, in *United States v. Andrews*, when deciding whether to adopt a new rule for the court as to whether the application of a Federal Sentencing Guidelines recommendation issued after the date of the offense, which would have yielded a higher sentence, raised ex post facto issues—something that had divided the appellate courts before the Supreme Court's decision in *Peugh v. United States*[320]—Judge Garland concluded that the D.C. Circuit need not choose which side of the debate to join because, under plain error review, "there is no plain error unless the district court failed to follow an absolutely clear legal norm."[321] In addition, when opining on the novel issue of "how to treat an unobjected-to *Booker* error when the original sentencing judge is no longer available to preside over remand,"[322] Judge Garland declined to grant the government's request to create a new rule granting a limited remand before a new district judge to determine whether the original sentencing judge would have imposed the same sentence had he known the Sentencing Guidelines were advisory rather than mandatory.[323] Instead, Judge Garland concluded that a plenary sentencing hearing was warranted because "district courts—no matter how collegial they may be—do not have a collective consciousness, one judge's conclusion as to what another would have done in a circumstance the latter never contemplated would truly be a legal fiction."[324]

With regard to statutory interpretation of criminal laws, Judge Garland has in divided cases tended to read criminal statutes more broadly than some of his colleagues on the D.C. Circuit to encompass the activities of charged defendants. For example, he sided with the government's position in several cases concerning whether a mens rea (i.e., mental state) element is required by a statute. In *United States v. Burwell*, Judge Garland joined the majority en banc opinion holding that the government need not prove that the defendant knew the firearm he carried was capable of firing automatically in a prosecution under Section 924(c)(1)(B)(iii) of Title 18 of the *U.S. Code*,[325] a result the majority concluded was in line with statute's purpose of deterring future "offenders more generally through the imposition of a particularly severe penalty" with respect to the use of a machine gun in a federal felony.[326] Judges Rogers, Kavanaugh, and David Tatel, however, dissented, arguing that the presumption that a mens rea element applies to every element of a criminal offense should apply to Section 924(c).[327] Similarly, in *United States v. Blalock*, Judge Garland authored an opinion holding that the fact the defendant was high on phencyclidine (PCP) did not negate the mens rea element in the statute, as there were attendant circumstances demonstrating that the defendant was sufficiently in control of his faculties to meet the mens rea requirement.[328] Nonetheless, Judge Garland has not uniformly sided with the government in mens rea cases, as he authored the majority opinion in *United States v. Project on Government Oversight*.[329] In that case, the court held a federal statute, which bars nongovernmental persons from compensating federal employees for performing government services, requires proof that the money was given with the *intent* to compensate the employee for government services.[330]

Outside of statutory interpretation cases concerning mens rea requirements, in one notable en banc case, *Valdes v. United States*,[331] Judge Garland, in dissent, supported a fairly broad reading of a federal criminal law, arguing that the federal antigratuity statute encompassed the actions of a police officer who agreed to use police databases to find contact information for certain individuals in exchange for money.[332] While the majority in *Valdes* interpreted the term "official act" in the relevant federal statute as including only those acts that are formally before a government agency, or responses to questions that the agency had authority to answer,[333] Judge Garland argued that the majority's narrow construction of the term "official act" would not only limit prosecutions under this statute, but "would [also] strike at the core of bribery prosecutions under [another statute]," which relies on the same definition of "official act."[334] He cautioned that, under the majority's approach, "successful bribery prosecutions under [this other statute] ... would not be possible."[335] Judge Garland's dissent here could be seen as evidencing an inclination to give broad effect to criminal statutes, especially those aimed at public corruption. If so, such an approach would mark a departure from Justice Scalia's often more favorable approach toward criminal defendants, which relied on the rule of lenity (i.e., the idea that persons must have sufficient notice of a law before they can be found in violation of it).[336]

Whether opinions like *Valdes* speak to a broader tendency of Judge Garland to favor the government systematically in criminal law matters, as has been suggested by some commentators,[337] remains to be seen, however. It is important to note that many aspects of criminal law and procedure upon which Justice Scalia deeply influenced the Court's jurisprudence[338]—including the scope of Fifth Amendment's double jeopardy and self-incrimination prohibitions and the Sixth Amendment's Confrontation and Jury Clauses—have simply not been addressed by Judge Garland in any manner that would meaningfully reveal how he would approach such issues if he were to be confirmed to the Supreme Court.[339] More broadly, while nearly two decades' worth of decisions in appeals on criminal law matters provides a large number of cases to examine in order to gauge Judge Garland's approach, the vast majority of these decisions have involved relatively straightforward applications of Supreme Court or circuit precedent,[340] or adherence to the uniform approaches of sister circuits.[341] This means that any absolute pronouncements about how Judge Garland would approach criminal law, if he were appointed to a position where he would not necessarily be constrained by precedent or the views of other judges, should be viewed with some skepticism.

ENVIRONMENTAL LAW

The D.C. Circuit hears a large number of environmental law cases, in part because several major environmental statutes require challenges to certain types of agency actions to be brought exclusively in that court.[342] As a consequence, Judge Garland has participated in dozens of environmental cases in his time on the D.C. Circuit.[343] Many environmental cases raise common issues of administrative law, such as standing to sue and standards for judicial review.[344] However, environmental law statutes and cases can also raise their own unique issues. Where a number of observers have suggested that Justice Scalia evidenced a certain degree of skepticism toward arguments emphasizing environmental values,[345] Judge Garland generally has been viewed as more receptive to such arguments,[346] even though he has not always ruled in favor of environmental protections.[347]

Judge Garland has often applied *Chevron* deference[348] in support of upholding agency interpretations of environmental statutes.[349] Indeed, some have singled out what they see as his "long-standing commitment to *Chevron* deference" as a defining characteristic of his environmental jurisprudence.[350] For example, in the 2002 case *American Corn Growers Association v. Environmental Protection Agency (EPA)*, which involved review of the EPA's Regional Haze Rule,[351] Judge Garland's partial dissent supported the position put forth by the agency. He wrote that, unlike the other two judges on the panel, who agreed with industry petitioners that language in the Clean Air Act (CAA) required each pollution source's control requirements to be based on assessments of that source's impact on haze, he would have deferred to the EPA's interpretation that the act allowed the agency to base controls on collective assessments of groups of sources.[352] Judge Garland was also in the majority of a divided panel that deferred to the EPA's interpretation of the phrase "appropriate and necessary" in a CAA provision on regulating hazardous emissions from power plants, and upheld the EPA's Mercury and Air Toxics (MATS) rule,[353] a holding that was overturned by the Supreme Court, by a vote of 5-4, in its 2015 decision in *Michigan v. EPA*.[354] Judge Garland has joined opinions applying *Chevron* deference to uphold agency interpretations against challenges from environmental groups as well.[355] However, where he has voted to vacate or remand environmental rules on *Chevron* grounds, he has more often,[356] but not exclusively,[357] done so in response to challenges from environmental groups rather than industry.

Judge Garland's application of the "arbitrary and capricious" standard for judicial review of agency actions found in the APA[358] and in environmental statutes such as the CAA[359] further illustrates his tendency to defer to agencies, especially on highly technical environmental matters.[360] For example, in *National Association of Home Builders v. EPA*, he wrote an opinion for the court that included a fairly in-depth review of the EPA's explanation and cost-benefit calculations, upholding a 2010 agency amendment that removed an "opt-out" provision from a Toxic Substances Control Act regulation on renovation and remodeling hazards from lead paint.[361] On the other hand, Judge Garland has ruled against agency actions on the facts of some cases. In a per curiam decision in *American Farm Bureau Federation v. EPA*, for example, a panel including Judge Garland agreed with state and environmental petitioners that the EPA's 2006 CAA standard for fine particulate matter was "unsupported by adequately reasoned decisionmaking," and remanded the rule to the EPA for "further consideration of whether it is set at a level requisite to protect the public health while providing an adequate margin of safety from the risk of short-term exposure...."[362]

The National Environmental Policy Act (NEPA), which imposes procedural requirements on agencies to take a "hard look" at environmental consequences,[363] has been a statutory vehicle for many challenges to agency actions and project approvals. It appears that where he has reached the merits of NEPA claims, Judge Garland has tended to uphold agencies' NEPA decisions unless they failed entirely to take a required step.[364] In *Sierra Club v. Van Antwerp*, he joined an opinion holding that when the Army Corps of Engineers issued a permit authorizing the discharge of dredge and fill material into specified wetlands for construction of a mall, the Corps "did not address the impacts of habitat fragmentation" on the endangered eastern indigo snake, and "the Corps must make some determination on the issue" under NEPA and the Endangered Species Act (ESA).[365]

In the environmental context, Judge Garland has required agencies to adhere to other statutory procedural requirements as well.[366] For example, in *Gerber v. Norton*, he authored an opinion agreeing with a plaintiff environmental group that the Fish and Wildlife Service (FWS) had violated the rather rigorous procedural requirements of the ESA[367] by, among other errors, failing to make a site map available during the comment period.[368] Other cases, though, appear to demonstrate more willingness to allow environmental agencies some procedural flexibility. Thus, in In re *Aiken County*, Judge Garland dissented from an opinion requiring the NRC to proceed to exhaust its previous appropriations to continue the Yucca Mountain licensing process.[369] The applicable statute provides that the NRC "shall issue a final decision approving or disapproving" the application filed by the

Department of Energy,[370] and the majority in In re *Aiken County* stated that "where previously appropriated money is available for an agency to perform a statutorily mandated activity, we see no basis for a court to excuse the agency from that statutory mandate," even where all agreed it was impossible for the agency to complete the licensing.[371] Judge Garland, in contrast, looked to the court's "discretion not to order the doing of," what he viewed to be, "a useless act."[372]

Access to courts has been another theme of recurring importance in environmental cases. One jurisdictional threshold that plaintiffs in federal courts must cross is establishing standing to sue under Article III of the Constitution.[373] In cases challenging federal agencies' environmental decisions, Judge Garland has been mindful of the constitutional requirements and prudential concerns of standing doctrines; he has authored[374] and joined[375] a number of opinions rejecting standing for environmental or industry plaintiffs or petitioners. However, he also has found standing in a number of cases,[376] including some in which other judges did not.[377] In addition to standing, would-be plaintiffs seeking to bring lawsuits or petitions raising environmental issues may also have to satisfy legal requirements relating to ripeness, the finality or binding nature of the agency action challenged, and their exhaustion of administrative remedies.[378] As with standing, in some cases Judge Garland has found causes of action ripe or otherwise appropriate to hear, even where other judges have disagreed.[379] However, some practitioners have noted[380] that he has fairly often written[381] or joined[382] opinions that applied these doctrines to bar challenges to agency environmental decisions before reaching the merits. In one notable example, in the 2014 case *Utility Air Regulatory Group (UARG) v. EPA*, Judge Garland wrote on exhaustion of administrative remedies that "the only objections that may immediately be raised upon judicial review are those that were raised during the public comment period. Objections raised for the first time in a petition for reconsideration must await EPA's action on that petition."[383] Judge Garland also has joined opinions holding NEPA claims, in particular, to be premature or improper on several occasions.[384]

Finally, environmental cases may also implicate other constitutional issues. Judge Garland generally has not favored constitutional arguments against environmental regulations. In *American Trucking Associations v. EPA*, a D.C. Circuit panel that did not include him held, among other things, that a section of the CAA unconstitutionally delegated legislative power to the EPA on the grounds that the agency had interpreted the statute in a manner that provided no "intelligible principle" to guide the agency's exercise of authority.[385] Judge Garland dissented from the denial of rehearing en banc and joined a statement of dissent emphasizing Supreme Court precedent on Congress's need to be able to delegate power to agencies "under broad general directives."[386] The panel's decision on the nondelegation issue was unanimously overturned by the Supreme Court in 2001 in *Whitman v. American Trucking Associations*, in a decision written by Justice Scalia.[387] Judge Garland similarly rejected a constitutional challenge to environmental protections in the 2003 case *Rancho Viejo, LLC v. Norton*, in which he wrote the opinion for the court finding that an agency's ESA determination—that a planned housing development was likely to jeopardize the continued existence of the arroyo southwestern toad— was a constitutional exercise of federal authority under the Commerce Clause.[388] More recently, Judge Garland joined the opinion in *Mississippi Commission on Environmental Quality v. EPA*, which rejected arguments that the EPA's designation of areas in Texas and elsewhere as "nonattainment" areas under the CAA exceeded federal authority under the Commerce Clause, the Due Process Clause, Spending Clause, and the Tenth Amendment.[389]

Overall, it appears that agencies defending environmental rules could find their odds somewhat more favorable in many cases if Judge Garland were to be confirmed to replace Justice Scalia on the Supreme Court. Any such shift could be key to the outcome of major environmental law challenges that could eventually reach the Supreme Court after working their way through lower courts at the time of Judge Garland's nomination. Perhaps most notable among these are the consolidated challenges to the EPA's Clean Power Plan rule, which was stayed by Justice Scalia in one of his last votes for the Court[390] and which is considered highly likely to be appealed to the Supreme Court by whichever side does not prevail before the current D.C. Circuit panel (this panel does not include Judge Garland).[391]

FEDERALISM

During his tenure on the D.C. Circuit,[392] Judge Garland has addressed issues of federalism and the scope of congressional power vis-à-vis the states in only a limited number of cases.[393] Issues raised by these cases include the constraints imposed upon Congress's legislative power by the anticommandeering principles of the Tenth Amendment;[394] the extent of the anticoercion principles undergirding the Supreme Court's jurisprudence on the Spending Clause;[395] the scope of the Commerce Clause;[396] and the limits upon states' ability to invoke Eleventh Amendment immunity.[397] Gleaning general trends from these few decisions is difficult, as it is unclear to what degree Judge Garland's conclusions may reflect his own approach to federalism questions, or what he perceives as adherence to Supreme Court precedent. However, it appears that in federalism cases in which there was some disagreement among the reviewing circuit judges, Judge Garland has tended to side with the federal government and narrowly construe judicial limits on Congress's power to act in a manner that could implicate the sovereign interests of the states.

In his judicial opinions, Judge Garland has had limited opportunity to assess the scope of the anticommandeering doctrine recognized by the Supreme Court. This doctrine posits that the Tenth Amendment prohibits Congress from "commandeering" states by compelling them to adopt laws[398] or enforce federal regulatory schemes,[399] by reserving to the states all powers not delegated to the federal government by the Constitution.[400] In the one case before Judge Garland where an anticommandeering argument was raised, the precise issue appears to have been squarely resolved by Supreme Court precedent on conditional preemption. In that case, Judge Garland joined a per curiam opinion in *Mississippi Commission on Environmental Equality v. EPA* that rejected the argument that the CAA commandeers state officials by compelling them to enforce federal environmental requirements, on the grounds that the Supreme Court had "repeatedly affirmed the constitutionality of federal statutes that allow States to administer federal programs but provide for direct federal administration if a State chooses not to administer [the program]."[401]

Arguably more telling, however, are the cases where Judge Garland has adjudicated claims concerning the constraints the Tenth Amendment may impose upon the exercise of Congress's power under the Spending Clause.[402] For example, the *Mississippi Commission* court, having rejected plaintiffs' commandeering argument, likewise dismissed an argument that the CAA constitutes an impermissible and coercive use of Congress's spending powers insofar as it permits the EPA to withdraw funding for transportation projects in areas determined not to have met federal air quality standards.[403] In so doing, the court examined the principle established by the Supreme Court in *South Dakota v. Dole*,[404] and more recently refined in *National Federation of Independent Business (NFIB) v. Sebelius*,[405] that when the "financial inducement offered by Congress [is] 'so coercive as to pass the point at which pressure turns into compulsion,'" the spending condition "runs contrary to our system of federalism."[406] Adopting an arguably narrower interpretation of

NFIB, the D.C. Circuit panel in *Mississippi Commission* distinguished the CAA provision in question from the provisions of the Affordable Care Act (ACA) at issue in *NFIB*. In particular, the court reasoned that, whereas the ACA called for the entirety of a state's Medicaid funding to be withheld if the state failed to meet expanded health insurance coverage requirements, under the CAA, a state would not lose *all* its federal transportation funding, but a lower amount, which did "not even approach the 'over 10 percent of a State's overall budget' at issue in *NFIB*."[407] Moreover, the per curiam opinion openly questioned in dicta whether a state could even challenge a spending condition as "unconstitutionally coercive" if it had "long accepted billions of dollars notwithstanding the challenged conditions," a possible limitation on state challenges to federal funding conditions not addressed by the Supreme Court in *Dole* and subsequent cases.[408]

In a slightly different context, Judge Garland more narrowly interpreted the *Dole* restrictions on the spending power in *Barbour v. WMATA*, affirming Congress's authority to condition federal transportation funding on a waiver of state sovereign immunity.[409] *Barbour* centered on a Spending Clause argument divorced from the issue considered by the Supreme Court in *NFIB*. Namely, the state defendants in *Barbour*—Maryland and Virginia—argued that Congress, in conditioning acceptance of federal transportation funds on a state's agreement to waive sovereign immunity with regard to disability discrimination lawsuits lodged by state employees, had exceeded its powers under the Spending Clause by conditioning the monetary grants to the states on something "unrelated to the federal interest in transportation funds."[410] In an opinion joined by D.C. Circuit Judge and future Supreme Court Chief Justice John Roberts, Judge Garland concluded that *Dole* 's requirement that the conditions relate to the purpose of the funding was satisfied because Congress "did not want *any* federal funds to be used to facilitate disability discrimination, and ... exposing recipient entities to the threat of a federal damages action was an effective deterrent."[411] Unlike Judge David Sentelle's dissent, [412]Judge Garland's majority opinion in *Barbour*, relying on Supreme Court precedent regarding spending conditions that imposed restrictions on *racial* discrimination by state governments,[413] gave considerable deference to Congress's judgment that a waiver of sovereign immunity was appropriate to protect federal funds from being used—even if only indirectly[414] for intentional *disability* discrimination.[415] In this sense, the conclusions reached in *Mississippi Commission* and *Barbour* may signal that Judge Garland believes that *Dole* and its progeny impose relatively limited restrictions on Congress's spending powers.

Of the various federalism cases interpreting the scope of federal powers granted by the Constitution, perhaps Judge Garland's most extensive writings have been with respect to Congress's power under the Commerce Clause.[416] The Supreme Court has established, in cases such as *United States v. Lopez*[417] and *United States v. Morrison*,[418] that the Commerce Clause provides Congress with broad power to regulate "channels of interstate commerce"; "instrumentalities of interstate commerce"; and "those activities that substantially affect interstate commerce."[419] In interpreting the scope of the third category, Judge Garland, citing to both Supreme Court and circuit precedent, has reasoned that in order to evaluate potential interstate effects, federal courts must "focus[] on the activity that the federal government seeks to regulate," as well as "activities that arise out of or are connected with a commercial transaction, which viewed in the aggregate, substantially affect[] interstate commerce."[420] In an opinion issued a little over a month after the Supreme Court decided *Morrison*, Judge Garland, writing on behalf of a unanimous circuit panel in *Allied Local & Regional Manufacturers Caucus v. EPA*, dismissed a challenge to a CAA provision authorizing the EPA to regulate architectural coatings for purposes of limiting volatile organic compound emissions.[421] In so doing, the court held that "none of the considerations" that had led the Supreme Court to find "Congress's authority wanting" in *Lopez* or *Morrison* had "any application to section 183(e) of the [CAA]."[422] In particular, Judge Garland concluded that the provisions in question were distinguishable from those legislative enactments recently invalidated in *Morrison* in that the CAA regulated economic activity; contained a jurisdictional element and express congressional findings describing the problems of "interstate transport of ozone"; and had a link to substantial effects on interstate commerce that was not "attenuated."[423]

In perhaps a closer case, Judge Garland wrote on behalf of a D.C. Circuit panel in *Rancho Viejo, LLC v. Norton*,[424] a case involving a challenge to a FWS determination that a developer's construction of a fence as part of a planned commercial development resulted in a "take" of arroyo southwestern toads in violation of the ESA.[425] Rejecting assertions that the federal government was regulating activities that were both wholly intrastate and noneconomic in nature,[426] Judge Garland wrote that the fact that certain toads' habitat did not extend beyond the state of California did not serve as a basis for invalidating the provisions of the ESA, as these provisions regulated "takings, not toads."[427] In Judge Garland's view, the "regulated activity" in question was not the harm to the toad, but rather the construction of the planned commercial development, an activity with a clear and substantial impact on interstate commerce.[428] In so concluding, Judge Garland rejected claims that the ESA provided the federal government with power over land-use decisions that the plaintiffs alleged were "an area of traditional state concern."[429] Relying heavily on an earlier decision by the U.S. Court of Appeals for the Fourth Circuit,[430] Judge Garland ultimately concluded that "the protection of endangered species cannot fairly be described as a power 'which the Founders denied the National Government and reposed in the States.'"[431] Judge Garland's opinion in *Rancho Viejo* was relied upon almost a decade later by a D.C. Circuit panel in *Mississippi Commission*, where the panel (of which Judge Garland was a member) rejected a Commerce Clause challenge to Congress's authority to regulate local nitrogen oxide emissions on the grounds that the "regulated activity" under the CAA was not the release of emissions, but rather "the *activities* that *produce* the emission."[432] Applying this reasoning, the court held that the entities producing the emissions were "indisputably [] engaged in substantial interstate commerce."[433]

Judge Garland's opinion in *Rancho Viejo* prompted criticism when the plaintiffs unsuccessfully petitioned the D.C. Circuit for en banc rehearing of the case.[434] In particular, Judge Sentelle disagreed that the Supreme Court's decisions in *Lopez* and *Morrison* could be read to allow Congress to "regulate any activity if the act of regulating catches an entity or an action that is itself commercial independent of the noncommercial nature of the regulated entity and activity."[435] Instead, Judge Sentelle contended that Judge Garland's approach could be seen to "continue[] [the D.C. Circuit's] divergence from contemporary Supreme Court Commerce Clause jurisprudence" because the "protection of a non-commercial, purely local toad is not within any of the *Lopez* categories."[436] Judge Roberts applied similar reasoning in a separate dissent, arguing that to sustain the ESA on the grounds that the "commercial development constitutes interstate commerce" seemed "inconsistent" with *Lopez* and *Morrison* insofar as the majority effectively "ask[ed] whether the challenged *regulation* substantially affects interstate commerce, rather than whether the *activity* being regulated does,"[437] "effectively obliberat[ing]" the "limiting purpose" of the Commerce Clause.[438] As a consequence, Judge Garland's Commerce Clause jurisprudence suggests that he has adopted a construction of the clause that provides the federal government with broad authority to regulate various forms of activity that others have viewed as noneconomic, intrastate activity not subject to federal regulation.

Finally, with respect to the doctrine of state sovereign immunity that the Supreme Court has recognized underlies the Eleventh Amendment,[439] Judge Garland has authored two arguably relevant opinions having divergent results.

In *Watters v. WMATA*, he wrote a unanimous panel opinion holding that the state signatories to the WMATA interstate compact were immune from the imposition or enforcement of an attorney's lien, narrowly reading the partial waiver of sovereign immunity contained in the compact.[440] Nonetheless, in *Barbour*, Judge Garland concluded that the states participating in WMATA had waived immunity through their acceptance of federal transit money, as the "language" of the Civil Rights Remedies Equalization Act of 1986 "unambiguously conditions a state agency's acceptance of federal funds on its waiver of Eleventh Amendment immunity."[441] Importantly, Judge Garland's majority opinion in *Barbour* held that a clear condition imposed in a federal statute suffices to waive sovereign immunity, and a state's beliefs when accepting federal funds are irrelevant in considering whether a waiver of sovereign immunity was "knowing."[442] Such an approach limits an alternate route to maintain an immunity defense recognized by another federal court of appeals.[443] As a result, *Barbour*, like some other federalism cases discussed here, could be seen to manifest some skepticism on Judge Garland's part about judicially imposed limits intended to protect the sovereign rights of states. However, because of the limited number of cases in which he ruled on the scope of federal power vis-à-vis the states, it is difficult to conclude with certainty that Judge Garland would, if appointed to the Supreme Court, be less receptive to federalism-based arguments than Justice Scalia had been.[444]

FREEDOM OF RELIGION

During Judge Garland's tenure on the D.C. Circuit, he has not authored any opinions indicating in any detail his substantive interpretation of constitutional or statutory religious freedom laws. However, he has joined opinions involving religious freedom issues, including constitutional and statutory challenges arising under the First Amendment and the Religious Freedom Restoration Act (RFRA).[445] Arguably the most significant religious freedom case in which Judge Garland had a role is *Priests for Life v. HHS*, a case currently under review by the Supreme Court.[446] The original decision in that case upheld a contraceptive coverage requirement of the Affordable Care Act that was generally applicable to employers, finding no violation of the protection for religious exercise by employers available under RFRA.[447] Although he did not serve on the panel that originally heard the case, Judge Garland participated in the court's decision to deny a petition for en banc rehearing in the case.[448] The decision to deny rehearing was issued per curiam, and Judge Garland did not join other judges' concurring or dissenting opinions for that decision.[449]

Although Judge Garland's role in *Priests for Life* provides little substantive insight into his legal reasoning on the issue of religious freedom,[450] it may be notable depending on the High Court's eventual disposition of the consolidated contraceptive coverage cases.[451] The Court appeared evenly divided following oral arguments, which could lead it to hold the cases over to its next term for rehearing.[452] If Judge Garland were to be confirmed prior to the Court's potential rehearing, he may play an important role in deciding these cases.[453]

FREEDOM OF SPEECH

While serving on the D.C. Circuit, Judge Garland has ruled in a number of major free speech cases. In particular, because the D.C. Circuit has exclusive jurisdiction over certain election law appeals,[454] the bulk of these matters have involved free speech issues arising in the context of campaign finance regulations and rules governing political parties.[455] Perhaps most significantly, Judge Garland wrote the opinion for a unanimous en banc court in *Wagner v. FEC*,[456] upholding the prohibition on campaign contributions by certain federal government contractors[457] against a challenge under the First Amendment and the Equal Protection clause of the Fifth Amendment. The court's ruling in *Wagner* was narrow in the sense that it was limited to a ban on contractors making contributions to candidates, parties, and traditional political action committees (PACs)[458] during the negotiation or performance of a government contract.[459] The *Wagner* court concluded that the federal ban serves "sufficiently important" government interests by guarding against quid pro quo corruption (and the appearance thereof) and protecting merit-based administration.[460] Relying on the Supreme Court's 2003 ruling in *FEC v. Beaumont*, Judge Garland's opinion applied the less rigorous "closely drawn" standard and rejected the argument that the Supreme Court's 2010 ruling in *Citizens United v. FEC* cast doubt on *Beaumont*.[461] Perhaps revealing aspects of Judge Garland's views on the constitutionality of campaign finance regulation more broadly, the opinion deferred to Congress's judgment on how best to serve the government's interests. Quoting from *Beaumont*, the opinion observed that "[j]udicial deference is particularly warranted where, as here, we deal with a congressional judgment that has remained essentially unchanged throughout a century of 'careful legislative adjustment.'"[462] In contrast, judicial deference to congressional determinations has arguably not been as evident in the Supreme Court's more recent campaign finance jurisprudence.[463] At the same time, because of the unanimity of the *Wagner* decision and the decision's relatively narrow scope, it may be difficult to draw any firm conclusions regarding Judge Garland's views on judicial deference toward congressional determinations respecting campaign restrictions from the *Wagner* decision, in and of itself.

Nonetheless, in another context, Judge Garland generally took a favorable view of the regulation of federal lobbyists. Specifically, in *National Association of Manufacturers (NAM) v. Taylor*,[464] he authored a unanimous opinion rejecting a First Amendment challenge to a federal lobbying disclosure law. The court found no evidence of harassment connected to lobbying disclosures[465] that might justify more skepticism with regard to the disclosure requirements, and, in a display of deference to Congress arguably like that in *Wagner*, ultimately concluded that there was "no reason why Congress cannot enact a scheme that plausibly yields a significant portion of the information it seeks."[466]

On the other hand, during Judge Garland's tenure on the D.C. Circuit, the appellate court issued a well-known campaign finance ruling that resulted in the establishment of super PACs, political committees that spend independently of any candidate or party and are permitted to receive unlimited contributions.[467] In *SpeechNow.org v. FEC*,[468] Judge Garland joined, but did not author, a unanimous en banc opinion holding that limits on contributions to groups that make only independent expenditures are unconstitutional.[469] Relying on the Supreme Court's ruling in *Citizens United*, the court reasoned that if independent expenditures do not give rise to corruption, then contributions to groups making only independent expenditures do not give rise to corruption.[470] Thus, the court held that contribution limits are unconstitutional as applied to such groups.[471] In view of the Supreme Court's binding precedent in *Citizens United*, the analysis in *SpeechNow.org* was necessarily "straightforward," in the court's view.[472] Therefore, although the ruling was consequential, it is difficult to infer Judge Garland's campaign finance philosophy from this case.[473]

Regarding the rights of political parties, Judge Garland's opinions have produced mixed results for the parties themselves, while generally interpreting the First Amendment as having limited import in deciding such disputes. In *Libertarian Party v. District of Columbia Board of Elections*,[474] he joined a unanimous opinion holding that a Washington, DC, law which prevented write-in votes for a third-party candidate from being officially tallied and reported did not amount to a severe burden on that individual's associational rights and, therefore, did not require the application of strict scrutiny.[475] On the other hand, in *LaRouche v. Fowler*,[476] Judge Garland's opinion favored a political party's right to decide its own nominees. Among other things, the court rejected a First Amendment challenge to a party's effort to limit who can run as a candidate of the party on the grounds that the party's effort was a rational means of advancing its interest in winning elections.[477] With possible relevance to the current presidential party nominating process, Judge Garland wrote, "A party may, of course, pay heavily at the polls for the perception that it treats its members, delegates, or candidates unfairly. But that is a matter for the party to weigh, and for the people to decide in the general election. It is not a basis upon which a court can intervene as long as the party's processes rationally advance its legitimate interests."[478]

Outside the election law context, Judge Garland has, relative to other areas of law, authored or joined few opinions analyzing the Free Speech Clause of the First Amendment.[479] Of these cases, his most notable majority opinion was perhaps the 2005 case[480] *Initiative and Referendum Institute (IRI) v. United States Postal Service.*[481] In that case, Judge Garland, on behalf of the court, held that a Postal Service regulation wholly prohibiting the solicitation of signatures outside postal buildings did not withstand First Amendment scrutiny as a valid "time, place, and manner" regulation of speech, as the rule was "neither ... narrowly tailored nor ensure[d] ample alternative channels of communication."[482] The Postal Service had defended the prohibition on the grounds that solicitors "at times" become disruptive, "occasionally" distracting postal employees from their duties.[483] In Judge Garland's opinion, this argument all but conceded that the "across-the-board" prohibition "necessarily bars much solicitation that is not disruptive," leading to the conclusion that a "substantial portion of the burden on speech does not serve to advance" the government's interest.[484] The ruling in *IRI* was not only unanimous, but rested on two separate and independent grounds casting doubt on the constitutionality of the underlying regulation,[485] suggesting that the case was not terribly controversial and may not provide any broad insights into Judge Garland's approach to free speech questions.

At the same time, a few trends do appear in Judge Garland's free speech rulings outside the context of election law. On the issue of commercial speech[486]—an area of law where narrow majorities of the Supreme Court have struck down state and federal regulations on the marketing of certain products in recent years[487]—he has joined majority opinions affirming the Federal Trade Commission's authority to prohibit commercial speech it finds to be misleading,[488] and otherwise protect certain consumer interests.[489] And in *American Meat Institute v. USDA,* an en banc ruling reviewing whether a regulation mandating disclosure of country-of-origin information for certain meat products was improperly compelled speech in violation of the First Amendment, Judge Garland joined a majority of the court in upholding the regulation.[490] In so doing, the D.C. Circuit concluded that the government can require disclosures not only to remedy potential consumer deception, but also in the context of a long history of consumer interest in the particular disclosure.[491] These decisions have led some to suggest that Judge Garland may prefer a more deferential approach to the government with respect to analyzing the constitutionality of commercial speech regulations.[492] In the context of public employee speech,[493] an area of First Amendment law in which—in contrast to commercial speech cases—narrow majorities of the High Court have, at times, tended to *favor* the authority of the government over the rights of employees,[494] Judge Garland has joined several majority opinions siding with public employees who alleged that their employers retaliated against them for engaging in protected speech.[495] And in *Mpoy v. Rhee*, Judge Garland authored an opinion that, while ultimately ruling for the government on qualified immunity grounds,[496] acknowledged that controlling D.C. Circuit precedent "could be in tension" with a recent Supreme Court case that may have "narrow[ed] ... the realm of employee speech left unprotected" by the Constitution.[497] Collectively, his rulings on commercial speech and public employee speech may signal areas of First Amendment law where he could, if elevated to the High Court, depart from recent majorities of the Court that have included Justice Scalia.

Perhaps Judge Garland's most noteworthy writings on free speech issues outside the context of election law involve the rights of the press to gather and maintain confidential sources.[498]

Specifically, in *Lee v. DOJ*,[499] he dissented from the denial of rehearing en banc in a case examining journalists' qualified privilege to refuse to testify in civil suits to which they are not parties.[500] While the panel had concluded that the plaintiff had overcome the journalists' qualified privilege,[501] Judge Garland, in dissenting from the denial of rehearing, argued that the "significance of the court's decision in [the] case should not be underestimated."[502] He contended that the standard applied by the panel gave insufficient weight to the public's interest in protecting the confidential sources of journalists.[503] In particular, Judge Garland argued that, without robust protections for journalists during civil discovery in cases to which they are not parties, potential sources will be reluctant to disclose information to the press.[504] Such a result, according to Judge Garland, would ultimately chill the speech of journalists, undermining the "Founders' intentions to protect the press 'so that it could bare the secrets of the government and inform the people.'"[505] Similarly, in *Boehner v. McDermott*,[506] he joined the dissenting opinion of Judge David Sentelle, which maintained that the government cannot, consistent with the First Amendment, punish thepublication of information that was *lawfully* obtained from a source who obtained it *unlawfully*.[50'] This position provides far more protection for the publication of information that is of public interest than the position asserted by Judge Raymond Randolph's majority opinion, which maintained that the government can "forbid individuals from disclosing information they have lawfully obtained" in certain contexts.[508] Judge Garland's decisions favoring stronger protections for the rights of journalists and the disclosure of information have led some observers to argue that he has a broad view of the First Amendment's free speech protections.[509] Nonetheless, because of the limited number of free speech cases outside the context of election law in which he has participated, the record may be too thin to make firm pronouncements about Judge Garland's overall views on free speech issues.

INTERNATIONAL AND FOREIGN LAW

Whereas Justice Scalia's written work and public speeches reflected distinct attitudes toward the use of contemporary foreign law and practice, ratified treaties, and international custom to inform understanding of the U.S. Constitution and federal statutes,[510] Judge Garland's jurisprudence offers comparatively little guidance as to his likely approach on such matters if appointed to the Supreme Court. For example, while Justice Scalia was a vociferous critic of using contemporary foreign law and practice to interpret the meaning of the Constitution, Judge Garland has not opined on the appropriateness of using foreign law as an interpretative aid beyond observing, in ruling that a federal judge had not committed misconduct by criticizing judicial reliance on foreign law to interpret the U.S. Constitution, that the practice was "the subject of a spirited debate among the Justices of the Supreme Court, and it cannot constitute misconduct for an appellate judge to choose one side or the other."[511] In other cases, Judge Garland appears to have eschewed reaching issues of international law when he believed it unnecessary to address such matters to resolve the case before the court.[512]

During his tenure on the D.C. Circuit, Judge Garland has decided a number of cases involving the primacy of conflicting requirements imposed by federal statutes and international legal agreements.[513] In adjudicating such cases, the circuit court often has been called upon to employ two canons of construction. One of these canons is the "last-in-time" rule, which generally provides that, if a conflict exists between a federal statute and a ratified treaty, then the requirements of the most recently enacted measure are controlling.[514] The other is the canon against abrogation, which recognizes that courts should, to the extent possible, construe ambiguous statutory language in a manner that does not abrogate international legal agreements.[515]

Judge Garland appears reluctant to construe statutory provisions in a manner that would abrogate earlier international agreements if another interpretation is possible. While he has written or joined opinions holding that provisions of a particular federal statute effectively abrogate provisions of a previously ratified treaty,[516] he has also joined panel opinions interpreting later-intime federal statutes in a manner that avoids abrogating earlier international agreements.[517] One notable example occurred in *Owner-Operator Independent Drivers Association, Inc. v. U.S. Department of Transportation*,[518] where Judge Garland joined another member of a three-judge panel in upholding the Federal Motor Carrier Safety Administration's (FMCSA's) exemption of commercial vehicle operators licensed by Mexico or Canada from generally applicable medical certification requirements. The exemption from statutory requirements was made by the FMCSA to avoid violating earlier reciprocal licensing agreements made by the United States with Mexico and Canada.[519] While the majority acknowledged that the federal statute spoke "in general yet textually unambiguous terms"[520] that could be construed to abrogate the earlier agreements, it found insufficient evidence that Congress intended the statute to have this effect. "[A]bsent some clear and overt indication from Congress," the court declared, "we will not construe a statute to abrogate existing international agreements even when the statute's text is not itself ambiguous."[521]

Judge Garland's approach in *Owner-Operator Independent Drivers Association*, where "general yet textually unambiguous terms" employed by a statute were presumed not to have been intended to abrogate an earlier agreement, might immediately appear to be in tension with Justice Scalia's textualist approach to statutory interpretation.[522] But Justice Scalia recognized that background presumptions may sometimes inform a court's interpretation of a statute, and he indicated his support for interpreting federal statutes in a manner consistent with international legal obligations whenever possible.[523]

Adding a further layer of uncertainty is the variation in contexts in which Judge Garland and Justice Scalia presumed that Congress did not intend for a legislative enactment to contravene an international legal norm or agreement. In *Owner-Operator Independent Drivers Association*, for example, Judge Garland joined an opinion that applied the canon against abrogation in a case that primarily concerned activities within the United States. On the other hand, Justice Scalia appeared to most forcefully advocate interpreting federal statutes consistently with international legal norms in cases where a federal statute potentially reached conduct recognized under international law as primarily subject to the jurisdiction of a foreign sovereign.[524] Justice Scalia was arguably less likely to interpret a statute addressing wholly domestic activities so as to avoid potential conflicts with international legal norms and agreements.[525]

The relatively limited number of cases considered by Justice Scalia and Judge Garland concerning arguably conflicting provisions in federal statutes and international agreements makes it difficult to assess whether they would have generally reached the same conclusions in similar circumstances. Judge Garland's jurisprudence suggests that, like Justice Scalia, he would strive to interpret federal statutes consistently with international legal obligations whenever statutory requirements were deemed ambiguous, though it seems possible that the two jurists' more general approach to statutory interpretation could lead to different conclusions on matters of statutory ambiguity.[526]

RIGHT TO BEAR ARMS

During his tenure on the D.C. Circuit, Judge Garland has not authored any judicial opinions or writings outside the court that directly address the Second Amendment or the constitutionality of firearms regulations.[527] He has, however, cast votes in cases addressing these issues, and some commentators have debated the extent to which they indicate his broader views on this area of law.[528] The most notable of these votes is arguably his 2007 vote dissenting from the denial of en banc review in *Parker v. District of Columbia*.[529] In *Parker*, a panel of the D.C. Circuit had held, by a vote of 2-1, that the Second Amendment protects an individual's right to possess a firearm and that the District of Columbia's laws—which functionally prevented handgun ownership— violated the Second Amendment.[530] The District sought en banc review of this decision, which the D.C. Circuit denied by a vote of 6-4.[531] Judge Garland was among those dissenting. However, the order denying en banc review gave no indication of the views of any voting judge as to why the D.C. Circuit should or should not reconsider the case.[532] Subsequently, the Supreme Court granted review,[533] and in a 2008 decision authored by Justice Scalia, affirmed the decision of the D.C. Circuit panel by a vote of 5-4.[534]

Earlier votes by Judge Garland also touched on Second Amendment issues. In 2005, he was among a majority of judges who voted against en banc review of *Seegars v. Ashcroft*, a case challenging the same D.C. gun restrictions that were eventually overturned in *Heller*.[535] Previously, in *National Rifle Association of America, Inc. (NRA) v. Reno*, Judge Garland voted as part of a three-judge panel to uphold a DOJ rule that permitted the federal government to retain temporarily firearms background check information, a regulation that had been promulgated after the enactment of the Brady Handgun Violence Prevention Act.[536] The *NRA* majority concluded that the Brady Act did not bar DOJ from temporarily retaining such information and that DOJ had permissibly construed the statute when it promulgated the rule.[537] However, neither the *NRA* court nor the *Seegars* court evaluated the constitutionality of the underlying firearm laws being challenged. As a result, these few cases would seem a tenuous basis for any firm conclusions as to Judge Garland's approach to the Second Amendment and firearms restrictions if he were to be confirmed to the Supreme Court.

SEPARATION OF POWERS

Judge Garland's writing from the bench to date has not revealed in express terms whether he approaches questions involving the separation of powers as resolvable mainly through an evaluation of strict delineations of governmental powers set forth in the Constitution (what scholars frequently term a "formalist" approach), or by determining whether a challenged law or action significantly upsets the equilibrium of powers the Framers hoped to achieve (a more flexible "functionalist" approach).[538] There may, however, be a few clues to be drawn from his written opinions, as well as his joining (or refusing to join) the opinions of his fellow judges. For example, in an order denying a petition to have the entire D.C. Circuit rehear a case challenging the Affordable Care Act on Origination Clause[539] grounds, Judge Garland did not join Judge Brett Kavanaugh's dissent, which articulated a formalist rationale for vacating the original panel decision[540] in order to reach the same result by interpreting the Clause in a way that Judge Kavanaugh viewed as truer to its text.[541] On the other hand, Judge Garland declined to sign on to a statement concurring in the denial of rehearing that endorsed the "purposive" test the original panel had applied and suggested the dissent's proposed test would turn the Origination Clause into an "empty formalism,"[542] which in itself reveals very little about Judge Garland's views.[543]

Why Judge Garland voted to stay out of this particular fray is impossible to discern from the record, but his silence could suggest his support for the original panel opinion and its functionalist approach, or perhaps a preference for avoiding the constitutional issue and leaving the matter to Congress, in contrast to the formalist view espoused by the dissent.[544] Or perhaps he simply regarded the issue as not sufficiently important to warrant a grant of rehearing. Supreme Court Justices may have had similar thoughts, as suggested by the denial of certiorari in this case.[545]

Judge Garland did not significantly participate in the *Zivotofsky* series of cases at the D.C. Circuit, which involved a statute that was ultimately viewed by the Supreme Court as impinging on executive branch power in the realm of foreign affairs, except to vote with the majority to deny en banc review of the circuit court's decision to decline to review the case on political question grounds.[546] That decision was subsequently reversed by the Supreme Court on the grounds that the judiciary has a duty to resolve significant separation of powers questions regarding Congress's authority to legislate in matters touching upon the executive power to recognize foreign sovereigns.[547] Judge Garland's vote to deny en banc review could indicate a preference for applying the political question doctrine to establish the proper role of the court in such cases—that is, to avoid its involvement—but there is no way of knowing from the record.

Perhaps less speculation is required to draw inferences from Judge Garland's dissent in In re *Aiken County*.[548] In that case, the majority considered the question of whether to require the NRC to fulfill a statutory mandate to process a license application for the construction of a permanent nuclear waste repository at Yucca Mountain as one to be resolved by applying a simple formula: absent any objection regarding the constitutionality of an act of Congress, the President is required to give it effect.[549] Stating that the NRC's failure to complete review of the application "raises significant questions about the scope of the Executive's authority to disregard federal statutes,"[550] the majority granted a petition for mandamus to order compliance. Judge Garland dissented, suggesting the court should take into account circumstances he believed made the NRC's noncompliance with the letter of the law reasonable.[551] Citing circuit precedent establishing that a court has discretion to withhold a writ of mandamus that would order the doing of a "useless thing" (albeit one that is technically required by law),[552] he contended that the court ought not to second-guess the NRC's determination that it had insufficient funds available to pursue further consideration of the license. In Judge Garland's view, forcing the NRC to expend what was left of the amounts previously appropriated to it for this purpose without any real chance of moving the project forward would "do nothing to safeguard the separation of powers."[553] In contrast to the majority's strict construction of the statute and adherence to constitutional roles, Judge Garland's pragmatic approach may suggest that he leans toward the functionalist school of separation of powers thought.

In re *Aiken County* may be indicative of another trend in Judge Garland's approach to separation of powers questions, namely, a hesitancy to have the court interfere with the executive branch. In interpreting the meaning of the term "agency records" in the context of the Freedom of Information Act (FOIA),[554] Judge Garland imputed separation of powers concerns to Congress in determining that White House access records are not releasable even if they are in the possession of the Secret Service.[555] To decide otherwise, he wrote, "could substantially affect the President's ability to meet confidentially with foreign leaders, agency officials, or members of the public. And that could render FOIA a potentially serious congressional intrusion into the conduct of the President's daily operations."[556]

In the decade and a half since September 11, 2001, the D.C. Circuit has confronted a host of issues touching on separation of powers principles regarding the wartime role of the judicial branch in relation to the political branches in cases brought by detainees held at the U.S. Naval Station, Guantanamo Bay, Cuba.[557] In *Al Odah v. United States*,[558] the court held itself to be without jurisdiction to examine the lawfulness of executive detention of foreign nationals held at Guantanamo, relying on Supreme Court precedent that enemy aliens held abroad are not entitled to pursue habeas writs, in part due to the interference with military operations such judicial examination would entail.[559] Judge Garland joined the majority opinion in that decision, which was later reversed by the Supreme Court in *Rasul v. Bush*.[560] After Congress altered the habeas statute to preclude jurisdiction[561] and the Supreme Court held that effort to be unconstitutional,[562] Al Odah's petition worked its way back to the D.C. Circuit. Judge Garland then voted with a unanimous three-judge panel to uphold a less rigorous evidentiary standard than the detainee urged—namely, a preponderance of the evidence standard with admission of reliable hearsay— and to affirm the denial of the writ.[563] While he also voted as part of a panel that found habeas jurisdiction available to challenge not only the legality of detention but also the conditions of detention at Guantanamo, rejecting the government's contention that Congress had effectively precluded such challenges,[564] the court in that case ultimately deferred to the government's view that the challenged prison procedures were "rationally related to security," reversing the court below.[565]

Judge Garland's opinion for a unanimous panel in *Parhat v. Gates*[566] may be read to suggest that his willingness to defer to the executive branch in military matters goes only so far, at least where Congress has prescribed a role for the courts. In that case, the court declined to validate the decision of a Combatant Status Review Tribunal (CSRT) based on the insufficiency of evidence proffered by the government to prove the petitioner's affiliation with an "associated force" fighting alongside Al Qaeda or the Taliban. To do otherwise, Judge Garland wrote, "would [] place a judicial imprimatur on an act of essentially unreviewable executive discretion. That is not what Congress directed us to do when it authorized judicial review of enemy combatant determinations under the [Detainee Treatment] Act."[567]

Noting the controversy still pending in *Bismullah v. Gates*[568] regarding the scope of evidence that the government was required to produce in CSRT challenges, the *Parhat* court evaluated the case on the record alone and found that the reliance on intelligence documents in question was unsupported.[569] While the Supreme Court's decision in *Boumediene v. Bush* effectively obviated reviews under the Detainee Treatment Act,[570] Judge Garland's *Parhat* opinion continues to be cited in detainee habeas cases for the proposition that evidence presented by the government must be in a form that permits a reviewing court to assess its reliability.[571] Still, in subsequent cases, no detainee has prevailed on the grounds that the evidence put forth by the government was unreliable.[572] Moreover, the court has repeatedly upheld the government's use of hearsay evidence, explaining that hearsay in such cases is always admissible, but that judges must assess its reliability.[573] It appears that the D.C. Circuit, after some prodding from the Supreme Court, has, to some degree, more closely scrutinized the executive branch in detainee habeas cases, but for detainees at Guantanamo, prevailing in court remains an uphill battle. Judge Garland's participation in these cases seems to indicate his position in the mainstream of D.C. Circuit judicial thought with respect to the court's role in evaluating executive branch detention, as approved by Congress.

In one notable case[574] interpreting the Military Commission Act (MCA) of 2006[575] and its enumerated charge of material support for terrorism, the D.C. Circuit declined to defer to Congress's assertion that the charge is one that has traditionally been triable by military commission and therefore may be tried even if the underlying conduct took place prior to the MCA's enactment.[576] The court explained its role where Congress's view on the subject was mistaken, stating "it is not our task to rewrite the statute to conform with the actual state of the law but rather to strike it down insofar as the Congress's mistake renders the statute unconstitutional."[577] Accordingly, assuming without deciding that the Ex Post Facto Clause of the Constitution[578] applies at Guantanamo,[579] the court vacated the accused's conviction for material support of terrorism and solicitation on ex post facto grounds, but sent his conspiracy conviction back to a three-judge panel to consider his other constitutional challenges to the MCA.[580] Judge Garland cast his vote with the majority and did not write separately. Although he did not join Judge Judith Rogers's concurring opinion emphasizing the separation of powers implications of delegating to the executive branch an arguably judicial role,[581] Judge Garland's vote with the majority might be viewed as an assertion of the judiciary's primacy in interpreting the law in this regard. On remand, the panel reversed the remaining charge for conspiracy, holding that Congress had encroached upon Article III judicial power by authorizing military commissions to try the purely domestic crime of inchoate conspiracy.[582] The full court vacated this decision and ordered rehearing en banc, possibly setting up another opportunity to consider Judge Garland's approach to separation of powers clashes.[583]

SUBSTANTIVE DUE PROCESS

Because the docket of the D.C. Circuit tends to focus less on social issues than the dockets of the regional circuit courts of appeals do,[584] Judge Garland has had few opportunities to express his views on the scope of the substantive component of the Due Process Clauses of the Fifth and Fourteenth Amendments, the source for various unenumerated rights that have been recognized by the Supreme Court over the years, including the right to privacy,[585] the right to an abortion,[586] and the right to marry.[587] As several commentators have noted, Judge Garland has never heard a case interpreting the propriety of an abortion regulation in his tenure on the D.C. Circuit.[588] In the few cases that have raised substantive due process issues in which the nominee has participated, Judge Garland's votes suggest an arguably moderate view of the scope of the doctrine. For example, in *Abigail Alliance for Better Access to Developmental Drugs v. Von Eschenbach*, he voted with the majority in an 8-2 en banc decision, reversing a panel decision and holding that the Due Process Clause does not include a substantive right for the terminally ill to access experimental drugs.[589] Moreover, in keeping with his writings prior to joining the D.C. Circuit wherein he voiced deep skepticism at the *Lochner* era[590] view that the Due Process Clauses protect economic liberties, such as freedom to contract,[591] Judge Garland joined a majority opinion that accorded the economic legislation in question—the Coal Industry Retiree Health Benefit Act of 1992—a "presumption of constitutionality."[592] Further, the majority opinion concluded that the presumption could not be overcome because the legislation, which retroactively imposed liability on certain mining companies, was justified by a rational legislative purpose to remedy a health care funding crisis in the coal industry."[593]

Nonetheless, in contrast to Justice Scalia, who openly questioned the substantive due process doctrine and criticized cases like *Roe v. Wade*,[594] Judge Garland does not appear to have rejected the concept wholly. He did not, for example, join Judge Laurence Silberman's concurrence in *Lightfoot v. District of Columbia*, in which the senior circuit judge described the doctrine of substantive due process as an "invention" of the Supreme Court with "unstable boundaries."[595] Potentially more telling, Judge Garland joined the panel opinion in *Butera v. District of Columbia*, a 2001 case which recognized that the substantive component of the Due Process Clauses can, in certain circumstances, impose affirmative duties to act on state officials when the officials create dangerous situations or render citizens more vulnerable to harm;[596] a rule creating an exception to the long-standing principle that the "Due Process Clauses generally confer no affirmative right to governmental aid, even where such aid may be necessary to secure life, liberty, or property interests...."[597] Moreover, in *Hutchins v. District of Columbia*, an en banc decision of the D.C. Circuit upholding the District of Columbia's juvenile curfew law,[598] Judge Garland, while voting to uphold the law and declining to strike the law down on due process grounds, did not join a key section of Judge Silberman's majority opinion.[599] In that section, Judge Silberman argued that judicial examinations of due process rights need to begin with a "careful description of the asserted right"[600]—a reference to a 1988 opinion by Justice Scalia which asserted that due process rights must be viewed narrowly by the courts in terms of the "most specific level at which a relevant tradition protecting, or denying protection to, the asserted right can be identified"[601]—and concluded that "juveniles do not have a fundamental right to be on the streets at night without adult supervision."[602] Instead, Judge Garland, joined by Judge Patricia Wald, concurred only in the ultimate result reached by Judge Silberman, arguing that while the curfew law implicated the "constitutional rights of children and their parents," the law passed "intermediate constitutional scrutiny."[603] In this sense, while very little is known about how Judge Garland might approach particular issues respecting substantive due process rights, like the right to an abortion, the nominee seems to have a broader view of the doctrine than the man whom he could succeed on the Court.

TAKINGS

Relative to Justice Scalia, who, during his tenure on the Supreme Court, authored and joined several opinions that can be interpreted as strengthening the protection of privateoperty rights afforded by the Takings Clause of the Fifth Amendment of the U.S. Constitution,[604] prJudge Garland has said little on the subject and adjudicated very few cases raising takings issues.[605] This is unsurprising, as the D.C. Circuit does not hear many takings claims since the Tucker Act vests the U.S. Court of Federal Claims (CFC) with jurisdiction over such claims when the plaintiff seeks more than $10,000 in compensation from the federal government.[606] With limited exceptions,[607] the CFC's jurisdiction over such claims is exclusive,[608] and appeals from the CFC are to the U.S. Court of Appeals for the Federal Circuit, not the D.C. Circuit.[609] While the Fifth Amendment has been construed to apply to states and localities, such as the District of Columbia,[610] there are few takings cases that have arisen against the District during Judge Garland's time on the court,[611] and none in which he has participated. As a result, there is an insufficient basis to predict with confidence Judge Garland's views regarding the extent to which the Takings Clause protects private property rights.

APPENDIX. JUDGE GARLAND AND THE D.C. CIRCUIT

Table A-1. Judges Who Have Served with Judge Garland on the D.C. Circuit Judges Listed Alphabetically by Their Last Names

Name	Years with Garland	Nominating President	Prior Position	Key Cases Noted in the Report Involving Judge Garland and One or More Colleagues
Janice Rogers Brown	11	George W. Bush	Associate justice, Supreme Court of California	Sissel v. U.S. Dep't of Health & Human Servs., 799 F.3d 1035 (D.C. Cir. 2015); United States v. Bigley, 786 F.3d 11 (D.C. Cir. 2015); Owner-Operator Indep. Drivers Ass'n, Inc. v. U.S. Dep't of Trans., 724 F.3d 230 (D.C. Cir. 2013); United States v. Askew, 529 F.3d 1119 (D.C. Cir. 2008) (en banc).
James Lane Buckley	19	Ronald W. Reagan	President, Radio Free Europe/Radio Liberty	n/a
Harry Thomas Edwards	19	Jimmy E. Carter	Chairman of the board, National Railroad Passenger Corporation	Fox v. Clinton, 684 F.3d 67 (D.C. Cir. 2012); United States v. Askew, 529 F.3d 1119 (D.C. Cir. 2008) (en banc); Levitan v. Ashcroft, 281 F.3d 1313 (D.C. Cir. 2002); United States v. Watson, 171 F.3d 695 (D. C. Cir. 1999).
Douglas Howard Ginsburg	19	Ronald W. Reagan	Assistant attorney general, Antitrust Division, U.S. DOJ	*In re* Johnson, 760 F.3d 66 (D.C. Cir. 2014); United States v. Askew, 529 F.3d 1119 (D.C. Cir. 2008) (en banc); Rancho Viejo LLC v. Norton, 323 F.3d 1062 (D.C. Cir. 2003).

Name	Years with Garland	Nominating President	Prior Position	Key Cases Noted in the Report Involving Judge Garland and One or More Colleagues
Thomas Beall Griffith	11	George W. Bush	General counsel, Brigham Young University	Sissel v. U.S. Dep't of Health & Human Servs., 799 F.3d 1035 (D.C. Cir. 2015); Hatim v. Obama, 760 F.3d 54 (D.C. Cir. 2014); Parhat v. Gates, 532 F.3d 834 (D.C. Cir. 2008); Boehner v. McDermott, 484 F.3d 573 (D.C. Cir. 2007).
Karen LeCraft Henderson	19	George H. W. Bush	Judge, U.S. District Court, District of South Carolina	Miss. Comm'n on Envtl. Quality v. EPA, 790 F.3d 138 (D.C. Cir. 2015); Sissel v. U.S. Dep't of Health & Human Servs., 799 F.3d 1035 (D.C. Cir. 2015); Al Bahlul v. United States, 767 F.3d 1 (D.C. Cir. 2014) (en banc); Trans Union, LLC v. FTC, 295 F.3d 42 (D.C. Cir. 2002); Levitan v. Ashcroft, 281 F.3d 1313 (D.C. Cir. 2002); Henderson v. Kennedy, 253 F.3d 12 (D.C. Cir. 2001); United States *ex rel.* Yesudian v. Howard Univ., 153 F.3d. 731 (D.C. Cir. 1998); Americable Int'l v. Dep't of Navy, 129 F.3d 1271 (D.C. Cir. 1997).
Brett Michael Kavanaugh	10	George W. Bush	Assistant to the President and staff secretary, George W. Bush	Sissel v. U.S. Dep't of Health & Human Servs., 799 F.3d 1035 (D.C. Cir. 2015); White Stallion Energy Ctr., LLC v. EPA, 748 F.3d 1222 (D.C. Cir. 2014) (per curiam); Util. Air Regulatory Grp.

Table A-1. (Continued)

Name	Years with Garland	Nominating President	Prior Position	Key Cases Noted in the Report Involving Judge Garland and One or More Colleagues
				(UARG) v. EPA, 744 F.3d 741 (D.C. Cir. 2014); *In re* Aiken Cty., 725 F.3d 255 (D.C. Cir. 2013); United States v. Burwell, 690 F.3d 500 (2012) (en banc); Sierra Club v. Van Antwerp, 661 F.3d 1147 (D.C. Cir. 2011); Am. Bird Conservancy, Inc. v. FCC, 516 F.3d 1027 (D.C. Cir. 2008) (per curiam); United States v. Askew, 529 F.3d 1119 (D.C. Cir. 2008) (en banc).
Patricia Ann Millett	2	Barack H. Obama	Private practitioner	People for the Ethical Treatment of Animals (PETA) v. Dep't of Agric. (USDA), 797 F.3d 1087 (D.C. Cir. 2015)
Cornelia Thayer Livingston Pillard	2	Barack H. Obama	Professor, Georgetown University Law Center	Sissel v. U.S. Dep't of Health & Human Servs., 799 F.3d 1035 (D.C. Cir. 2015).
Arthur Raymond Randolph	19	George H. W. Bush	Special assistant attorney general	Boehner v. McDermott, 484 F.3d 573 (D.C. Cir. 2007); Henderson v. Kennedy, 253 F.3d 12 (D.C. Cir. 2001).
John Glover Roberts Jr.	2	George W. Bush	Private practitioner (currently Chief Justice of the Supreme Court)	United States *ex rel.* Totten v. Bombardier Corp., 380 F.3d 488 (D.C. Cir. 2004; Barbour v. Washington Metropolitan Transit Authority (WMATA), 374 F.3d 1161 (D.C. Cir. 2004);

Name	Years with Garland	Nominating President	Prior Position	Key Cases Noted in the Report Involving Judge Garland and One or More Colleagues
				Rancho Viejo LLC v. Norton, 323 F.3d 1062 (D.C. Cir. 2003).
Spottswood William Robinson III	1	Lyndon B. Johnson	Judge, U.S. District Court for the District of Columbia	n/a
Judith Ann Wilson Rogers	19	William J. Clinton	Chief Judge, District of Columbia Court of Appeals	Sissel v. U.S. Dep't of Health & Human Servs., 799 F.3d 1035 (D.C. Cir. 2015); Al Bahlul v. United States, 767 F.3d 1 (D.C. Cir. 2014) (en banc).
David Bryan Sentelle	19	Ronald W. Reagan	Judge, U.S. District Court, Western District of North Carolina	Owner-Operator Indep. Drivers Ass'n, Inc. v. U.S. Dep't of Trans., 724 F.3d 230 (D.C. Cir. 2013); Al- Bihani v. Obama, 619 F.3d 1 (D.C. 2010) (denying reh'ing en banc); Parhat v. Gates, 532 F.3d 834 (D.C. Cir. 2008); United States v. Askew, 529 F.3d 1119 (D.C. Cir. 2008) (en banc); Boehner v. McDermott, 484 F.3d 573 (D.C. Cir. 2007) (en banc); Barbour v. WMATA, 374 F.3d 1161 (D.C. Cir. 2004); Rancho Viejo, LLC v. Norton, 334 F.3d 1158 (D.C. Cir. 2003) (denying reh'ing en banc); Sec'y of Labor v. Excel Mining, LLC, 334 F.3d 1 (D.C. Cir. 2003); Navegar, Inc. v. United States, 200 F.3d 868 (D.C. Cir. 2000);

Table A-1. (Continued)

Name	Years with Garland	Nominating President	Prior Position	Key Cases Noted in the Report Involving Judge Garland and One or More Colleagues
				Nat'l Rifle Ass'n of Am., Inc. v. Reno, 216 F.3d 122 (D.C. Cir. 2000); *In re* Sealed Case No. 97-312, 181 F.3d 128, 144 (D.C. Cir. 1999).
Laurence Hirsch Silberman	19	Ronald W. Reagan	Senior fellow, American Enterprise Institute; private practitioner	Hutchins v. District of Columbia, 188 F.3d 531 (D.C. Cir. 1999).
Padmanabhan Srikanth "Sri" Srinivasan	3	Barack H. Obama	Principal deputy solicitor general, U.S. DOJ	Miss. Comm'n on Envtl. Quality v. EPA, 790 F.3d 138 (D.C. Cir. 2015).
David S. Tatel	19	William J. Clinton	William J. Clinton	United States v. Burwell, 690 F.3d 500 (D.C. Cir. 2012) (en banc); United States v. Askew, 529 F.3d 1119 (D.C. Cir. 2008) (en banc); Nat'l Rifle Ass'n of Am., Inc. v. Reno, 216 F.3d 122 (D.C. Cir. 2000); Am. Trucking Ass'ns, Inc. v. EPA, 195 F.3d 4 (D.C. Cir. 1999) (denial of reh'ing en banc); Kolstad v. Am. Dental Ass'n, 139 F.3d 958 (D.C. Cir. 1998) (en banc).
Patricia McGowan Wald	2	Jimmy E. Carter	Assistant Attorney General for Legislative Affairs, U.S. DOJ	Hutchins v. District of Columbia, 188 F.3d 531 (D.C. Cir. 1999).

Name	Years with Garland	Nominating President	Prior Position	Key Cases Noted in the Report Involving Judge Garland and One or More Colleagues
Robert Leon Wilkins	2	Barack H. Obama	Judge, U.S. District Court for the District of Columbia	Sissel v. U.S. Dep't of Health & Human Servs., 799 F.3d 1035 (D.C. Cir. 2015).
Stephen Fain Williams	19	Ronald W. Reagan	Professor of law, University of Colorado	Fox v. Clinton, 684 F.3d 67 (D.C. Cir. 2012); Navab-Safavi v. Glassman, 637 F.3d 311 (D.C. Cir. 2011).

Source: Congressional Research Service, based on information from the Federal Judicial Center database, available at http://www.fjc.gov/history/home.nsf/page/judges.html.

End Notes

[1] *See, e.g., Transcript: Obama Announces Nomination of Merrick Garland to Supreme Court*, WASH. POST (March 16, 2016), https://www.washingtonpost.com/news/post-politics/wp/2016/03/16/transcript-obama-announces-nominationof-merrick-garland-to-supreme-court/. *See also* CRS Legal Sidebar WSLG1518, *Merrick Garland's Nomination to the Supreme Court: Initial Observations*, by Andrew Nolan.

[2] *See Garland, Merrick B.,* FED. JUDICIAL CTR., http://www.fjc.gov/servlet/nGetInfo?jid=820 (last visited April 15, 2016) [hereinafter "FJC Garland"]. Judge Garland was initially nominated to the D.C. Circuit in 1995, but the Senate did not vote on that nomination. *Id.*

[3] *Id.*

[4] *See* U.S. COURT OF APPEALS FOR THE D.C. CIRCUIT, HANDBOOK OF PRACTICE AND INTERNAL PROCEDURES, UNITED STATES COURT FOR THE DISTRICT OF COLUMBIA CIRCUIT, AS AMENDED THROUGH MARCH 1, 2016, 2, https://www.cadc.uscourts.gov/internet/home.nsf/Content/VL%20-%20RPP%20-%20Handbook%202006%20Rev%202007/$FILE/HandbookMarch2016Final.pdf (last visited April 20, 2016).

[5] *See, e.g., Confirmation Hearings on Federal Appointments: Hearings before the Committee on the Judiciary, United States Senate, Part 2*, 104th Congress, 1st sess., 1058 (1995).

[6] FJC Garland, *supra* note 2.

[7] *See, e.g.*, David M. Herszenhorn, *Senator Grassley and Judge Garland Meet, and Rehash the Obvious*, N.Y. TIMES (April 12, 2016), http://www.nytimes.com/2016/04/13/us/politics/senator-chuck-grassley-merrick-garland-meet.html? _r=0; Todd Ruger, *Grassley: I Haven't Changed My Mind on Garland Hearings*, ROLL CALL (April 7, 2016), http://www.rollcall.com/news/home/grassley-havent-changed-mind-garland-hearings.

[8] *See* S. COMM. ON RULES AND ADMIN., STANDING RULES OF THE SENATE, S. Doc. No. 113-18 (2013) (Rule XXXI), https://www.gpo.gov/fdsys/pkg/CDOC-113sdoc18/html/CDOC-113sdoc18.htm; CRS Report RL31980, *Senate Consideration of Presidential Nominations: Committee and Floor Procedure*, by Elizabeth Rybicki.

[9] These areas are noted in CRS Report R44419, *Justice Antonin Scalia: His Jurisprudence and His Impact on the Court*, coordinated by Kate M. Manuel, Brandon J. Murrill, and Andrew Nolan [hereinafter referred to as the "CRS Scalia report"].

[10] *See* 28 U.S.C. §2284(a) ("A district court of three judges shall be convened when otherwise required by Act of Congress, or when an action is filed challenging the constitutionality of the apportionment of congressional districts or the apportionment of any statewide legislative body.").

[11] *See, e.g.*, *Confirmation Hearings on Federal Appointments*, *supra* note 5, at 1109 (listing Judge Garland's publications prior to joining the D.C. Circuit).

[12] *See* Jonathan H. Adler, *What Happened When Merrick Garland Wrote for Himself*, VOLOKH CONSPIRACY (March 21, 2016), https://www.washingtonpost.com/news/volokh-conspiracy/wp/2016/03/21/what-happened-when-merrickgarland-wrote-for-himself/ ("The best way to get a handle on a circuit judge's judicial philosophy is to look at the judge's concurrences and dissents.").

[13] Christine Kexel Chabot & Benjamin Remy Chabot, *Mavericks, Moderates, or Drifters? Supreme Court Voting Alignments, 1838-2009*, 76 MO. L. REV. 999, 1040 (2011) ("[U]ncertainty is empirically well-founded. It is borne out by Justices' overall voting records since at least 1838. The president's odds of appointing a Justice who sides with appointees of his party have been no better than a coin flip."); *id.* at 1021 (listing Justices Brennan, Clark, Frankfurter, Holmes, McLean, McReynolds, Reed, Souter, Stevens, Warren, and Wayne as examples of jurists who "disappointed" the expectations of the President who appointed them to the Court); *see also The Judicial Nomination and Confirmation Process: Hearings Before the Subcommittee on Administrative Oversight & the Courts, Senate Committee on the Judiciary*, 107th Cong., 1st sess., 195 (2001) (statement of Douglas W. Kmiec, Dean & St. Thomas More Professor of Law, The Catholic University of America) ("Nominee selection—as a matter of fact—is seldom sufficient to predict accurately the philosophical direction of a particular judicial candidate, once appointed to a lifetime job with no salary diminution. Eisenhower had his Earl Warren; Nixon had his Blackmun; Bush had his Souter. In each case, it is either popularly speculated or actually articulated that the nominee's service was at some considerable variance to the philosophy of the nominating president. A recent study for the LBJ Journal of Public Affairs estimates that one Justice in four disappointed his appointing president.").

[14] *See* Joseph L. Rauh, Jr., *An Unabashed Liberal Looks at a Half-Century of the Supreme Court*, 69 N.C. L. REV. 213, 220 (1990) ("When Frankfurter took his seat on the Supreme Court in January 1939, almost everyone assumed that he would become the dominant spirit and intellectual leader of the new liberal Court. After all, he had been, in the words of Brandeis, 'the most useful lawyer in the United States': defender of Tom Mooney, the alien victims of the Palmer Red Raids, the striking miners of Bisbee, Arizona, Sacco and Vanzetti, and too many others to mention."); JAMES F. SIMON, THE ANTAGONISTS: HUGO BLACK, FELIX FRANKFURTER AND CIVIL LIBERTIES IN MODERN AMERICA 13-16, 46-47 (1989) (noting fears in some political circles that Frankfurter was a Communist or Communist sympathizer, "inspir[ing] American conservatives to label Frankfurter a dangerous radical"); *see generally* NOAH FELDMAN, SCORPIONS: THE BATTLES AND TRIUMPHS OF FDR'S GREAT SUPREME COURT JUSTICES 14, 21-27 (2010).

[15] *See, e.g.*, Rauh, *supra* note 14, at 220 ("But ... a deep belief in judicial restraint in all matters overtook even [Frankfurter's] lifelong dedication to civil liberties.").

[16] *See, e.g.*, W. Va. State Bd. of Educ. v. Barnette, 319 U.S. 624, 646 (1943) (Frankfurter, J., dissenting) (arguing for the constitutionality of a World War II-era law requiring students to

salute the flag); Korematsu v. United States, 323 U.S. 214, 225 (1944) (Frankfurter, J., concurring) (contending that the propriety of the Japanese-American civilian exclusion order was the "business" of Congress and the Executive, not the Court).

[17] *See, e.g.*, Dennis v. United States, 341 U.S. 494, 556 (1951) (Frankfurter, J., concurring) (upholding the conviction of three defendants under the Smith Act for conspiracy to organize the Communist Party as a group advocating the overthrow of the U.S. government by force).

[18] *See Blackmun, Harry Andrew,* FED. JUDICIAL CTR., http://www.fjc.gov/servlet/nGetInfo?jid=187&cid=0&ctype=sc& instate=na (last visited April 15, 2016).

[19] *See* BOB WOODWARD & SCOTT ARMSTRONG, THE BRETHREN: INSIDE THE SUPREME COURT 97 (1979) ("Nixon found Blackmun's moderate conservatism perfect.... [Blackmun] had a ... predictable, solid body of opinions that demonstrated a levelheaded, strict-constructionist philosophy.... Blackmun was a decent man, consistent, wedded to routine, unlikely to venture far.").

[20] *See generally* 410 U.S. 113 (1973) (Blackmun, J.).

[21] *See* LINDA GREENHOUSE, BECOMING JUSTICE BLACKMUN 235 (2005) (noting that, by 1994, "Harry Blackmun was, by wide consensus, the most liberal member of the Supreme Court").

[22] Judge Garland has served for nearly 20 years on the D.C. Circuit. *See* FJC Garland, *supra* note 2. By comparison, of the current members of the Supreme Court, Justice Alito had served the longest on the federal court of appeals—16 years—prior to being elevated to the High Court. *See Alito, Samuel A., Jr.*, FED. JUDICIAL CTR., http://www.fjc.gov/servlet/nGetInfo?jid=26 (last visited April 15, 2016).

[23] *See* Brewster v. Comm'r of Internal Revenue, 607 F.2d 1369, 1373-74 (D.C. Cir. 1979) (explaining that future panels are bound to follow precedent set by previous panels until the en banc court or Supreme Court overrules that precedent); *see generally* Tuan Samahon, *The Judicial Vesting Option: Opting Out of Nomination and Advice and Consent*, 67 OHIO ST. L.J. 783, 816 n.160 (2006) ("Vertical stare decisis binds hierarchically inferior federal appellate judges to follow the Supreme Court's on-point precedent. The relationship is vertical, or between inferior and superior. Horizontal stare decisis merely constrains justices to follow their own precedent—decisions made by their co-equal predecessors—until a five-vote majority decides to overrule it. Once there are five votes to overrule, it merely becomes a matter of prudence whether the Court will revise what was once established precedent.").

[24] *See* HON. RICHARD A. POSNER, THE FEDERAL COURTS: CHALLENGE AND REFORM 367 (2009) ("Supreme Court decisions bind the courts of appeals in a way in which they do not bind the Court itself, and therefore narrow considerably the scope for those courts to exercise choice."); *see also* DAVID ALISTAIR YALOF, PURSUIT OF JUSTICES: PRESIDENTIAL POLITICS AND THE SELECTION OF SUPREME COURT NOMINEES 171 (1999) (noting that the nature of a judge's work on a federal appellate court allows "most circuit judges [to] chart a course of moderation" and "more often than not, a circuit judge's opinions tend to betray outsiders' perceptions of that judge as a sharp ideological extremist").

[25] Louis J. Sirico, Jr., *The Citing of Law Reviews by the United States Courts of Appeals: An Empirical Analysis*, 45 U. MIAMI L. REV. 1051, 1052 n.8 (1991); *see generally* POSNER, *supra* note 24, at 367 (2009) (observing that "more of the work of [the federal appellate] courts really is technical.... Most of the appeals they get can be decided uncontroversially by the application of settled principles.").

[26] *See* FRANK B. CROSS, DECISION MAKING IN THE U.S. COURTS OF APPEALS 160 (2007) (noting the "relative paucity of circuit court panel dissents").

[27] *See, e.g.*, Hon. Douglas H. Ginsburg, *Remarks Upon Receiving the Lifetime Service Award of the Georgetown Federalist Society Chapter Georgetown University Law Center, April 26, 2011*, 10 GEO. J.L. & PUB. POL'Y 1, 7 (2012) (noting that in 2010, panels of the D.C. Circuit "disposed of 873 cases, 191 of them with published opinions, but our nine active and four senior judges ... issued a total of only nineteen dissenting opinions"); *see also* Hon. Douglas H. Ginsburg & Brian M. Boynton, *The Court En Banc: 1991-2002*, 70 GEO. WASH. L. REV. 259, 265 (2002) (noting that, from FY1995 through FY2001, a dissent was filed in only 9% of published decisions of the D.C. Circuit).

[28] *See* YALOF, *supra* note 24, at 170 ("Although hardly dispositive, federal appellate opinions offer perhaps the best gauge available for predicting an individual's future voting behavior on the Supreme Court.").

[29] *See* Bert I. Huang & Tejas N. Narechania, *Judicial Priorities*, 163 U. PA. L. REV. 1719, 1754-55 (2015) (suggesting that the "presence of a concurrence or dissent serves as a signal" that the case before the court is a "hard case"); *see generally* Hon. Patricia M. Wald, *The Rhetoric of Results and the Results of Rhetoric: Judicial Writings*, 62 U. CHI. L. REV. 1371, 1412-15 (1995) (noting the motivations that prompt judges to write concurring or dissenting opinions); Hon. Diane P. Wood, *When to Hold, When to Fold, When to Reshuffle: The Art of Decisionmaking on a Multi-Member Court*, 100 CAL. L. REV. 1445, 1451-57 (2012) (describing the considerations that prompt judges to publish separate opinions).

[30] *See* Hon. Ruth Bader Ginsburg, as quoted in Irin Carmon, *Opinion, Justice Ginsburg's Cautious Radicalism*, N.Y. TIMES (October 24, 2015), http://www.nytimes.com/2015/10/25/opinion/sunday/justice-ginsburgs-cautiousradicalism.html (noting that "an opinion of the court very often reflects views that are not 100 percent what the opinion author would do, were she writing for herself").

[31] *See* Sanford Levinson, *Trash Talk at the Supreme Court: Reflections on David Pozen's Constitutional Good Faith*, 129 HARV. L. REV. F. 166, 174 (2016) (declaring the assumption that "all adjudicators are splendidly isolated" to be "foolish," and arguing that it may be "incumbent" upon judges to engage in "intellectual compromise[s]" "to serve the public weal"); *see, e.g.*, Gerald W. Heaney, *Judge Martin Donald Van Oosterhout: The Big Judge from Orange City, Iowa*, 79 IOWA L. REV. 1, 16 (1993) (discussing former Eighth Circuit Judge Van Oosterhout's judicial philosophy).

[32] *See* Steven D. Smith, *Lessons from Lincoln: A Comment on Levinson*, 38 PEPP. L. REV. 915, 924 (2011).

[33] *Cf.* Mathes v. Comm'r of Internal Revenue, 788 F.2d 33, 35 (D.C. Cir. 1986) (noting that the "substantive merits of a claim" are irrelevant when a claim is prosecuted in an untimely manner).

[34] *See, e.g.*, Priests for Life v. Dep't of Health & Human Servs. (HHS), 808 F.3d 1 (D.C. Cir. 2015) (voting to deny a petition for en banc hearing in a matter arising under the Religious Freedom Restoration Act); Parker v. District of Columbia, No. 04-7041, 2007 U.S. App. LEXIS 11029 (D.C. Cir. May 8, 2007) (dissenting from a vote denying a petition for rehearing en banc in a Second Amendment case). For further discussion of these votes, see *infra* "Freedom of Religion" and "Right to Bear Arms," respectively.

[35] *See* Hon. Patricia M. Wald, *The Problem with the Courts: Black-Robed Bureaucracy, or Collegiality Under Challenge?*, 42 MD. L. REV. 766, 784 (1983) (noting that "[s]ome judges vote routinely for rehearings en banc on all cases with which they disagree...."); *see*

also Hon. Antonin Scalia, *Submitted Testimony to the Commission on Structural Alternatives for the Federal Courts of Appeals* 1 (August 21, 1998), http://www.library.unt.edu/gpo/csafca/ hearings/submitted/pdf/Scalia1.pdf ("[T]he function of en banc hearings ... is not only to eliminate intra-circuit conflicts, but also to correct and deter panel opinions that are pretty clearly wrong.").

[36] *See* United States v. Weitzenhoff, 35 F.3d 1275, 1293 (9th Cir. 1993) (Kleinfeld, J., dissenting from denial of reh'ing en banc); *see also* Bartlett v. Bowen, 824 F.2d 1240, 1244 (D.C. Cir. 1987) (Edwards, J., concurring in the denial of reh'ing en banc) ("By declining to rehear a case, 'we do not sit in judgment on the panel; we do not sanction the result it reached'.... We decide merely that ... review by the full court is not justified."). This more limited view of the nature of a vote for or against a rehearing aligns with the plain text of the Federal Rules of Appellate Procedure, which state that an en banc hearing is "not favored and ordinarily will not be ordered" unless en banc consideration is necessary to "secure or maintain" the uniformity of a court's decisions, or the proceeding involves a question of "exceptional importance." *See* FED. R. APP. P. 35(a).

[37] *See* Mitts v. Bagley, 626 F.3d 366, 370 (6th Cir. 2010) (Sutton, J., concurring in the reh'ing en banc) ("No one thinks a vote against rehearing en banc is an endorsement of a panel decision....").

[38] See CRS Legal Sidebar WSLG533, *Why is the D.C. Circuit "So" Important?*, by Andrew Nolan.

[39] *See* Hon. Brett M. Kavanaugh, *The Courts and the Administrative State,* 64 CASE W. RES. L. REV. 711, 715 (2014) ("[T]he bread and butter of our docket, is our administrative law docket. What I mean by that is determining in a particular case whether an administrative agency, like the EPA, the NLRB, or the FCC, exceeded statutory limits on their authority or violated a statutory prohibition on what they can do. These are the cases that come up to our court constantly. We see very complicated administrative records, and we adjudicate very complex statutes."); *see also* Hon. Harry T. Edwards, *A Conversation with Judge Harry T. Edwards*, 16 WASH. U. J.L. & POL'Y 61, 64 (2004) ("The D.C. Circuit docket largely consists of very dense administrative law cases in appeals that often include huge records and numerous parties with their numerous briefs."); Eric M. Fraser et al., *The Jurisdiction of the D.C. Circuit,* 23 CORNELL J.L. & PUB. POL'Y 131, 152 (2013) ("The modern D.C. Circuit hears a disproportionate share of administrative petitions and other cases involving the federal government....").

[40] *See* Jason J. Czarnezki, *An Empirical Investigation of Judicial Decisionmaking, Statutory Interpretation, and the* Chevron *Doctrine in Environmental Law*, 79 U. COLO. L. REV. 767, 790 (2008) (noting that, in a data set of 347 judicial votes cast in the federal courts of appeals from 2003 to 2005 on environmental law matters, "cases involving environmental statute interpretation tend to occur in the D.C. Circuit"); Hon. Patricia M. Wald, *Regulation at Risk: Are Courts Part of the Solution or Most of the Problem?*, 67 S. CAL. L. REV. 621, 623, 633 (1994) (stating that the D.C. Circuit has decided a number of significant environmental law cases).

[41] *See* David G. Savage, *Supreme Court Nominee Merrick Garland Has a Record of Restraint, Not Activism*, L.A. TIMES, (March 18, 2016), http://www.latimes.com/nation/la-na-garland-legal-analysis-20160318-story.html.

[42] *See generally* CRS Scalia report, *supra* note 9, at 2-4.

[43] *See, e.g.*, Hon. Antonin Scalia, *Originalism: The Lesser Evil*, 57 U. CIN. L. REV. 849 (1989) (an address delivered on September 16, 1988, at the University of Cincinnati as the William Howard Taft Constitutional Law Lecture); Hon. Antonin Scalia, *Common-Law Courts in a*

Civil-Law System: The Role of United States Federal Courts in Interpreting the Constitution and Laws, in A MATTER OF INTERPRETATION: FEDERAL COURTS AND THE LAW 3-47 (Amy Gutmann ed., 1997) (containing Justice Scalia's Tanner Lectures on Human Values delivered at Princeton University on March 8 and 9, 1995).

[44] *See, e.g.*, Obergefell v. Hodges, --- U.S. ---, 135 S. Ct. 2584, 2629 (2015) (Scalia, J., dissenting); King v. Burwell, --- U.S. ---, 135 S. Ct. 2480, 2496 (2015) (Scalia, J., dissenting).

[45] Judge Garland was initially nominated by President Clinton to serve on the D.C. Circuit in 1995. *See* FJC Garland, *supra* note 2. No vote was ever taken on his nomination then, and he was subsequently renominated in 1997 and confirmed to his current office soon after. *Id.*

[46] *See Confirmation Hearings on Federal Appointments*, *supra* note 5, at 1128 (submission of Senate Judiciary Committee Questionnaire for Judicial Nominees for Merrick Brian Garland).

[47] *See* Hon. Merrick B. Garland, *Remarks by the President Announcing Judge Merrick Garland as His Nominee to the Supreme Court* (March 16, 2016), https://www.whitehouse.gov/the-press-office/2016/03/16/remarks-presidentannouncing-judge-merrick-garland-his-nominee-supreme ("People must be confident that a judge's decisions are determined by the law, and only the law. For a judge to be worthy of such trust, he or she must be faithful to the Constitution and to the statutes passed by the Congress. He or she must put aside his personal views or preferences, and follow the law—not make it.").

[48] 1 Cranch (5 U.S.) 137 (1803).

[49] *See Confirmation Hearings on Federal Appointments*, *supra* note 5, at 1064 (submission of Senate Judiciary Committee Questionnaire for Judicial Nominees for Merrick Brian Garland). As one commentator has noted, to the extent that Judge Garland's opinions on the court can be seen to reflect the judges whom he admires, he cites most often to Judge Harry Edwards, followed by Justice William Rehnquist and Judge David Sentelle. *See What Data Science Tells Us About Merrick Garland*, RAVEL LAW'S BLOG (March 17, 2016), http://blog.ravellaw.com/what-datascience-tells-us-about-merrick-garland.

[50] *See Independence of Federal Prosecutors: A Panel Discussion at the Federalist Society 2007 National Lawyers Convention*, 7 AVE MARIA L. REV. 207 (2008) (moderator).

[51] See (In)effective Assistance of Counsel for Criminal Defendants: Constitutional Standards and Practical Solutions: A Panel Discussion at the 2008 American Constitution Society Convention (June 13, 2008), http://acslaw.org/pdf/ ACS%20National%20Convention%20 Schedule.pdf.

[52] *See Changing the Federal Rules of Civil Procedure: Has the Time Come?: Litigation Practice Group for the Federalist Society* (December 9, 2010), http://www.fed-soc.org/multimedia/detail/changing-the-federal-rules-of-civilprocedure-has-the-time-come-event-audiovideo (moderator).

[53] *See* Adams v. Clinton, 90 F. Supp. 2d 35 (D.D.C. 2000) (three-judge panel). *Adams* was a 2-1 decision with Judge Garland and Judge Colleen Kollar-Kotelly of the D.C. district court joining the per curiam opinion and Judge Louis Oberdorfer of the D.C. district court dissenting.

[54] *See, e.g., id.* at 50 ("We conclude from our analysis of the text that the Constitution does not contemplate that the District may serve as a state for purposes of the apportionment of congressional representatives.").

[55] *See, e.g., id.* at 50 n.25 (quoting from James Madison's notes from the federal convention in 1787).

[56] *See, e.g., id.* at 51 ("At the New York ratifying convention, for example, Thomas Tredwell argued that '[t]he plan of the federal city ... departs from every principle of freedom ... subjecting the inhabitants of that district to the exclusive legislation of Congress, in whose appointment they have no share or vote.'").

[57] *Id.* at 37 ("[W]e are constrained to agree with defendants that the remedies plaintiffs request are beyond this court's authority to grant.").

[58] *See id.* at 55-56 ("In sum, we conclude that constitutional text, history, and judicial precedent bar us from accepting plaintiffs' contention.")

[59] As a lower court judge, Judge Garland has, of course, relied on precedent from the Supreme Court and the D.C. Circuit as a necessary guide for his opinions. *See, e.g.*, United States v. Weathers, 186 F.3d 948, 957 n.12 (D.C. Cir. 1999) (Garland, J.) (noting that lower courts should "follow the case which directly controls, leaving to [the Supreme] Court the prerogative of overruling its own decisions.") (internal citations and quotations omitted).

[60] *See, e.g.*, Savage, *supra* note 41 (describing Judge Garland's record as being "cautious" and "centrist"); Karen Dunn, as quoted in Josh Gerstein, *Garland's Lack of Standout Opinions a Boon in Confirmation Fight*, POLITICO (March 16, 2016), http://www.politico.com/story/2016/03/merrick-garland-supreme-court-opinions-220902#ixzz45CGt5Vcb ("When he crafts opinions, he's just extremely meticulous.").

[61] *See* RAVEL'S LAW BLOG, *supra* note 49 (noting that *Trudeau* had been cited in nearly 500 other cases as of March 2016).

[62] 456 F.3d 178 (D.C. Cir. 2006).

[63] *Id.* at 180.

[64] On the question of whether the Administrative Procedure Act's (APA's) requirement of "final agency action" is jurisdictional, compare *Nulankeyutmonen Nkihtaqmikon v. Impson*, 503 F.3d 18, 33 (1st Cir. 2007) (holding that the APA's finality requirement is nonjurisdictional) with *Flue-Cured Tobacco Coop. Stabilization Corp. v. Envtl. Prot. Agency (EPA)*, 313 F.3d 852, 857 (4th Cir. 2002) (holding that, because the agency action being challenged did not constitute final agency action under Section 704 of the APA, the court lacked subject-matter jurisdiction). With regard to the question of whether the APA's waiver of sovereign immunity is contingent on the existence of final agency action, compare *Presbyterian Church (U.S.A.) v. United States*, 870 F.2d 518, 525-26 (9th Cir. 1989) (holding that the waiver of sovereign immunity provided in 5 U.S.C. §702 is not limited to "final agency actions" as defined in Section 704) with In re *Secs. & Exch. Comm'n (SEC)* ex rel. *Glotzer,* 374 F.3d 184, 190 (2d Cir. 2004) (holding that "the federal government, in enacting the APA, waived its immunity with respect to those 'action[s] in a court of the United States' which seek review of 'agency action'").

[65] *Trudeau*, 456 F.3d at 184 (holding that the APA's requirement of final agency action is not jurisdictional); *id.* at 187 (holding that the APA's waiver of sovereign immunity permits both a cause of action brought under that act as well as nonstatutory and constitutional claims).

[66] *Id.* at 191 (assuming without deciding that a press release by an agency constitutes final agency action under the APA).

[67] *Id.* at 189 (noting criticism of the holding of *Hearst Radio v. Fed. Commc'n Comm'n (FCC)*, 167 F.2d 225 (D.C. Cir. 1948), which concluded that agency publications do not constitute "agency action").

[68] *Id.* at 191.

[69] *See* Allan Smith, *Supreme Court Pick Merrick Garland's Most Cited Decision Involved an Informercial Star*, BUS. INSIDER (March 18, 2016), http://www.businessinsider.com/merrick-garland-infomercial-star-2016-3 (quoting Daniel Lewis of Revel Law).

[70] *See, e.g.*, Bismullah v. Gates, 514 F.3d 1291, 1298-99 (D.C. Cir. 2008) (Garland, J., concurring in the reh'ing en banc) (reserving judgment on the merits of the dispute and arguing that the D.C. Circuit should not grant en banc review in *Bismullah v. Gates*, a Guantanamo Bay detainee case, when the Supreme Court had already granted certiorari in *Boumediene v. Bush*, as en banc review would "plainly delay" the resolutions of the two cases by the D.C. Circuit and the Supreme Court); United States v. Linares, 367 F.3d 941, 953 (D.C. Cir. 2004) (Garland, J., concurring) (concluding that the appeal of a criminal defendant could have been resolved on harmless error grounds alone, and the majority of the court did not need to reach a "substantially more difficult question" respecting whether the admission of certain evidence violated the Federal Rules of Evidence); Citizens for Responsibility & Ethics in Wash. v. Fed. Election Comm'n (FEC), 475 F.3d 337, 341 (D.C. Cir. 2007) (Garland, J., concurring) (agreeing with the majority opinion on the sole ground that the instant case could not be distinguished from controlling circuit precedent); McDonnell Douglas Corp. v. Dep't of the Air Force, 375 F.3d 1182, 1194 (D.C. Cir. 2004) (Garland, J., dissenting) (arguing that the majority opinion unnecessarily "come[s] perilously close" to imposing a "per se rule that line-item prices [in a public contract] may never be revealed to the public"); Pub. Citizen Health Research Grp. v. Food & Drug Admin. (FDA), 185 F.3d 898, 907 (D.C. Cir. 1999) (Garland, J., concurring in judgment) (noting that while the "court exercises appropriate discretion in declining to decide" whether the Federal Food, Drug and Cosmetic Act's prohibition on the disclosure of certain trade secrets is "congruent with" Exemption 4 of the Freedom of Information Act, the court "errs ... in not exercising similar restraint with respect to an issue regarding the meaning of Exemption 4 itself").

[71] By comparison, Judge David Tatel, who has served on the D.C. Circuit for roughly as long as Judge Garland (Tatel was appointed in 1994, and Garland in 1997), has authored at least five opinions that have been reviewed by the Supreme Court. *See* Hoffman Plastic Compounds, Inc. v. Nat'l Labor Relations Bd., 237 F.3d 639 (D.C. Cir. 2001) (en banc), *rev'd*, 535 U.S. 137 (2002); NextWave Pers. Commc'ns, Inc. v. FCC, 254 F.3d 130 (D.C. Cir. 2001), *aff'd*, 537 U.S. 293 (2003); Omar v. Harvey, 479 F.3d 1 (D.C. Cir. 2007), *vacated sub nom.*, Munaf v. Geren, 553 U.S. 674 (2008); Nw. Austin Mun. Util. Dist. No. One v. Mukasey, 573 F. Supp. 2d 221 (D.D.C. 2008) (three-judge panel), *rev'd & remanded sub nom.*, Nw. Austin Mun. Util. Dist. No. One v. Holder, 557 U.S. 193 (2009); Shelby Cty. v. Holder, 679 F.3d 848 (D.C. Cir. 2012), *rev'd*, --- U.S. ---, 133 S. Ct. 2612 (2013).

[72] *See* Bert I. Huang & Tejas N. Narechania, *Judicial Priorities*, 163 U. PA. L. REV. 1719, 1756 n.129 (2015) ("Court observers routinely use reversal rates only among published opinions to measure the quality of a particular court.").

[73] *See* William M. Landes, Lawrence Lessig & Michael E. Solimine, *Judicial Influence: A Citation Analysis of Federal Courts of Appeals Judges*, 27 J. LEGAL STUD. 271, 325-26 (1998) (hypothesizing that the Supreme Court "rarely takes cases" from certain "top-ranked" federal appellate judges because these judges "get things 'right'"); Frank B. Cross & Stefanie Lindquist, *Judging the Judges*, 58 DUKE L.J. 1383, 1405 (2009) ("[The] Supreme Court selectively reviews the most important decisions rendered by circuit courts, making it reasonable to use these important decisions as a metric.... [T]o the degree that evaluation of circuit court judges is employed as a standard for Supreme Court appointments, it seems appropriate to consider the fate of their decisions at the Supreme Court level."); *cf.* Scalia, *Submitted Testimony*, *supra* note 35 (suggesting that the Supreme

Court's discretionary docket reflects, in part, cases where errors have occurred); *but see* Cross & Lindquist, *supra*, at 1405 (noting that the rate of Supreme Court review may not fully gauge the quality of a federal appellate judge's work, as "[m]any incorrect circuit court rulings may go unexamined by the Supreme Court, which is not a court of 'error correction'").

[74] *See* Table 1. Four of the decisions were affirmed by the Supreme Court; *Kolstad v. Am. Dental Ass'n*, 139 F.3d 958 (D.C. Cir. 1998), in which Judge Garland joined the dissent, was ultimately reversed by the Supreme Court, in a complicated result that could be interpreted in various ways regarding its take on the position of the dissenting judges in the D.C. Circuit. 527 U.S. 526 (1999). For more on *Kolstad*, see *infra* "*Civil Rights*."

[75] *See Stat Pack Archive*, SCOTUSblog, http://www.scotusblog.com/reference/stat-pack/ (last visited April 16, 2016) (indicating reversal rates of 72% for the October 2014 Term; 73% for the October 2013 Term; 72% for the October 2012 Term; 63% for the October 2011 Term; and 72% for the October 2010 Term).

[76] *See* Cross & Lindquist, *supra* note 73, at 1402-05 (discussing why the "success of judges' opinions before the Supreme Court ... is a legitimate factor to be considered" when evaluating circuit court judges); *cf.* Wendy E. Long, counsel to the Judicial Confirmation Network, as quoted in Keith Perine, CONG. Q. TODAY ONLINE NEWS (May 26, 2006), http://www.cq.com/doc/news-3125545?0 (arguing that the high rate at which then Judge Sonia Sotomayor had been reversed by the Supreme Court indicated that she was a "liberal activist"); *but see* Guy-Uriel Charles et al., *Sonia Sotomayor and the Construction of Merit*, 61 EMORY L.J. 801, 811 (2012) (arguing that "the rate at which the Supreme Court reverses a judge" is a poor metric to gauge judicial activism). Another means by which academics assess federal circuit judges has been the frequency with which a judge is cited by his peers. *See* Stephen J. Choi & G. Mitu Gulati, *Choosing the Next Supreme Court Justice: An Empirical Ranking of Judge Performance*, 78 S. CAL. L. REV. 23 (2004). In a 2004 study by Professors Choi and Gulati, Judge Garland ranked among the lowest-scoring judges in an assessment based, in part, on the number of times a federal judge was cited in other cases. *Id.* at 77. However, those assessing the Choi and Gulati study have suggested that the study may indicate how inclined a particular judge is toward "judicial entrepreneurship," with judges that "strive to make law" being more frequently cited. *See* Cross & Lindquist, *supra* note 73, at 1412. As a result, the findings regarding Judge Garland in the Choi and Gulati study could be seen to confirm the hypothesis that Judge Garland has a more cautious approach to judging than many other federal appellate judges.

[77] 793 F.3d 1 (D.C. Cir. 2015) (en banc).

[78] *Id.* at 3.

[79] *Id.* at 10-18.

[80] *Id.* at 22.

[81] *Id.* at 3.

[82] 475 F.3d 1319, 1333 (D.C. Cir. 2007) (Garland, J., dissenting).

[83] *Id.* at 1323 ("*Sun-Diamond's* interpretive gloss, like the rule of lenity, thus works to protect a citizen from punishment under a statute that gives at best dubious notice that it has criminalized his conduct.").

[84] *Id.* at 1330.

[85] *Id.* at 1346 (Garland, J., dissenting).

[86] *See* Adler, *supra* note 12.

[87] *See* Merrick B. Garland, *Antitrust and State Action: Economic Efficiency and the Political Process*, 96 YALE L.J. 486, 488 (1987).

[88] *See* Adler, *supra* note 12 (predicting that Judge Garland would be unlikely to follow Justice Scalia's formalist approach); *see generally* HON. RICHARD POSNER, HOW JUDGES THINK 30-31 (2010) (describing Justice Scalia as "our most prominent legalist judge," in contrast to those judges that may "trade off principle against effectiveness").

[89] *See, e.g.*, Jess Bravin & Brent Kendall, *For Supreme Court Nominee Merrick Garland, Law Prevails Over Ideology*, WALL STREET J. (March 16, 2016), http://www.wsj.com/articles/judge-garland-had-been-considered-for-seat-on-highcourt-before-1458138973 ("Judge Garland has been part of consensus rulings joined by judges appointed by both Democrats and Republicans."); Laurence H. Tribe, *From Judge to Justice: The Case for Merrick Garland*, BOSTON GLOBE (March 29, 2016), https://www.bostonglobe.com/opinion/2016/03/29/from-judge-justice-case-for-merrickgarland/gHBtdYos4vjZTUmtVDfsVL/story.html ("As chief judge of the D.C. Circuit, a court that has often witnessed bitter divisions, Garland has presided over a collegial court and gained universal respect among his colleagues, whatever their philosophical bent. And he has long been able to write opinions that win votes from judges with views quite different from his own.").

[90] While noted for his humor, outgoing personality, and friendships with persons who could be seen as his ideological opposites, *see* Nadine Strossen, *Tribute to Justice Antonin Scalia*, 62 N.Y.U. ANN. SURV. AM. L. 1, 9 (2006) ("Nino Scalia's warm and ebullient personality has won him many friends, across the ideological spectrum. To cite one prominent example, Ruth Bader Ginsburg refers to him as her closest friend on the Court...."), Justice Scalia's colleagues and legal scholars have noted that his approach at oral argument and sharp tone of his opinions, at times, were perceived to be counterproductive to persuading others to agree with him. *See, e.g.* Hon. Sandra Day O'Connor, as quoted in Joan Biskupic, SANDRA DAY O'CONNOR: HOW THE FIRST WOMAN ON THE SUPREME COURT BECAME ITS MOST INFLUENTIAL JUSTICE 277 (stating that with respect to Justice Scalia's criticism of her opinion, that it "probably isn't true" that "[s]ticks and stones will break my bones, but words will never hurt me"); *see generally* DAVID A. SCHULTZ & CHRISTOPHER E. SMITH, THE JURISPRUDENTIAL VISION OF JUSTICE ANTONIN SCALIA 99-100 (1996) (arguing that Scalia's approach to his colleagues at times "diminished his ability to persuade other justices to join in his opinions"); JEFFREY ROSEN, THE SUPREME COURT: THE PERSONALITIES AND RIVALRIES THAT DEFINED AMERICA 199-200 (2006) (arguing that Scalia's "relentless personal attacks on O'Connor and Kennedy dissuaded them from overturning *Roe v. Wade*"); William K. Kelley, *Justice Antonin Scalia and the Long Game,* 80 GEO. WASH. L. REV. 1601, 1602 (2012) ("It is fair to say ... that Justice Scalia's judicial style and sometimes caustic pen alienated some of his colleagues, particularly Justice Sandra Day O'Connor.... Justice Scalia famously characterized Justice O'Connor's separate opinion in *Webster v. Reproductive Health Services* as 'irrational' and not to be taken 'seriously'—and in the process was said to have fairly seriously alienated Justice O'Connor. Other Justices were also put off by Justice Scalia's style."); Tinsley E. Yarborough, THE REHNQUIST COURT AND THE CONSTITUTION 44 (2000) (quoting Justice O'Connor regarding Scalia's *Webster* opinion and noting that "O'Connor's alienation from Scalia probably worked to undermine further whatever influence he might otherwise have enjoyed among the justices"); *but see* Steven G. Calabresi & Justin Braga, *The Jurisprudence of Justice Antonin Scalia: A Response to Professor Bruce Allen Murphy and Professor Justin Driver*, 9 NYU J.L. & LIBERTY 793, 820 (2015) ("David Souter, like Sandra Day O'Connor and Anthony M. Kennedy, was not 'driven to the left' by Justice Scalia's dissents and his ebullient, joyful personality. Souter, O'Connor, and Kennedy were ALWAYS well to the left of Justice Scalia, and this fact was

widely known to many people at the time they were appointed."). Because Justices are "reluctant to reveal the inner workings of the Supreme Court, let alone reveal any interpersonal problems," the impact of Justice Scalia's personality and approach toward his colleagues "will never be known," *see* SCHULTZ & SMITH, *supra* at 101, and, as a result, this report's discussion of Justice Scalia's personality and temperament is focused on what can be demonstrated—Justice Scalia's ability to garner support among his colleagues on the Court for opinions that he wrote.

[91] *See, e.g.,* Obergefell v. Hodges, --- U.S. ---, 135 S. Ct. 2584, 2630 (2015) ("If, even as the price to be paid for a fifth vote, I ever joined an opinion for the Court that began: 'The Constitution promises liberty to all within its reach, a liberty that includes certain specific rights that allow persons, within a lawful realm, to define and express their identity,' I would hide my head in a bag. The Supreme Court of the United States has descended from the disciplined legal reasoning of John Marshall and Joseph Story to the mystical aphorisms of the fortune cookie."); Holland v. Illinois, 493 U.S. 474, 486 (1990) (Scalia, J.) ("Justice [Marshall's] dissent rolls out the ultimate weapon, the accusation of insensitivity to racial discrimination—which will lose its intimidating effect if it continues to be fired so randomly."); Webster v. Reprod. Health Servs., 492 U.S. 490, 532 (1989) (Scalia, J., concurring in part and concurring in the judgment) ("Justice [O'Connor's] assertion ... that a 'fundamental rule of judicial restraint' requires us to avoid reconsidering *Roe*, cannot be taken seriously").

[92] *See, e.g.,* Kerry v. Din, --- U.S. ---, 135 S. Ct. 2128, 2139 (2015) (Kennedy, J., concurring in the judgment) (declining to join Justice Scalia's opinion that held that a citizen does not have a protected liberty interest in the visa application of her alien spouse); Hudson v. Michigan, 547 U.S. 586, 602 (2006) (Kennedy, J., concurring in part and concurring in judgment) (declining to provide the fifth vote for a Justice Scalia's opinion openly questioning the continued viability of the exclusionary rule); Capitol Square Review & Advisory Bd. v. Pinette, 515 U.S. 753, 764 (1995) (Scalia, J.) (receiving only four votes for the proposition that "it is no violation [of the Establishment Clause] for government to enact neutral policies that happen to benefit religion"); Planned Parenthood v. Casey, 505 U.S. 833, 846 (1992) (joint opinion of Kennedy, O'Connor, & Souter, JJ.) (rejecting Justice Scalia's argument to overturn *Roe* entirely); Lujan v. Defenders of Wildlife, 504 U.S. 555, 580 (1992) (Kennedy, J., concurring) (declining to join part of Justice Scalia's opinion holding that an injury for purposes of Article III standing needed to equate with injuries found at common law); Harmelin v. Mich., 501 U.S. 957, 996 (1991) (Kennedy, J., concurring) (refusing to join Justice Scalia's opinion arguing that the Eighth Amendment contains no proportionality guarantee); Michael H. v. Gerald D., 491 U.S. 110, 127-128, n.6 (1989) (Scalia, J.) (delivering the opinion of the court except for footnote six which broadly argued that due process rights should be viewed with heightened specificity); *see generally* SCHULTZ & SMITH, *supra* note 90 at 99-100 (contending that Justice Scalia's "clear, fixed vision of how cases should be decided" may have prevented other Justices from joining his opinions).

[93] *See* Jeffrey Toobin, *Holding Court,* NEW YORKER (March 26, 2012), http://www.newyorker.com/magazine/2012/03/ 26/holding-court ("If a Republican ... wins in November, his most likely first nominee to the Supreme Court will be Brett Kavanaugh.").

[94] *See* Hon. Brett M. Kavanaugh, at *The Court: Power, Policy, and Self-Government,* AM. ENTER. INST. (March 31, 2016), http://www.aei.org/events/the-court-power-policy-and-self-government/.

[95] *See Merrick B. Garland*, 2 ALMANAC OF THE FED. JUDICIARY, 2016 WL 15131 ("Lawyers were unanimous in their praise of Garland's legal ability. 'His legal ability is the best.' 'He's very smart.' 'I have a high regard for him; he's very bright and very able.' 'His legal ability is extraordinary.' 'He has excellent legal ability.' 'His legal ability is superb.' 'He's a brilliant judge.' 'He's one of the great judges in the country; he's a spectacular judge.' 'He's very bright.' 'He's a very, very smart guy; he has very strong legal ability.' Garland is very courteous to litigants, lawyers interviewed said. 'His courtroom demeanor is excellent.' 'He's very nice.' 'He has an excellent temperament.' 'He's courteous to litigants.' 'It's very good; he's very even tempered.' 'He's a judge's judge.' 'It's pretty good, an A-minus.' 'He's no-nonsense.' 'He's very courteous.'").

[96] *See Garland Citation List of Dissenting Opinions*, CONG. RES. SERV., http://www.crs.gov/products/Documents/Garland%20Citation%20List%20of%20 Dissenting%20Opinions/pdf (listing 16 dissenting opinions for Judge Garland). By comparison, an April 2016 Lexis search indicates that Judge Kavanaugh, who has served on the D.C. Circuit since 2006, has authored 48 dissenting opinions, averaging nearly five dissents per year. Judge Tatel, who has served on the D.C. Circuit since 1994, has written 56 dissents in his tenure on the court, averaging around two and a half dissents per year.

[97] Lee Epstein, William M. Landes, & Hon. Richard A. Posner, *Why (and When) Judges Dissent: A Theoretical and Empirical Analysis*, 3 J. LEGAL ANALYSIS 101, 135 (2011) (arguing that the frequency with which a judge dissents may be a product of the costs of "impaired collegiality" versus the benefits of influencing or clarifying the law).

[98] An April 2016 Lexis search of Judge Garland's majority opinions on the D.C. Circuit indicate that in 21 out of 329 (6.4%), a concurrence or dissent was written in response to the majority. By comparison, an April 2016 Lexis search showed that Judge Kavanaugh, who has served on the D.C. Circuit since 2006, authored 36 majority opinions that prompted a concurrence or dissent out of approximately 162 majority opinions (22.2%). Judge Tatel, who has served on the D.C. Circuit since 1994, has written approximately 447 majority opinions of which 75 prompted a concurrence or dissent (16.8%).

[99] *See* Epstein, Jeffrey A. Segal & Harold J. Spaeth, *The Norm of Consensus on the U.S. Supreme Court*, 45 AM. J. POL. SCI. 362, 362, 364-65 (2001) (arguing that Justices, driven by a norm of suppressing dissent in order to preserve consensus, will write broad unanimous opinions).

[100] *See* Nina Totenberg, *Merrick Garland Has a Reputation of Collegiality, Record of Republican Support,* NAT'L PUB. RADIO (March 16, 2016), http://www.npr.org/2016/ 03/16/126614141/merrick-garland-has-a-reputation-of-collegialityrecord-of-republican-support ("But Garland also has been a persuasive voice for liberals, managing to bring conservatives over to his side on issues ranging from the environment to national security."); Jaime Gorelick, as quoted in Ed Shanahan, *Does D.C. Circuit Court Judge Merrick Garland Have Supreme Potential?,* AM. L. LITIG. DAILY (November 17, 2008), http://amlawdaily.typepad.com/amlawdaily/2008/11/the-am-law-li-9.html ("If you look at [Judge Garland's] opinion in the Uighur case, he brought along judges from very different parts of the political and judicial spectrum.... That is precisely what one would want on the Supreme Court.").

[101] *See supra* "Predicting Nominees' Future Decisions on the Court."

[102] As such, the fact that judges of differing ideologies might agree in *any* case is—in and of itself—unremarkable, , as the D.C. Circuit tends to issue unanimous opinions in many cases. *See supra* note 27 and accompanying text. What is notable is that Judge Garland has been able to author unanimous opinions in number of cases on often contentious matters

like the scope of Congress's power vis-á-vis the states, the rights of detainees at Guantanamo Bay, or the limits the First Amendment imposes on campaign finance restrictions.

[103] *See* Rancho Viejo LLC v. Norton, 323 F.3d 1062 (D.C. Cir. 2003).

[104] 532 F.3d 834 (D.C. Cir. 2008).

[105] *Parhat*, 532 F.3d at 836-37.

[106] *See* Thomas B. Colby & Peter J. Smith, *The Return of* Lochner, 100 CORNELL L. REV. 527, 575 (2015) (noting the judicial leanings of Judges Sentelle and Griffith on economic issues).

[107] *See* Janet Cooper Alexander, *The Law-Free Zone and Back Again*, 2013 U. ILL. L. REV. 551, 595 (2013) (arguing that Guantanamo Bay detainee cases in the D.C. Circuit tend to be divisive with judges with perceived conservative leanings "rul[ing] against the detainee in every case that has come before" the court); *see generally* CRS Report R41156, *Judicial Activity Concerning Enemy Combatant Detainees: Major Court Rulings*, by Jennifer K. Elsea and Michael John Garcia (discussing decisions by D.C. Circuit in litigation concerning Guantanamo detainees).

[108] *See* Wagner v. FEC, 793 F.3d 1 (D.C. Cir. 2015) (en banc).

[109] *See, e.g.,* NFIB v. Sebelius, --- U.S. ---, 132 S. Ct. 2566 (2012) (5-4 decision on scope of the Commerce Clause); Boumediene v. Bush, 553 U.S. 723 (2008) (5-4 decision on Guantanamo Bay detainees' ability to seek habeas review of the legality of their detention); Citizens United v. FEC, 558 U.S. 310 (2010) (5-4 decision on limits of the First Amendment imposes on a campaign finance regulation).

[110] *See supra* notes 97 and 99.

[111] For further discussion of Justice Scalia's approach to statutory interpretation, as well as questions about the degree to which he applied textualism and canons of interpretation in his own decisions while on the Court, see CRS Scalia report, *supra* note 9, at 4-7.

[112] William N. Eskridge, Jr., *The New Textualism and Normative Canons*, 113 COLUM. L. REV. 531, 532 (2013) ("[Justice Scalia's] judicial opinions, speeches, articles, and books have generated great debates, which have (ironically) revealed a substantial consensus about the ground rules for statutory interpretation.... [V]irtually all theorists and judges are 'textualists,' in the sense that all consider the text the starting point for statutory interpretation and follow statutory plain meaning if the text is clear.... [V]irtually all theorists and judges are also 'purposivists,' in the sense that all believe that statutory interpretation ought to advance statutory purposes, so long as such interpretations do not impose on words a meaning they will not bear. And virtually all theorists and judges insist the statutory context is important in discerning the meaning of statutory texts. So what has the debate been all about? Doctrinally, the big debate has been whether interpretative context can include internal 'legislative history' preceding a statute's enactment into law.... Theoretically, the big debate has focused on what the role of judges should be."). For more on the latter, see *supra* "Role of the Judiciary."

[113] In some cases, Judge Garland seems to have viewed the consideration of these factors to be required by Supreme Court or circuit precedents. *See, e.g.*, United States v. Cassell, 530 F.3d 1009, 1013 (D.C. Cir. 2008) (citing Supreme Court precedent when looking at the "language, structure, context, history, and such other factors as typically help courts determine a statute's objectives" in construing particular statutory text); Pub. Citizen, Inc. v. HHS, 332 F.3d 654, 662 (D.C. Cir. 2003) (citing circuit precedent when looking at the "text, structure, legislative history, and purpose" of the statute in question). In other cases, Judge Garland invokes similar factors without expressly noting that he is relying upon Supreme Court or circuit precedents when applying them to construe statutory text. *See,*

e.g., Holland v. Williams Mountain Coal Co., 496 F.3d 670, 672-76 (D.C. Cir. 2007); United States *ex rel.* Totten v. Bombardier Corp., 380 F.3d 488, 502-13 (D.C. Cir. 2004) (Garland, J., dissenting).

[114] *Totten*, 380 F.3d at 503.

[115] *Id.* at 506, 510-11.

[116] *Id.* at 511-13.

[117] *Id.* at 503 (citing, among other things, United States *ex rel.* Yesudian v. Howard University, 153 F.3d 731 (D.C. Cir. 1998)).

[118] For more on Justice Scalia's approach here, see CRS Scalia report, *supra* note 9, at 4-7.

[119] 572 F.3d 912 (D.C. Cir. 2009).

[120] 332 F.3d 654, 662 (D.C. Cir. 2003).

[121] *Id.*; *see also id.* at 663 ("We expect that litigants, including the parties to this appeal, would be both surprised and puzzled if all we told them at the end of the day was that 'the case has been decided'—without telling them what the decision was."). For other examples of a similar approach to statutory interpretation by Judge Garland, see Sottera, Inc. v. FDA, 627 F.3d 891, 899 (D.C. Cir. 2010) (Garland, J., concurring) ("On its face, the natural meaning of the term 'tobacco product' is a product—like cigarettes or chewing tobacco—that contains tobacco."); Bennett v. Islamic Republic of Iran, 618 F.3d 19, 24 (D.C. Cir. 2010) (Garland, J., concurring) ("No one would say that property a tenant uses as a gin joint is being used exclusively for educational purposes, even if the landlord uses the rent to send his children to college."); United States v. Cassell, 530 F.3d 1009, 1017 (D.C. Cir. 2008) (finding that the use of the phrase "convicted of a violation" makes clear that the provisions of 18 U.S.C. §924(c)(1) apply only at sentencing); *Totten*, 380 F.3d at 503 (Garland, J., dissenting) ("The court's interpretation of that subsection as *requiring* presentment is ... inconsistent with its plain text," since the word "presentment" does not appear there).

[122] *Public Citizen*, 332 F.3d at 662-63; *Se. Ala. Med. Ctr.*, 572 F.3d at 917; Grand Canyon Air Tour Coal. v. Fed. Aviation Admin. (FAA), 154 F.3d 455, 474-75 (D.C. Cir. 1998) (resorting to dictionaries on the question of whether "substantial" means more than half); Fin. Planning Ass'n v. SEC, 482 F.3d 481, 496 (D.C. Cir. 2007) (Garland, J., dissenting) (resorting to the dictionary definition of "other" in construing the phrase "other persons").

[123] *See, e.g.*, MCI Telecomm. Corp. v. Am. Tel. & Tel. (AT&T) Co., 512 U.S. 218, 228-30 (1994) (discussing the definitions of the term "modify" given in various dictionaries when determining whether certain proposed changes were within the FCC's authority under a statutory provision that authorized the FCC to "modify any requirement" of the Federal Communications Act).

[124] *See, e.g.*, *id.* at 228 (rejecting the definition of "modify" given in *Webster's Third New International Dictionary* on the grounds that "[i]n 1934, when the Communications Act became law—the most relevant time for determining a statutory term's meaning ...—*Webster's Third* was not yet even contemplated.").

[125] It would appear that Judge Garland has authored only one opinion that uses the words "ordinary meaning" in a context that does not involve a clear quotation or paraphrase of another court decision or a party's arguments. *See* Initiative & Referendum Inst. v. U.S. Postal Serv., 417 F.3d 1299, 1314 (D.C. Cir. 2005) (noting, in construing a Postal Service regulation, that "[t]he ordinary meaning of 'solicit' is merely to request, without reference to whether an immediate response is expected"); *see also id.* at 1317 (also referring to the "ordinary meaning" of the term "solicit"). In the few other cases where an opinion authored by Judge Garland uses the phrase "ordinary meaning," the opinion either is quoting or paraphrasing another opinion or a party, or is construing text that is not a statute or

regulation. *See Se. Ala. Med. Ctr.*, 572 F.3d at 916-17 (using the phrase "ordinary meaning" in paraphrasing the district court's decision and in quoting a Supreme Court opinion); McDonnell Douglas Corp. v. Dep't of the Air Force, 375 F.3d 1182 (D.C. Cir. 2004) (Garland, J., dissenting) (referring to "ordinary meaning" when discussing the text of a prior Supreme Court opinion); Global Crossing Telecomm., Inc. v. FCC, 259 F.3d 740 (D.C. Cir. 2001) (noting that the agency had relied on the "ordinary meaning" of the term "certify," as defined in *Black's Law Dictionary*); *In re* Sealed Case No. 96-3167, 153 F.3d 759, 771 (D.C. Cir. 1998) (noting that the Supreme Court had, in an earlier decision, held that Congress intended "carry" to have its "ordinary meaning" in the statute in question).

[126] For more on Justice Scalia's approach here, see CRS Scalia report, *supra* note 9, at 4-7.

[127] *See, e.g.*, Miranda O. McGowan, *Do as I Do, Not as I Say: An Empirical Investigation of Justice Scalia's Ordinary Meaning Method of Statutory Interpretation*, 78 MISS. Li. 129, 148-49 (2009) (noting that subtle differences in judges' use of terms like "ordinary meaning," "plain meaning," etc., can reflect more fundamental differences in their approaches to statutory interpretation).

[128] *See infra* notes 129-139 and accompanying text. In his dissenting opinion in *Totten*, Judge Garland did suggest that the various canons of statutory interpretation employed by the majority "serve here as 'cannons' of statutory destruction." United States *ex rel.* Totten v. Bombardier Corp., 380 F.3d 488, 503 (D.C. Cir. 2004). However, immediately thereafter, he clarified that he had "no quarrel with the canons the court has chosen," but rather with the conclusion they were used to support in *Totten*. *Id.*

[129] *See, e.g.*, United States v. Cassell, 530 F.3d 1009, 1017 (D.C. Cir. 2008); *In re* Sealed Case No. 97-312, 181 F.3d 128, 133 (D.C. Cir. 1999).

[130] *See, e.g.*, *Totten*, 380 F.3d at 505 (Garland, J., dissenting); Pub. Citizen, Inc. v. HHS, 332 F.3d 654, 665 (D.C. Cir. 2003) (quoting Russello v. United States, 464 U.S. 16, 23 (1983)); Allied Local & Reg'l Mfrs. Caucus v. EPA, 215 F.3d 61, 71 (D.C. Cir. 2000).

[131] *See, e.g.*, *Totten*, 380 F.3d at 505, 509 (Garland, J., dissenting); *Public Citizen*, 332 F.3d at 670 (quoting Moskal v. United States, 498 U.S. 103, 109-110 (1990)).

[132] *See, e.g.*, Sec'y of Labor v. Excel Mining, LLC, 334 F.3d 1, 9 (D.C. Cir. 2003).

[133] *See, e.g.*, Mittleman v. Postal Regulatory Comm'n, 757 F.3d 300, 306 (D.C. Cir. 2014).

[134] *See, e.g.*, *id.* at 307.

[135] *See, e.g.*, Holland v. Williams Mountain Coal Co., 496 F.3d 670, 675 (D.C. Cir. 2007).

[136] *See, e.g.*, *id.*

[137] *In re* Sealed Case No. 97-312, 181 F.3d 128, 132 (D.C. Cir. 1999).

[138] United States *ex rel.* Totten v. Bombardier Corp., 380 F.3d 488, 509 (D.C. Cir. 2004) (Garland, J., dissenting).

[139] *See, e.g.*, William D. Popkin, *An "Internal" Critique of Justice Scalia's Theory of Statutory Interpretation*, 76 MINN. L. REV. 1133, 1156 (1991/1992) (discussing Justice Scalia's concern that judicial discretion in interpreting statutes is inconsistent with a government of rules).

[140] *See* Chevron U.S.A., Inc. v. Nat. Res. Def. Council, 467 U.S. 837, 843 (1984); *infra* "Administrative Law."

[141] *See generally* CRS Congressional Distribution Memorandum, *Judge Merrick Garland and His Approach Towards Administrative Law*, by Jared P. Cole, Michael John Garcia, and Andrew Nolan (noting that Judge Garland voted to uphold the agency's interpretation in all but five of the 21 cases in which he participated (either as part of a three-judge panel or in en banc proceedings) that (1) raised *Chevron* issues and (2) prompted a concurring or

dissenting opinion by a member of the court). Copies of this memorandum are available upon request from its authors.

[142] 482 F.3d 481 (D.C. Cir. 2007).

[143] *Id.* at 484-85.

[144] *Id.* at 488 ("The word 'any' is usually understood to be all inclusive.").

[145] *Id.* at 489 ("[T]he word 'other' connotes 'existing besides, or distinct from, that already mentioned or implied.'"). *See also id.* ("There is nothing to suggest that Congress did not intend the words 'any' or 'other' to have their 'ordinary or natural meaning.'").

[146] Fin. Planning Ass'n v. SEC, 482 F.3d 481, 495 (D.C. Cir. 2007) (Garland, J., dissenting).

[147] *Id.*

[148] *Id.* at 496. *But see id.* at 492 (majority opinion) ("First, [a]mbiguity is a creature not of definitional possibilities but of statutory context.... Second, the absence of a statutory definition of 'intent of this paragraph' and 'other persons' does not necessarily render their meaning ambiguous."). Other cases manifest a similar approach to statutory interpretation by Judge Garland. *See, e.g.*, Se. Ala. Med. Ctr. v. Sebelius, 572 F.3d 912, 917, 923 (D.C. Cir. 2009); (noting that the statute in question does not define "wages," "wage-related," or "geographic area"); Am. Corn Growers Ass'n v. EPA, 291 F.3d 1, 19 (D.C. Cir. 2002) (Garland, J., dissenting) ("There is nothing in the statutory language that requires a source-by-source application of the fifth factor."); Arizona v. Thompson, 281 F.3d 248, 257 (D.C. Cir. 2002) (noting that there is nothing in the statutory phrase "authorized to use" that dictates that funds be used under a state plan, as opposed to a state cost allocation); Serono Labs., Inc. v. Shalala, 158 F.3d 1313, 1319-20 (D.C. Cir. 1998) (noting that the statute in question did not define the phrase "same as" or indicate whether chemical or clinical identity was contemplated); Allied Local & Reg'l Mfrs. Caucus v. EPA, 215 F.3d 61, 70-71 (D.C. Cir. 2000) (noting that nothing in the statute specifies that the only way to determine reactivity was through the agency's own studies); Grand Canyon Air Tour Coal. v. FAA, 154 F.3d 455, 466-67 (D.C. Cir. 1998) ("There is nothing in the Overflights Act's reference to 'natural quiet' that requires the FAA to define the term by survey results rather than decibel level."); *id.* at 467 (noting that there is nothing in the statute requiring the agency to create one or a few "quiet" zones); *id.* at 474 (observing that the statute does not say "noise free").

[149] Chevron U.S.A., Inc. v. Nat. Res. Def. Council, 467 U.S. 837, 843 (1984). Notably, in *Grand Canyon Air Tour Coalition*, Judge Garland paraphrased *Chevron* as saying that "where Congress leaves a statutory term undefined, it makes an implicit 'delegation of authority to the agency to elucidate a specific provision of the statute' through reasonable interpretation." 154 F.3d at 474 (quoting *Chevron*, 467 U.S. at 843-44). However, the cited passage of *Chevron* refers to the "unambiguously expressed intent of Congress," not congressionally established definitions per se.

[150] Sec'y of Labor v. Excel Mining, LLC, 334 F.3d 1, 14 (D.C. Cir. 2003) (Sentelle, J., dissenting). *See also In re* Sealed Case No. 97-312, 181 F.3d 128, 144 (D.C. Cir. 1999) (Sentelle, J., concurring) (stating, of the majority opinion by Judge Garland, which had found the statutory language in question ambiguous, "I write separately only to say that I think this is not nearly so close a case as the very thoroughness of the majority opinion might imply").

[151] *See supra* "Role of the Judiciary."

[152] *See, e.g.*, Mittleman v. Postal Regulatory Comm'n, 757 F.3d 300, 305 (D.C. Cir. 2014); Nat'l Res. Def. Council v. Nuclear Reg. Comm'n (NRC), 216 F.3d 1180, 1193-94 (D.C. Cir. 2000); Pub. Citizen, Inc. v. HHS, 332 F.3d 654, 668 (D.C. Cir. 2003); *Grand Canyon Air*

Tour Coal., 154 F.3d at 467. It is important to note that, in at least some cases, Judge Garland would appear to have viewed the consideration of legislative history materials as required by Supreme Court or circuit precedent. *See supra* note 113 and accompanying text. However, in other cases, he does not expressly indicate that he views precedent as requiring the consideration of legislative history materials when resorting to such materials. *See id. See also* Merrick B. Garland, *Antitrust and Federalism: A Response to Professor Wiley*, 96 YALE L. REV. 1291, 1292 n.4 (1987) ("There is nothing wrong with a court looking at legislative history in order to interpret the meaning of a statute.").

[153] *See* United States *ex rel.* Totten v. Bombardier Corp., 380 F.3d 488, 511-12 (D.C. Cir. 2004) (Garland, J., dissenting).

[154] *Id.* at 502.

[155] *Id.* at 504 (Garland, J., dissenting) (quoting Lamie v. U.S. Trustee, 540 U.S. 526, 534 (2004)).

[156] *See, e.g., id.* at 495. Chief Justice Roberts subsequently acknowledged the "difficulty" of this case, as well as the possibility that the majority "didn't get it right" in his own confirmation hearings to the High Court. *See Confirmation Hearing on the Nomination of John G. Roberts, Jr. To Be Chief Justice of the United States: Hearing Before the Committee on the Judiciary, United States Senate*, 109th Congress, 1st Sess., 320-21 (2005). However, while acknowledging the possibility that *Totten* might have been wrongly decided, Chief Justice Roberts continued to maintain that the *Totten* majority was correct. *Id.* at 321.

[157] *See, e.g.*, Mittleman v. Postal Regulatory Comm'n, 757 F.3d 300, 305 (D.C. Cir. 2014) (taking the view that a text-based interpretation is "confirmed by the legislative history of the section").

[158] *See, e.g.*, United States v. Cassell, 530 F.3d 1009, 1017 (D.C. Cir. 2008) (looking at the actual words of the statute last, but characterizing the statutory text as the "most significant" factor in construing the statute); Pub. Citizen, Inc. v. HHS, 332 F.3d 654, 662 (D.C. Cir. 2003) (characterizing the statutory text as "the most important manifestation of Congressional intent").

[159] *See, e.g.*, *Cassell*, 530 F.3d at 1017 (characterizing legislative history materials as "inconclusive" on the question at issue); Arizona v. Thompson, 281 F.3d 248, 257 (D.C. Cir. 2002) (rejecting the view that the word "activities," as used in a conference report, necessarily indicated an intent to preclude the use of funds to reimburse administrative costs common to both the funded program and other related programs); Grand Canyon Tour Coalition v. FAA, 154 F.3d 455, 467 (D.C. Cir. 1998) (noting Supreme Court precedents on the lack of weight to be given to the statements of a single legislator, even if that legislator was the bill's sponsor); *id.* at 474 (noting that parties with opposing interests in the litigation had cited the same legislative history materials as supporting differing positions).

[160] When Judge Garland does refer to "congressional purpose," his understanding of that purpose would appear to be based on the statutory text, not extrinsic considerations. *See, e.g.*, *Thompson*, 281 F.3d at 255 ("There is no doubt that Congress imposed a 15% cap in order to limit administrative expenditures; what other purpose could such a limit have?"). In his dissenting opinion in *Financial Planning Association*, Judge Garland does note that his interpretation of the statute in question would permit the statute to serve its purpose as to a population that did not exist when the statute was enacted in 1940. Fin. Planning Ass'n. v. SEC, 482 F.3d 481, 500 (D.C. Cir. 2007) (Garland, J., dissenting). However, he also viewed the statute in question in that case as ambiguous. *See supra* notes 142-148; *infra* notes 191 200 and accompanying text.

[161] *See, e.g.*, United States v. Mead Corp., 533 U.S. 218, 257 (2001) (Scalia, J., dissenting) ("*Chevron* sets forth an across-the-board presumption, which operates as a background rule

of law against which Congress legislates: Ambiguity means Congress intended agency discretion."); Hon. Antonin Scalia, *Judicial Deference to Administrative Interpretations of Law*, 1989 DUKE L.J. 511, 517 (1989) (similar).

[162] *See, e.g.*, Immigration & Naturalization Serv. (INS) v. Cardozo-Fonseca, 480 U.S. 421, 453 (1987) (Scalia, J., concurring) ("Since the Court quite rightly concludes that the INS's interpretation is clearly inconsistent with the plain meaning of that phrase and the structure of the Act, there is simply no need and thus no justification for a discussion of whether the interpretation is entitled to deference.") (internal citations omitted); Hon. Antonin Scalia, *The Rule of Law as a Law of Rules*, 56 U. CHI. L. REV. 1175, 1183 (1989) ("It is rare ... that even the most vague and general text cannot be given some precise, principled content—and that is indeed the essence of the judicial craft.").

[163] Zedner v. United States, 547 U.S. 489, 511 (2006) (Scalia, J., concurring) ("[T]he use of legislative history is illegitimate and ill advised in the interpretation of any statute—and especially a statute that is clear on its face....").

[164] *See supra* note 39 (discussing the prominence of administration law cases on the docket of the D.C. Circuit).

[165] Although beyond the scope of this report, another major issue might be judicial review of agency compliance with the procedural requirements of the APA, 5 U.S.C. §§551 *et seq.*

[166] *See* CRS Congressional Distribution Memorandum, *Judge Merrick Garland*, *supra* note 141.

[167] The Constitution establishes that the judicial power of the federal courts extends to "Cases" and "Controversies." U.S. CONST. art. III, §2, cl. 1. *See also* Lujan v. Defenders of Wildlife, 504 U.S. 555, 560 (1992) ("[T]he core component of standing is an essential and unchanging part of the case-or-controversy requirement of Article III."); United Pub. Workers of Am. (C.I.O.) v. Mitchell, 330 U.S. 75, 89 (1947) ("As is well known, the federal courts established pursuant to Article III of the Constitution do not render advisory opinions. For adjudication of constitutional issues, concrete legal issues, presented in actual cases, not abstractions are requisite.") (internal quotations and citations omitted).

[168] *See* Bennett v. Spear, 520 U.S. 154, 162 (1997) ("In addition to the immutable requirements of Article III, the federal judiciary has also adhered to a set of prudential principles that bear on the question of standing.") (internal citations and quotations omitted).

[169] *See, e.g.*, 5 U.S.C. §704 (providing for the availability of judicial review of administrative action under the APA when such action is "final").

[170] *See Bennett*, 520 U.S. at 162 ("To satisfy the 'case' or 'controversy' requirement of Article III, which is the 'irreducible constitutional minimum' of standing, a plaintiff must, generally speaking, demonstrate that he has suffered 'injury in fact,' that the injury is 'fairly traceable' to the actions of the defendant, and that the injury will likely be redressed by a favorable decision.") (quoting *Lujan*, 504 U.S. at 560-61).

[171] The requirement that a plaintiff exhaust administrative remedies before seeking judicial review of agency action is commonly the result of a judicial doctrine premised on prudential concerns, but may also be statutorily required in some circumstances. *See generally* Avocados Plus Inc. v. Veneman, 370 F.3d 1243, 1247-48 (D.C. Cir. 2004).

[172] Consideration of whether a legal claim is ripe for review often involves both constitutional elements—namely, whether a petitioner has alleged an imminent or impending injury-in-fact—as well as prudential concerns relating to "the fitness of the issues for judicial decision and the hardship to the parties of withholding court consideration." Nat'l Treasury Emps. Union v. United States, 101 F.3d 1423, 1427 (D.C. Cir. 1996) (quoting Abbott Labs. v. Gardner, 387 U.S. 136, 149 (1967)).

[173] For a general overview of the mootness doctrine and relevant exceptions thereto, see, generally, archived CRS Report RS22599, *Mootness: An Explanation of the Justiciability Doctrine*, by Brian T. Yeh.

[174] *See, e.g.*, Ctr. for Sustainable Econ. v. Jewell, 779 F.3d 588, 596-99 (D.C. Cir. 2015) (Garland, J.) (holding that an environmental advocacy group had associational standing to represent members affected by a lease program permitting drilling in the Outer Continental Shelf); Cohen v. United States, 578 F.3d 1, 13 (D.C. Cir. 2009) (in majority opinion joined by Judge Garland, concluding that the petitioners' challenge to an Internal Revenue Service (IRS) refund mechanism satisfied the requirements for ripeness), *reh'g en banc granted in part, vacated in part*, 599 F.3d 652 (D.C. Cir. 2010); Devia v. NRC, 492 F.3d 421, 422 (D.C. Cir. 2007) (Garland, J.) (holding that a petition for review of an NRC decision to grant a license that permitted construction of a spent nuclear fuel storage facility was prudentially unripe); PPL Wallingford Energy LLC v. Fed. Energy Regulatory Comm'n (FERC), 419 F.3d 1194, 1200 (D.C. Cir. 2005) (Garland, J.) (holding that the petitioners had standing to challenge FERC's rejection of agreements they had reached to provide electric power to certain locations, but lacked standing to challenge the agency's rejection of agreements made by other energy providers); La. Envtl. Action Network v. EPA, 172 F.3d 65, 67-69 (D.C. Cir. 1999) (in a majority opinion joined by Judge Garland, holding that an organization had prudential standing to challenge an EPA regulation that would allow variances from normal treatment standards for excavated waste).

[175] Citizens for Responsibility & Ethics in Wash. v. FEC, 475 F.3d 337, 341 (D.C. Cir. 2007) (Garland, J., concurring in judgment) (in a case where the petitioner sought information on campaign contribution activity from a previous presidential election, concurring with the majority's dismissal of the case on standing grounds because there was "no meaningful distinction" between the case and a prior D.C. Circuit case dismissed on standing grounds); Fin. Planning Ass'n. v. SEC, 482 F.3d 481, 493 (D.C. Cir. 2007) (Garland, J., dissenting) (dissenting on the grounds that the agency action was based on a reasonable interpretation of the governing statute in a case where the majority, after finding that the petitioners had standing, ruled that the agency action was contrary to that statute); Am. Corn Growers Ass'n v. EPA, 291 F.3d 1, 15 (D.C. Cir. 2002) (per curiam) (Garland, J., concurring in part and dissenting part) (dissenting based on a disagreement with the majority's characterization of the agency's interpretation of the statute as unreasonable in a case where the majority upheld certain aspects of a challenged agency action and struck down others, while also finding some claims unripe for review).

[176] *See, e.g.*, People for the Ethical Treatment of Animals (PETA) v. Dep't of Agric. (USDA), 797 F.3d 1087, 1097 (D.C. Cir. 2015) (concluding that PETA had standing to sue the USDA for failure to promulgate bird-specific animal welfare regulations under the Animal Welfare Act); Holistic Candlers & Consumers Ass'n v. FDA, 664 F.3d 940 (D.C. Cir. 2014) (upholding the dismissal of a suit against the FDA by manufacturers of candles intended to remove ear wax, who had sought to enjoin a possible FDA determination that the candles were unapproved medical devices, because the warning letters sent to the manufacturers did not constitute "final agency action" subject to judicial review under the APA). *But see* Util. Air Regulatory Grp. (UARG) v. EPA, 744 F.3d 741, 751 (D.C. Cir. 2014) (Kavanaugh, J., concurring) (concurring in full with the majority opinion authored by Judge Garland, but suggesting that the majority's characterization of the statute as constraining judicial review might not be in accordance with developments in Supreme Court case law, despite being consistent with existing D.C. Circuit jurisprudence); Am. Bird Conservancy, Inc. v. FCC, 516 F.3d 1027, 1035 (D.C. Cir. 2008) (per curiam) (Kavanaugh, J., dissenting) (disagreeing

with the majority's view that the case was ripe for review in a panel decision in which Judge Garland was in the majority, but the majority opinion was not credited to a particular author).

[177] *See, e.g.*, *Holistic Candlers*, 664 F.3d at 941-42 (upholding dismissal of a suit against the FDA by candle manufacturers, because the warning letters sent to the manufacturers did not constitute "final agency action" subject to judicial review under the APA); Conservation Force, Inc. v. Jewell, 733 F.3d 1200 (D.C. Cir. 2013) (dismissing various claims raised against the Fish and Wildlife Service (FWS) regarding purported violations of the Endangered Species Act on mootness and ripeness grounds); Chamber of Commerce v. EPA, 642 F.3d 192 (D.C. Cir. 2011) (in a challenge brought by the Chamber of Commerce and an automobile dealership organization to an EPA decision to waive federal preemption under the Clean Air Act (CAA) and allow California to adopt more stringent emission standards, dismissing the claims on various grounds including lack of standing and mootness); Ranger Cellular v. FCC, 348 F.3d 1044 (D.C. Cir. 2003) (dismissing applicants' challenge to the validity of FCC-issued cellular telephone licenses due to lack of standing because a judicial ruling in the plaintiffs' favor would not provide redress because it would result in an open auction for licenses in which the applicants would almost certainly be outbid); Klamath Water Users Ass'n v. FERC, 534 F.3d 735 (D.C. Cir. 2008) (dismissing a challenge by a water users association to review of FERC orders concerning an electric utility's license, when the association had not demonstrated that court action would likely provide redress to its purported injuries); Grand Canyon Air Tour Coalition v. FAA, 154 F.3d 455 (D.C. Cir. 1998) (deeming unripe for judicial review various claims raised in a challenge to an FAA final rule for the reduction of aircraft noise from Grand Canyon sightseeing tours).

[178] *See, e.g.*, *Ctr. for Sustainable Econ.*, 779 F.3d at 612-14 (Sentelle, J., dissenting) (disagreeing with the panel majority's finding that an environmental organization had standing to challenge the EPA permit process on behalf of two affected members, and arguing that the organization had not satisfied the requirements previously recognized by the D.C. Circuit as necessary for associational standing); Cohen v. United States, 578 F.3d. at 15-22 (Kavanaugh, J., dissenting in part) (disputing the panel majority's conclusion that the petitioners could proceed in a judicial challenge to an IRS refund mechanism on the grounds that the plaintiffs had failed to exhaust their administrative remedies, as required by statute, and the case was unripe for review), *accord* Cohen v. United States, 650 F.3d 717 (D.C. Cir. 2011) (en banc) (Kavanaugh, J., dissenting) (dissenting on similar grounds in en banc reconsideration of an earlier decision); Animal Legal Def. Fund, Inc. v. Glickman, 154 F.3d 426, 442 (D.C. Cir. 1998) (en banc) (Sentelle, J., dissenting) (arguing, in response to the majority opinion—which had found that the plaintiff challenging USDA regulations as contrary to the Animal Welfare Act had standing on account of suffering an aesthetic injury based on viewing affected animals in animal exhibitions—that "the majority significantly weakens existing requirements of constitutional standing"). *See also PETA*, 797 F.3d at 1099 (Millett, J., dubitante) (acknowledging that the majority opinion, which found that PETA had standing to bring suit against the USDA for failing to promulgate bird-specific animal welfare regulations, was consistent with D.C. Circuit jurisprudence, but expressing concern that the ruling was "in grave tension with Article III precedent and principles, such as the principle that an individual's interest in having the law property enforced against others is not, without more, a cognizable [] injury").

[179] *See, e.g.*, Summers v. Earth Island Inst., 555 U.S. 488 (2009) (environmental organizations lacked standing to challenge U.S. Forest Service regulations exempting small fire-

rehabilitation and timber-salvage projects from the notice, comment, and appeal process); Steel Co. v. Citizens for Better Env't, 523 U.S. 83 (1998) (organization lacked standing to employ the citizen suit provision of an environmental statute against a private party for violating reporting requirements; the complaint alleged only past infractions and not a continuing violation or the likelihood of a future violation, meaning that court-ordered injunctive relief would not redress the organization's injuries). For a more extensive discussion of Justice Scalia's views on standing, see CRS Scalia report, *supra* note 9, at 7-10.

[180] *See generally* Margaret McDonald, Summers v. Earth Island Institute*: Overhauling the Injury-in-Fact Test for Standing to Sue*, 71 LA. L. REV. 1053, 1066 (2011) (cataloging the recent standing cases before the Supreme Court and noting typical division among the Justices as to their outcome).

[181] See Merrick B. Garland, Deregulation and Judicial Review, 98 HARV. L. REV. 505, 585 (1985) (examining the evolution of administrative law in response to deregulation by executive agencies).

[182] 5 U.S.C. §706(2)(A), (C).

[183] United States v. Mead Corp., 533 U.S. 218, 226-27, 229 (2001). In a series of cases, the Supreme Court has limited Chevron's applicability by introducing a threshold inquiry that looks at a multi-factor balancing test to determine whether the two-step Chevron analysis is appropriate; see Barnhart v. Walton, 535 U.S. 212, 222 (2002); Christensen v. Harris Cty., 529 U.S. 576, 587 (2000), often referred to as Chevron "step zero." See Cass R. Sunstein, Chevron Step Zero, 92 VA. L. REV. 187 (2006). One critical factor in determining Chevron's applicability to a particular agency interpretation is the formality of the agency procedures when issuing the operative interpretation. See Mead, 533 U.S. at 226-27.

[184] 467 U.S. 837 (1984).

[185] Id. at 842.

[186] Id. at 842-43.

[187] Id. at 843.

[188] *See* Nat'l Cable & Telecomm. Ass'n v. Brand X Internet Servs., 545 U.S. 967, 981 (2005) ("Only a judicial precedent holding that the statute unambiguously forecloses the agency's interpretation, and therefore contains no gap for the agency to fill, displaces a conflicting agency construction.").

[189] For purposes of this section, the term "divided court" refers to a case that prompted a concurrence or dissent. For a defense of relying on such opinions, see CRS Congressional Distribution Memorandum, *Judge Merrick Garland, supra* note 141 (discussing why cases with concurrences or dissents typically signal "closer" cases). *See also* supra note 29.

[190] *See* CRS Congressional Distribution Memorandum, *Judge Merrick Garland, supra* note 141 (studying 21 cases in which Judge Garland voted that raised *Chevron* issues, and finding that Judge Garland deferred to the agency in 16 of these cases).

[191] 482 F.3d 481, 493 (2007). *See supra* "Statutory Interpretation."

[192] 15 U.S.C. §§80b–3 to –6.

[193] 15 U.S.C. §80b-2(a)(11)(C).

[194] 15 U.S.C. §80b-2(a)(11)(F).

[195] SEC, Certain Broker–Dealers Deemed Not to be Investment Advisers, 70 Fed. Reg. 20424 (April 19, 2005).

[196] *Fin. Planning*, 482 F.3d at 487-93.

[197] *Id.* at 501 (Garland, J., dissenting).

[198] *Id.* at 495.

[199] *Id.*

[200] *Id.* at 500.

[201] *See* United States v. Mead Corp., 533 U.S. 218, 226-27 (2001).

[202] *See* Nat'l Cable & Telecomm. Ass'n v. Brand X Internet Servs., 545 U.S. 967, 981 (2005).

[203] *Id. See supra* "Statutory Interpretation."

[204] 627 F.3d 891 (D.C. Cir. 2010).

[205] *Id.* at 904 (Garland, J., concurring).

[206] *Id.*

[207] *See, e.g.*, Miller v. Clinton, 687 F.3d 1332, 1335, 1341-42 (D.C. Cir. 2012) (ruling that, notwithstanding language potentially favorable to the agency in the Basic Authorities Act, the Age Discrimination in Employment Act applied to State Department employees overseas, in part, because the department's view to the contrary had been articulated in a contract between the department and a private party and thus lacked the formality to suggest that it possessed the force of law); Fox v. Clinton, 684 F.3d 67, 78 (D.C. Cir. 2012) (Edwards, J., joined by Garland & Williams, JJ.) (joining a majority opinion that refused to defer broadly to the State Department's interpretation of a section of the Immigration and Nationality Act because that interpretation was rendered in an informal decision letter rather than in a manner "clearly intended to have general applicability and the force of law").

[208] *See* 5 U.S.C. §706(2)(A).

[209] Motor Vehicle Mfrs. Ass'n of U.S., Inc. v. State Farm Mut. Auto. Ins. Co., 463 U.S. 29, 43 (1983) (quoting Burlington Truck Lines, Inc. v. United States, 371 U.S. 156, 168 (1962)). The Court explained that a decision will be arbitrary if "the agency has relied on factors which Congress has not intended it to consider, entirely failed to consider an important aspect of the problem, offered an explanation for its decision that runs counter to the evidence before the agency, or is so implausible that it could not be ascribed to a difference in view or the product of agency expertise." *Id.* at 43. The doctrine is often referred to as "hard look" review. Thomas J. Miles & Cass R. Sunstein, *The Real World of Arbitrariness Review*, 75 U. CHI. L. REV. 761, 763 (2008) ("In its seminal decision in *Motor Vehicle Manufacturers Association v. State Farm Auto Mutual Insurance Co.*, the Court entrenched hard look review and clarified its foundations.").

[210] *See State Farm*, 463 U.S. at 43.

[211] TC Ravenswood, LLC v. FERC, 741 F.3d 112, 118 (D.C. Cir. 2013); *see also* Nat'l Tel. Coop. Ass'n v. FCC, 563 F.3d 536, 541 (D.C. Cir. 2009) (cataloging the "many times" when the D.C. Circuit has noted the "highly deferential" nature of arbitrary and capricious review).

[212] *See State Farm*, 463 U.S. at 43.

[213] *See* CRS Congressional Distribution Memorandum, *Judge Merrick Garland*, *supra* note 141.

[214] See infra "Environmental Law." See, e.g., Grand Canyon Air Tour Coal. v. FAA, 154 F.3d 459-60 (D.C. Cir. 1998) (Garland, J.) ("We ... uphold the rule ... not because we necessarily believe the rule is 'just right,' but because we defer to the agency's reasonable exercise of its judgment and technical expertise....").

[215] 706 F.3d 438, 452 (D.C. Cir. 2013).

[216] Id. at 450 (internal quotations omitted). See 21 U.S.C. §812(b)(3)-(5); Drug Enf't Admin. (DEA), Denial of Petition to Initiate Proceedings to Reschedule Marijuana, 76 Fed. Reg. 40552 (July 8, 2011).

[217] Transcript of Oral Argument, Americans for Safe Access v. DEA, 706 F.3d 438 (D.C. Cir. 2013),
https://www.cadc.uscourts.gov/recordings/recordings2013.nsf/8D0A87D269BCD0C285257

BC90058DF5D/$file/ 10161211-1265.mp3/ ("Don't we have to defer to the agency, defer doesn't mean they win, but defer in the sense of ... we're not scientists, they are, to the definition of what is an adequate and well-controlled study.").

[218] 725 F.3d 255, 257 (D.C. Cir. 2013). For background and analysis on other issues raised with regards to Yucca Mountain, see CRS Report R44151, Yucca Mountain: Legal Developments Relating to the Designated Nuclear Waste Repository, by Todd Garvey and Alexandra M. Wyatt.

[219] In re Aiken Cty., 725 F.3d at 268-69 (Garland, J., dissenting).

[220] *Id.* at 269.

[221] *Id.*

[222] Del. Dep't. of Nat. Res. & Envtl. Control v. EPA, 785 F.3d 1, 10-19 (2015) (panel holding that the EPA acted arbitrarily and capriciously when it modified CAA rules allowing backup generators to operate without emissions controls for up to 100 hours per year as part of an emergency demand-response program); Fox v. Clinton, 684 F.3d 67, 80 (D.C. Cir. 2012) (panel finding that because "the Department failed to provide any coherent explanation for its decision regarding the applicability of Section 1, the agency's action was arbitrary and capricious for want of reasoned decisionmaking"); Int'l Union, United Mine Workers of Am. (UMWA) v. Mine Safety & Health Admin., 626 F.3d 84, 93 (D.C. Cir. 2010) (panel finding that "[t]he training provision is nonetheless arbitrary and capricious because, as the UMWA contends, it defies the expert record evidence and is unexplained"); Am. Farm Bureau Fed'n v. EPA, 559 F.3d 512, 524 (D.C. Cir. 2009) (concluding that the EPA failed reasonably to explain why it believes its standard will provide an appropriate degree of protection from the health effects of short-term exposure to particulate matter); Dep't of State v. Coombs, 482 F.3d 577, 581 (D.C. Cir. 2007) (panel finding that "[t]he Board does not appear to have even considered whether it is reasonable to require reinstatement of such an employee, in light of the demands of the Foreign Service. We think such an omission makes the Board's decision arbitrary and capricious").

[223] 460 F.3d 1, 9-12 (D.C. Cir. 2006).

[224] *Id.* at 9. In particular, the *Alpharma* court found that the agency's choice of the appropriate dosage used in its study contradicted agency statements that a bioequivalence study must use the highest approved dosage. *Id.* at 10. In addition, in the view of the majority, the agency failed to explain why its choice of dosage was appropriate. *Id.* at 11.

[225] *See supra* "Statutory Interpretation."

[226] *See* Scalia, *Judicial Deference to Administrative Interpretations*, *supra* note 161, at 521 ("One who finds *more* often (as I do) that the meaning of a statute is apparent from its text and from its relationship with other laws, thereby finds less often that the triggering requirement for *Chevron* deference exists. It is thus relatively rare that *Chevron* will require me to accept an interpretation which, though reasonable, I would not personally adopt.") (emphasis in original). This is not to imply that Justice Scalia was necessarily less likely to defer to agencies when he did find statutory ambiguity, or skeptical of affording deference to agency decisions. *See* Thomas W. Merrill, *Textualism and the Future of the* Chevron *Doctrine*, 72 WASH. U. L. Q. 351, 353 (1994) ("Although *Chevron* itself was decided before Justice Scalia joined the Court, he has long been perceived as the Court's most enthusiastic partisan of the two-step method associated with the decision."); Michael Herz, *Textualism and Taboo: Interpretation and Deference for Justice Scalia*, 12 CARDOZO L. REV. 1663, 1663 (1991) ("Justice Scalia is a fierce, sometimes strident defender of *Chevron*."). *But see* Perez v. Mortg. Bankers Ass'n, --- U.S. ---, 135 S. Ct. 1199, 1211 (2015) (Scalia, J., concurring)

("Heedless of the original design of the APA, we have developed an elaborate law of deference to agencies' interpretations of statutes and regulations.").

[227] *See, e.g.*, Baze v. Rees, 553 U.S. 35, 87 (2008) (Scalia, J., concurring in judgment) ("This conclusion [that the death penalty violates the Eight Amendment] is insupportable as an interpretation of the Constitution, which generally leaves it to democratically elected legislatures rather than courts to decide what makes significant contribution to social or public purposes."); Ring v. Arizona, 536 U.S. 584, 610 (2002) (Scalia, J., concurring) ("What compelled Arizona (and many other states) to specify particular 'aggravating factors' that must be found before the death penalty can be imposed was the line of this Court's cases beginning with *Furman v. Georgia*. In my view, that line of decisions had no proper foundation in the Constitution."). For further discussion of Justice Scalia's jurisprudence on capital punishment, see CRS Scalia report, *supra* note 9, at 10-12.

[228] Glossip v. Gross, --- U.S. ---, 135 S. Ct. 2726, 2776-77 (2015) (Breyer, J., dissenting). Justice Ginsburg joined in Justice Breyer's dissent in *Glossip*. Previously, certain other Justices on the Court shared similar views. *See, e.g.*, *Baze*, 553 U.S. at 86 (Stevens, J., concurring) ("I have relied on my own experience in reaching the conclusion that the imposition of the death penalty represents 'the pointless and needless extinction of life with only marginal contributions to any discernible social or public purposes. A penalty with such negligible returns to the State [is] patently excessive and cruel and unusual punishment violative of the Eighth Amendment.'") (quoting Furman v. Georgia, 408 U.S. 238, 312 (1972)).

[229] *See, e.g.*, *District of Columbia: General Information*, DEATH PENALTY INFO. CENTER, (2016), http://www.deathpenaltyinfo.org/district-columbia.

[230] 18 U.S.C. §3235 ("The trial of offenses punishable with death shall be had in the county where the offense was committed, where that can be done without great inconvenience.").

[231] *See generally supra* "Administrative Law" and *infra* "Environmental Law."

[232] *See, e.g.*, *Confirmation Hearings on Federal Appointments*, *supra* note 5, at 1062 (1995) (Judge Garland noting his prior work as a prosecutor in death penalty cases in the 1995 hearing on his nomination). He did not specify which cases were involved, but Oklahoma City bomber Timothy McVeigh was executed. *See, e.g.*, *Defiant McVeigh Dies in Silence*, BBC NEWS (June 11, 2001), http://news.bbc.co.uk/2/hi/1382602.stm.

[233] *Confirmation Hearings on Federal Appointments*, *supra* note 5, at 1062.

[234] *See* CRS Scalia report, *supra* note 9, at 12-15.

[235] *See, e.g.*, Comcast Corp. v. Behrend, --- U.S. ---, 133 S. Ct. 1426 (2013); Wal-Mart v. Dukes, 564 U.S. 338 (2011); AT&T Mobility v. Concepcion, 563 U.S. 333 (2011).

[236] *See, e.g.*, Mut. Pharm. v. Bartlett, --- U.S. ---, 133 S. Ct. 2466, 2480 (2013); PLIVA, Inc. v. Mensing, 564 U.S. 604, 606 (2011); Bruesewitz v. Wyeth LLC, 562 U.S. 223, 232 (2011).

[237] *See, e.g.*, Janus Capital Grp., Inc. v. First Derivative Traders, 564 U.S. 135 (2011); Schindler Elevator Corp. v. United States *ex rel.* Kirk, 563 U.S. 401 (2011).

[238] *See, e.g.*, Lee Epstein, William M. Landes, & Hon. Richard A. Posner, *How Business Fares in the Supreme Court*, 97 MINN. L. REV. 1431, 1472 (2013) ("Whether measured by decisions or Justices' votes, a plunge in warmth toward business during the 1960s (the heyday of the Warren Court) was quickly reversed; and the Roberts Court is much friendlier to business than either the Burger or Rehnquist Courts, which preceded it, were.").

[239] *See* James B. Stewart, *On Business Issues, Republicans Might Want a Justice Garland*, N.Y. TIMES (March 24, 2016), http://www.nytimes.com/2016/03/25/business/on-business-issues-republicans-might-want-a-justicegarland.html?_r=0 ("Memo to the Republican senators who refuse to consider President Obama's Supreme Court nominee, Merrick Garland: When it comes to business issues, Judge Garland is about as good as you could

hope for. That's because if there is any overriding philosophy in Judge Garland's writing and opinions, dating to his earliest law review articles, it is judicial restraint—a deference to decisions by elected officials and those they appoint.").

240 One study noted that in 22 appeals involving decisions of the National Labor Relations Board (NLRB), Judge Garland sided with the agency to find that an employer had committed an unfair labor practice in all but four cases. *See* Hannah Belitz, *The Supreme Court Vacancy and Labor: Merrick Garland*, ON LABOR (February 23, 2016), https://onlabor.org/2016/02/23/the-supreme-court-vacancy-and-labor-merrick-garland-2/.

241 *See* Juanita Duggan, *We Oppose Judge Garland's Confirmation*, WALL STREET J. (March 16, 2016), http://www.wsj.com/articles/we-oppose-judge-garlands-confirmation-1458169299 ("After studying his extensive record, the National Federation of Independent Business believes that Judge Garland would be a strong ally of the regulatory bureaucracy, big labor and trial lawyers.").

242 *See* Stewart, *supra* note 239; *see also supra* "Predicting Nominees' Future Decisions on the Court."

243 *See generally* Stewart, *supra* note 239 (noting that many of Judge Garland's labor law decisions were unanimous and had the support of more conservative or even libertarian members of the D.C. Circuit).

244 *See generally* "Predicting Nominees' Future Decisions on the Court."

245 *See In re* Rail Freight Fuel Surcharge Antitrust Litig., 725 F.3d 244, 255 (D.C. Cir. 2013); *see also* DL v. District of Columbia, 713 F.3d 120, 125-26 (D.C. Cir. 2013).

246 *See In re* Johnson, 760 F.3d 66, 76 (D.C. Cir. 2014).

247 Similar conclusions can be made with respect to Judge Garland's votes on substantive issues of civil liability. For example, he has participated in several unanimous cases that interpreted D.C. law with mixed results for the plaintiffs. *E.g.*, Sigmund v. Starwood Urban Retail VI, LLC, 617 F.3d 512 (D.C. Cir. 2010) (finding that a parking garage did not have increased awareness of violent, armed assault for purposes of a negligence claim); Kassem v. Wash. Hosp. Ctr., 513 F.3d 251 (D.C. Cir. 2008) (finding that a discharged employee had successfully stated a claim for intentional infliction of emotional distress under DC law); Daskalea v. District of Columbia, 227 F.3d 433 (D.C. Cir. 2000) (finding that DC law would not authorize the imposition of punitive damages for negligent supervision on the facts before the court).

248 *E.g.*, Oneok, Inc. v. Learjet, Inc., --- U.S. ---, 135 S. Ct. 1591 (2015); Mut. Pharm. Co., Inc. v. Bartlett, --- U.S. ---, 133 S. Ct. 2466 (2013); Kurns v. R.R. Friction Prods. Corp., --- U.S. ---, 132 S. Ct. 1261 (2012); PLIVA, Inc. v. Mensing, 564 U.S. 604 (2011); Wyeth v. Levine, 555 U.S. 555 (2009).

249 580 F.3d 1, 17 (D.C. Cir. 2009) (Garland, J., dissenting), *cert. denied*, 564 U.S. 1037 (2011).

250 *Id.* at 2.

251 *Id.*

252 *Id.* at 3.

253 *Id.* at 4.

254 28 U.S.C. §§2671-2680.

255 28 U.S.C. §2680(a), (j).

256 28 U.S.C. §2671.

257 Saleh v. Titan Corp., 580 F.3d 1, 5 (D.C. Cir. 2009); *see also* Boyle v. United Techs. Corp., 487 U.S. 500, 507-08 (1988); CRS Report R43462, *Tort Suits Against Federal Contractors: Selected Legal Issues*, by Rodney M. Perry. The suit in *Boyle* alleged that the manufacturer of a helicopter for the government was liable for a design defect that resulted in the death of

a U.S. Marine. 487 U.S. at 502-03. Noting that the alleged defect was part of the product specifications the government had provided to the contractor, the Court determined that allowing the suit to proceed against the contractor would conflict with a federal requirement set forth in the contract. *Id.* at 511-12. Notably, the *Boyle* Court found that a lesser degree of conflict between state and federal law is required to find preemption in areas involving "uniquely federal interests" such as the procurement of equipment by the government. *Id.* at 504-07. Writing for a majority of the Court, Justice Scalia found that allowing the suit against the contractor would have the same effect as allowing the plaintiff to sue the government for its decision to require the defective design. *Id.* at 511-12. However, as evidenced by the discretionary function exception to the FTCA, the government has not waived sovereign immunity with respect to these claims. *Id.* at 511. Therefore, preemption of the state cause of action is required; to permit otherwise would, in the opinion of the Court, frustrate the purpose of Congress's choice to exclude these suits from its waiver of sovereign immunity. *Id.* at 512.

[258] *Saleh*, 580 F.3d at 32.

[259] 28 U.S.C. §2680(j).

[260] *Saleh*, 580 F.3d at 7.

[261] *Id.* at 32 (Garland, J., dissenting).

[262] *Id.* at 24 (distinguishing Koohi v. United States, 976 F.2d 1328 (9th Cir. 1992), which had found a tort suit against the manufacturer of a weapons system that shot down a civilian aircraft during authorized military action to be preempted). If the military had authorized or directed the defendants' actions at Abu Ghraib, Judge Garland acknowledged that preemption of the state claims may be warranted. *Id.* at 34.

[263] *Id.* at 23-24 (citing Wyeth v. Levine, 555 U.S. 555, 565 (2009)).

[264] *See, e.g.*, PLIVA, Inc. v. Mensing, 564 U.S. 604, 621 (2011) (plurality opinion) (Thomas, J., joined by Roberts, C.J., & Scalia & Alito, JJ.) (arguing that the presumption against preemption is inappropriate in implied preemption matters); Cipollone v. Liggett Grp., 505 U.S. 504, 548 (1992) (Scalia, J., dissenting) (arguing against the use of the presumption to foreclose implied preemption where Congress provides an express preemption clause).

[265] *Saleh*, 580 F.3d at 21.

[266] *See* Garland, *Antitrust and State Action*, *supra* note 87, at 488. In this vein, it might be argued that Judge Garland, who was unpersuaded by the argument that federal antitrust law should be read to preempt economically inefficient state laws, *id.* at 487-88 ("The judiciary should not interfere under the aegis of the antitrust laws with a state's political decision, however misguided it may be, to substitute regulation for the operation of the market."), may similarly find unconvincing arguments that federal law should displace state laws, such as the common law tort system, that may interfere with optimal market conditions. *See, e.g.*, *Wyeth*, 555 U.S. at 626 (Alito, J., dissenting) (arguing that state juries are "ill equipped" to perform the necessary cost-benefit-balancing function necessary to determine whether a human drug should be introduced into commerce).

[267] 42 U.S.C. §1981a(b)(1).

[268] Kolstad v. Am. Dental Ass'n, 139 F.3d 958, 964-65 (D.C. Cir. 1998) (en banc), *rev'd* 527 U.S. 526 (1999).

[269] *Id.* at 964-65.

[270] *Id.* at 973 (Tatel, J., dissenting). The dissent acknowledged that common law principles of agency may result in a finding that the employer is not liable for the employee's discriminatory conduct. *Id.* at 974.

[271] 153 F.3d. 731 (D.C. Cir. 1998).

[272] *Id.* at 748 (Henderson, J., dissenting).

[273] *Id.* at 742. Instead, the majority held that the plaintiff must provide evidence that the defendant "know[s] ... that [the] plaintiff is engaged in protected activity as defined above—that is, in activity that reasonably could lead to a False Claims Act case." *Id.* On this point, Judge Henderson dissented. *Id.* at 748 ("Such a showing requires a plaintiff to have put the employer on notice not only that he is investigating fraud but also that the fraud is *against the federal government*, so as to potentially support a *qui tam* suit or a direct suit by the government.") (emphasis in original).

[274] 380 F.3d 488, 490 (D.C. Cir. 2004).

[275] *Id.* at 502 (Garland, J., dissenting).

[276] *See* CRS Scalia report, *supra* note 9, at 15-16; *see also* Obergefell v. Hodges, --- U.S. ---, 135 S. Ct. 2584, 2626 (2015) (Scalia, J., dissenting); United States v. Windsor, --- U.S. ---, 133 S. Ct. 2675, 2698 (2013) (Scalia, J., dissenting); Parents Involved in Cmty. Sch. v. Seattle Sch. Dist. No. 1, 551 U.S. 701 (2007); Grutter v. Bollinger, 539 U.S. 306, 378 (2003) (Scalia, J., dissenting).

[277] Kolstad v. Am. Dental Ass'n, 139 F.3d 958 (1998) (en banc).

[278] *Id.* at 60. Title VII, which prohibits employment discrimination on the basis of race, color, national origin, sex, or religion, is codified as amended at 42 U.S.C. §§2000e *et seq.*

[279] *Kolstad*, 139 F.3d at 970-71.

[280] 527 U.S. 526, 534-35 (1999).

[281] *Id.* at 536. The Court, however, also found that "in the punitive damages context, an employer may not be vicariously liable for the discriminatory employment decisions of managerial agents where these decisions are contrary to the employer's good-faith efforts to comply with Title VII." *Id.* at 545 (internal citations omitted).

[282] *See, e.g.*, Steele v. Schafer, 535 F.3d 689 (2008) (reinstating an employee's Title VII hostile work environment and retaliation claims); Czekalski v. Peters, 475 F.3d 360 (2007) (reviving an employee's Title VII claim that her reassignment was due to sex discrimination); Sparrow v. United Air Lines, Inc., 216 F.3d 1111 (2000) (reversing a lower court's decision to dismiss a plaintiff's race discrimination claim for failure to establish a prima facie case); Aka v. Wash. Hosp. Ctr., 156 F.3d 1284 (1998) (allowing an employee's age and disability discrimination claims to proceed); *but see*, Duncan v. Washington Metro. Area Transit Author. (WMATA), 240 F.3d 1110 (2001) (vacating a jury's verdict in favor of an employee's claim under the Americans with Disabilities Act).

[283] *See, e.g.*, Crawford v. Washington, 541 U.S. 36, 61 (2004) (recognizing broad Confrontation Clause rights for criminal defendants); Johnson v. United States, --- U.S. ---, 135 S. Ct. 2551, 2555 (2015) (invalidating a federal criminal statute in the face of a Due Process challenge).

[284] *See, e.g.*, Maryland v. Shatzer, 559 U.S. 98, 110 (2010) (limiting the right to counsel rule for confined prisoners); Hudson v. Michigan, 547 U.S. 586, 599 (2006) (holding that a violation of the knock-and-announce rule does not require suppression of evidence).

[285] *See generally* CRS Scalia report, *supra* note 9, at 16-19.

[286] FJC Garland, *supra* note 2.

[287] *See* David A. Graham, *How Did the Oklahoma City Bombing Shape Merrick Garland?*, ATLANTIC (March 17, 2016), http://www.theatlantic.com/politics/archive/2016/03/merrick-garland-oklahoma-city-bombing-supreme-court/ 474090/; Nina Totenberg, *Out of the Horror in Oklahoma City, Merrick Garland Forged the Way Forward,* (April 19, 2016), http://www.npr.org/2016/04/19/474689286/out-of-the-horror-in-oklahoma-city-merrick-garland-forged-theway-forward.

[288] *See, e.g.*, Eric Posner, *Merrick Garland Would Shift the Court Decisively Leftward*, SALON (March 17, 2016), http://www.slate.com/articles/news_and_politics/jurisprudence/2016/03/merrick_garland_would_shift_the_supreme_court_left_a_lot.html ("Garland was a prosecutor, and may well be less sympathetic to criminal defendants than most liberal are."); Lincoln Caplan, *Merrick Garland, President Obama's Sensible Supreme Court Choice*, NEW YORKER (March 16, 2016), http://www.newyorker.com/news/news-desk/president-obamas-sensible-supreme-court-choice (noting how Judge Garland's time as a prosecutor has influenced his work as a judge); Dara Lind, *One Tweet That Shows Why Some Liberals Are Worried About Merrick Garland*, VOX (March 16, 2016), http://www.vox.com/2016/3/16/11246258/merrick-garland-prosecutor ("In Garland's case, the issue that gives him so much cred with conservatives is the very issue that gives liberals pause: criminal justice. Garland is a former prosecutor with a tough-on-crime record.").

[289] Charlie Savage, *In Criminal Rulings, Garland Has Usually Sided with Law Enforcement*, N.Y. TIMES (March 22, 2016), http://www.nytimes.com/2016/03/23/us/politics/merrick-garland-supreme-court-nominee.html?_r=0 ("Of 14 criminal cases identified by the *New York Times* in which Judge Garland voted differently from at least one fellow judge, he came down in favor of law enforcement 10 times."); Tom Goldstein, *The Potential Nomination of Merrick Garland*, SCOTUSblog (April 26, 2010), http://www.scotusblog.com/2010/04/the-potential-nomination-of-merrickgarland/ (noting that "in ten criminal cases, Judge Garland ha[d] disagreed with his more-liberal colleagues; in each, he adopted the position that was more favorable to the government or declined to reach a question on which the majority adopted the more favorable position"); Daniel Denvir, *Inside Merrick Garland's Troubling Record: Why He Could Take the Supreme Court Right in One Very Important Regard*, SALON (Mar. 17, 2016), http://www.salon.com/2016/03/ 17/ inside_merrick_garlands_bleak_record_why_he_could_take_the_supreme_court_right_in_one_very_important_regard/ ("Garland's record is particularly troubling when it comes to his deference to police and prosecutors, including the suppression of evidence allegedly obtained by way of an unconstitutional police search."); Totenberg, *supra* note 100 ("On the appeals court, Garland has been a moderate liberal, with a definite pro-prosecution bent in criminal cases. Indeed, his views in the area of criminal law are considerably more conservative than those of the man he would replace, Justice Antonin Scalia.").

[290] Perhaps countering the viewpoint that Judge Garland has been visibly supportive of the government's position in criminal procedure cases, in 2010, Judge Garland voted not to rehear the government's appeal in the Global Positioning System tracking case, *United States v. Jones*. *See* 625 F.3d 766 (D.C. Cir. 2010). Nonetheless, Judge Garland has, at times, been more sympathetic to the government's position in criminal cases than colleagues whom some view as more liberal or libertarian in their judicial philosophies. In the context of sentencing decisions, in at least two cases, a colleague criticized Judge Garland for deferring too much to the government's position in at least two cases. *See, e.g.*, United States v. Bigley, 786 F.3d 11, 17 (D.C. Cir. 2015) (Brown, J., concurring); United States v. Riley, 376 F.3d 1160, 1176-78 (D.C. Cir. 2004) (Rogers, J., dissenting). Judge Garland also once authored an opinion dissenting from the majority's decision (authored by Judge Rogers and joined by Judge Edwards) to grant the defendant a new trial on the grounds that the prosecutor had substantially misstated the evidence during closing argument, and the jury instructions had not adequately cured the resulting prejudice. *See* United States v. Watson, 171 F.3d 695, 703 (D. C. Cir. 1999). In dissent, Judge Garland asserted that the prosecutor's mistake was not sufficiently egregious to warrant reversing the defendant's conviction because, at the time of the trial in 1999, transcripts of witness

testimony were unavailable during closing arguments, making "[i]nnocent mistakes of recollection ... inevitable and hardly uncommon[;]" "[i]n the end, the jury's memory of what a witness actually said provides the corrective for errors made by the parties." *See id.* at 703-04 (Garland, J., dissenting). Yet Judge Garland also recognized that "[i]t may well be that in the not-too-distant future even routine criminal trials will have the benefit of real-time transcripts of witness testimony," and "[w]hen that day comes, disputes over testimony will be resolved by reference to transcripts rather than memories." *See id.* at 708-09. Thus, given recent advances in technology, it is hard to predict whether Judge Garland would continue to give the prosecution the benefit of doubt if a prosecutor made similar misstatements today or in the future.

291 In 2015, for example, according to DOJ statistics, the federal government prevailed in 6,777 of 7,191 criminal appeals. *See generally* U.S. DOJ, Office of the United States Attorneys, *Annual Statistical Reports (Years 2013-2015)*, https://www.justice.gov/usao/resources/ annual-statistical-reports (click on links for 2013, 2014, and 2015 and go to Table 7). In 2014, the government prevailed in 7,197 of 7,622 criminal appeals. *Id.* For an examination of this trend in federal criminal law, see Hon. Alex Kozinski, *Criminal Law 2.0*, 44 GEO, L.J. ANN. REV. CRIM PROC. iii (2015) ("[W]e like to boast that our criminal justice system is heavily tilted in favor of criminal defendants because we'd rather that ten men go free than an innocent man be convicted. There is reason to doubt it."); Angela J. Davis, *Federal Proscutors* [sic] *Have Way Too Much Power*, NY TIMES (January 14, 2015), http://www.nytimes.com/roomfordebate/2012/08/19/ do-prosecutors-have-too-much-power/federal-proscutors-have-way-too-much-power (alleging that government prosecutors "control the criminal justice system"; the "Supreme Court has consistently deferred to prosecutors in a series of cases"; and charges are "rarely" brought against misbehaving prosecutors); Cassandra Burke Robertson, *The Right to Appeal*, 91 N.C. L. REV. 1219, 1227 (2013) (noting that most criminal defendants lose on direct appeal); Christopher M. Johnson, *Post-Trial Judicial Review of Criminal Convictions: A Comparative Study of the United States and Finland*, 64 ME. L. REV. 425, 472-73 (2012) ("[T]he United States requires courts engaged in [appellate] review of a conviction to enter upon the task in a spirit of substantial deference to the trial court fact-finder.").

292 For a discussion on why nonunanimous opinions may provide more insight into a nominee's prior judicial record, see "Predicting Nominees' Future Decisions on the Court."

293 334 F.3d 1161, 1173 (2003) (Rogers, J., dissenting).

294 *See* U.S. CONST. amend. IV.

295 *Brown*, 343 F.3d at 1162-63. In *Brown*, two officers, arriving at the scene where a shooting had reportedly occurred several hours earlier, noticed a suspicious-looking car in the parking lot where the shooting is said to have occurred. *Id.* at 1162. Although this vehicle was not the one pointed out by a witness, the officers approached the vehicle after its occupants made several movements that the officers viewed as suspicious. *Id.* at 1162-63. Hearing no response when he tapped on the rear window, one officer opened the vehicle door, purportedly to ensure the officers' safety. *Id.* at 1163. Subsequently, the officer opened the car's locked trunk, finding a firearm that became the basis for the defendant's prosecution for being a felon in possession of a firearm in violation of federal statute. *Id.*

296 392 U.S. 1 (1967). In *Terry*, the Supreme Court construed the Fourth Amendment as permitting police officers to undertake investigatory stops if they have a reasonable suspicion of criminal activity, and to conduct protective searches for weapons if they have a reasonable fear for their safety. *See id.at* 30.

297 *Id.* at 1165-68.

[298] In dissent, Judge Rogers argued that, while the officers might have had a *generalized* suspicion that the car's occupants posed a danger to police, they did not have a sufficiently *particularized* suspicion of danger, as required under *Terry*. *Id.* at 1173 (Rogers, J., dissenting).

[299] *Id.* at 1166.

[300] *Id.* (citing Whren v. United States, 517 U.S. 806, 813 (1996)).

[301] *See, e.g.*, Janet Koven Levit, *Pretextual Traffic Stops:* United States v. Whren *and the Death of* Terry v. Ohio, 28 LOY. U. CHI. L.J. 145, 174 (1996) (arguing that the objective standard set forth in *Whren* increased the risk that the police will be able to conduct suspicionless stops through post-hoc pretexual justifications).

[302] 187 F.3d 663, 669 (D.C. Cir. 1999).

[303] *Id.* ("To the contrary, we must defer to his 'quick decision as to how to protect himself and others from possible danger.'") (quoting *Terry*, 392 U.S. at 28).

[304] *Id.* at 670 ("Thus, [the police officer's] actual motives for conducting the search were not relevant as long as his actions were objectively reasonable.").

[305] *See supra* "Role of the Judiciary" (noting that Judge Garland's jurisprudence strives not to have the court overreach in any particular case).

[306] 483 F.3d 836 (D.C. Cir. 2007).

[307] *See* United States v. Robinson, 414 U.S. 218, 236 (1973).

[308] 483 F.3d at 837.

[309] *Id.* at 843-44 (Rogers, J., dissenting).

[310] Knowles v. Iowa, 525 U.S. 113 (1998).

[311] *Powell*, 483 F.3d at 839-40 (quoting Rawlings v. Kentucky, 448 U.S. 98, 111 (1980)).

[312] This interpretation is supported by a passage from the majority opinion which noted that, even if subsequent Supreme Court jurisprudence could be read to undermine *Rawlings*, "[i]f a precedent of [the Supreme] Court has direct application in a case, yet appears to rest on reasons rejected in some other line of decisions, the Court of Appeals should follow the case which directly controls, leaving to [the Supreme] Court the prerogative of overruling its own decisions." *Id.* at 841-42.

[313] 529 F.3d 1119 (D.C. Cir. 2008) (en banc).

[314] *Id.* at 1127 (Edwards, J., joined by Brown, Griffith, Rogers, & Tatel, JJ.).

[315] *Id.* at 1149 (Kavanaugh, J., dissenting, joined by Henderson, Randolph, & Sentelle, JJ.).

[316] *Id.* at 1141 (Edwards, J., joined by Garland & Ginsburg, JJ.).

[317] *Id.* at 1149 (Kavanaugh, J., dissenting) ("Unlike the other nine judges on the en banc panel, Judges Ginsburg and Garland have not reached that legal question: In their view, the facts of this case do not present it. They thus do not join Part III(A)-(C) of Judge Edwards's opinion on the show-up issue; but they also do not join Part II(B) of our opinion. On the show-up issue, they join only the single, fact-bound paragraph in Part III(D) of Judge Edwards's opinion, thereby making Part III(D) the entirety of the majority's opinion on that issue.").

[318] *See, e.g.*, United States v. Caso, 723 F.3d 215, 219 (D.C. Cir. 2013) (assuming, without deciding, two legal questions before ruling on a narrower third ground); United States v. Andrews, 532 F.3d 900, 909 (D.C. Cir. 2008) (declining to create a new circuit rule post-*United States v. Booker*, 543 U.S. 220 (2005), concerning whether the Ex Post Facto Clause prohibits the use of the version of the Guidelines Manual in effect at the time of sentencing if that manual would yield a sentence higher than that under the Guidelines Manual that was in effect at the time of the illegal conduct, and concluding that no plain error occurred).

[319] *Caso*, 723 F.3d at 219.

[320] --- U.S. ---, 133 S. Ct. 2072 (2013) (holding that the Ex Post Facto Clause is violated when a defendant is sentenced under the version of the Guidelines that provides a higher sentencing range than the Guidelines in effect at the time when the defendant committed the illegal act).

[321] *See* United States v. Andrews, 532 F.3d 900, 909 (D.C. Cir. 2008) (internal quotation marks, alterations, and citations omitted).

[322] The term *"Booker* error" refers to the Supreme Court's landmark 2005 ruling in *United States v. Booker*, 543 U.S. 220 (2005), which held that the Sixth Amendment right to jury trial generally requires that only facts admitted by a defendant, or proved beyond a reasonable doubt to a jury, be used to calculate a sentence, making the sentencing guidelines functionally discretionary for trial judges. *Id.* at 226-27.

[323] *See* United States v. Branham, 515 F.3d 1268, 1277-79 (D.C. Cir. 2008).

[324] *See id.* at 1278.

[325] United States v. Burwell, 690 F.3d 500, 515 (2012) (en banc).

[326] *Id.* at 513. Nonetheless, while Judge Garland voted for the government's position in these cases, his vote in *Burwell* could be attributable to the fact that the defendant had requested the court to overturn long-standing circuit precedent, rather than a penchant to agree with the government's position. *Id.* at 515 (noting *stare decisis* concerns with the dissent's position).

[327] *Id.* at 519 (Rogers, J., dissenting); *id.* at 527 (Kavanaugh, J., dissenting, joined by Tatel, J.).

[328] 571 F.3d 1282, 1288 (D.C. Cir. 2009).

[329] 616 F.3d 544 (D.C. Cir. 2010).

[330] *Id.* at 560.

[331] 475 F.3d 1319 (D.C. Cir. 2007) (en banc).

[332] *Id.* at 1333 (Garland, J., dissenting).

[333] *Id.* at 1324.

[334] *Id.* at 1338 (Garland, J., dissenting).

[335] *Id.*

[336] *See, e.g.*, Johnson v. United States, --- U.S. ---, 135 S. Ct. 2551, 2555 (2015) (invalidating the residual clause of the Armed Career Criminal Act); United States v. Santos, 553 U.S. 507, 524 (2008) (interpreting a federal money-laundering statute narrowly to avoid constitutional infirmity).

[337] *See supra* notes 288-289.

[338] *See* CRS Scalia report, *supra* note 9, at 16-19.

[339] *See, e.g.*, United States v. Coughlin, 610 F.3d 89, 93 (D.C. Cir. 2010) (concluding, for a unanimous court, that the Double Jeopardy Clause barred the retrial of certain mail fraud claims); United States v. Ginyard, 511 F.3d 203, 204 (D.C. Cir. 2008) (holding, for a unanimous court, that a defendant can be retried on lesser-included charges without transgressing the Fifth Amendment's double jeopardy prohibition); United States v. Jones, 567 F.3d 712, 717 (D.C. Cir. 2009) (a unanimous ruling written by Judge Garland concluding that the public safety exception to *Miranda* applied to the defendant's statements); United States v. Miller, 738 F.3d 361, 375 (D.C. Cir. 2013) (a unanimous ruling joined by Judge Garland resolving a Sixth Amendment Confrontation Clause claim in a single paragraph); United States v. Gurr, 471 F.3d 144, 153 (D.C. Cir. 2006) (same); United States v. Pettigrew, 346 F.3d 1139, 1140 (D.C. Cir. 2003) (resolving an *Apprendi* claim on behalf of a unanimous court on harmless error grounds); United States v. Lafayette, 337 F.3d 1043, 1044 (D.C. Cir. 2003) (same).

[340] *See, e.g.*, United States v. Law, 806 F.3d 1103, 1107 (D.C. Cir. 2015) (concluding that the defendant's argument— that a life sentence violates Eighth Amendment—was foreclosed by *Harmelin v. Michigan*, 501 U.S. 957 (1991), and D.C. Circuit precedents following *Harmelin*); United States v. Swangin, 726 F.3d 205, 208 (D.C Cir. 2013) (noting that Supreme Court and circuit precedents foreclosed the defendant's argument that he should receive the benefit of the Fair Sentencing Act's lower mandatory minimum sentence even though he was sentenced before its passage); United States v. Blackson, 709 F.3d 36, 40-42 (D.C. Cir. 2013) (collecting cases and reiterating the circuit's rules regarding the scope of remand); United States v. Motley 587 F.3d 1153, 1156-60 (2009) (noting that the Supreme Court decision in *Melendez v. United States*, 518 U.S. 120 (1996), foreclosed the defendant's argument that a district court must depart from the mandatory minimum sentence under the relevant federal statute when the government requests a downward variance under the sentencing guidelines); United States v. Adewani, 467 F.3d 1340, 1341-43 (D.C. Cir. 2006) (rejecting the defendant's request to ignore circuit precedent concerning the definition of "crime of violence" under the guidelines).

[341] *See, e.g.*, United States v. Salahmand, 651 F.3d 21, 27-28 (2011) (joining nine circuits in concluding that the guidelines' definition of "vulnerable victim" extends to victims of the defendant's relevant conduct, as well as to victims of the crime of conviction); United States v. Jones, 567 F.3d 712, 719 (D.C. Cir. 2009) (joining the majority of circuits in remanding for resentencing in the first instance, instead of forcing the defendant to file a petition under the relevant federal statute, after the Sentencing Commission retroactively lowered guidelines ranges for certain crack-cocaine offenses.

[342] *See, e.g.*, 42 U.S.C. §300j-7(a) (petitions for review of EPA actions pertaining to the establishment of national primary drinking water regulations); 42 U.S.C. §6976 (petitions for review of EPA regulatory actions under the Resource Conservation and Recovery Act (RCRA)); 42 U.S.C. §7607(b)(1) (petitions for review of various EPA actions under the CAA).

[343] For example, a search of the Lexis databases for cases involving Judge Garland whose text included at least five instances of the terms "EPA," "FWS," "NEPA," or "environmental" gives 105 results; other search parameters give more or fewer results.

[344] *See supra* "Administrative Law."

[345] *See, e.g.*, Rebecca Wilhelm, *Standing, Administrative Law Define Scalia's Legacy*, DAILY ENVTL. REP. (February 17, 2016), http://www.bna.com/standing-administrative-law-n57982067391/ (subscription required) (quoting environmental law professors Jonathan Z. Cannon, Jonathan A. Adler, Richard J. Lazarus, Richard B. Flatt, and Jody Freeman); *see also* CRS Scalia report, *supra* note 9, at 19-22.

[346] *See generally, e.g.*, Rebecca Wilhelm, *Observers: Judge Garland Typically Deferential to EPA*, DAILY ENVTL. REP. (March 17, 2016), http://www.bna.com/observers-judge-garland-n57982068626/ (subscription required); Keith Goldberg, *Garland Could Be Agency Ally In Energy, Enviro Rule Fights*, LAW360, (March 16, 2016), http://www.law360.com/articles/ 772367/ garland-could-be-agency-ally-in-energy-enviro-rule-fights (subscription required).

[347] *See generally discussion and citations infra*, "Environmental Law."

[348] *See generally* Chevron U.S.A. Inc. v. Nat. Res. Def. Council, Inc., 467 U.S. 837 (1984); *supra* "Administrative Law."

[349] *See, e.g.*, Miss. Comm'n on Envtl. Quality v. EPA, 790 F.3d 138 (D.C. Cir. 2015) (per curiam) (affirming "EPA's reasonable interpretation of the ambiguous statutory term 'nearby'"); Cement Kiln Recycling Coal. v. EPA, 493 F.3d 207, 215-26 (D.C. Cir. 2007) (Garland, J.)

(upholding an EPA interpretation of RCRA); UARG v. EPA, 471 F.3d 1333 (2006) (upholding EPA's 2005 Regional Haze Rule); Allied Local & Reg'l Mfrs. Caucus v. EPA, 215 F.3d 61, 70 (D.C. Cir. 2000) (Garland, J.) (upholding an EPA interpretation allowing a "category-by-category" basis for regulating emissions).

[350] *See* Scott Fulton, president of the Environmental Law Institute, as quoted in Wilhelm, *Observers*, *supra* note 346 (quoting).

[351] 291 F.3d 1 (D.C. Cir. 2002) (per curiam) (remanding the 1999 Regional Haze Rule to the EPA for reconsideration of certain issues, but rejecting challenges to certain other aspects of the rule).

[352] *Id.* at 15-16 ("[T]he court adopts an interpretation of the Act that, in the view of [EPA] and the National Academy of Sciences, will prevent the achievement of Congress' goal. If that interpretation were required by the statutory language, we would of course be compelled to adopt it. But such an interpretation is not required.").

[353] White Stallion Energy Ctr., LLC v. EPA, 748 F.3d 1222, 1229-45 (D.C. Cir. 2014).

[354] 576 U.S.—, 135 S. Ct. 2699 (2015). Justice Scalia wrote the opinion for the Court requiring the EPA to consider the costs of compliance and other costs in deciding whether the regulation was appropriate and necessary. Some viewed this holding as a narrowing of the *Chevron* doctrine. *See, e.g.*, Jonathan R. Nash, Michigan v. EPA *and the Future of* Chevron *Deference*, THE HILL (July 16, 2015), http://thehill.com/blogs/pundits-blog/the-judiciary/248040-michigan-vepa-and-the-future-of-chevron-deference. The Supreme Court left intact the D.C. Circuit's other rulings upholding other aspects of the rule, 748 F.3d at 1229-45; on remand, Judge Garland's panel unanimously remanded the rule to the agency for a cost determination without vacating it. White Stallion Energy Ctr., LLC v. EPA, No. No. 12-1100, 2015 U.S. App. LEXIS 21819 (D.C. Cir. December 15, 2015) (per curiam) (unpub. order).

[355] *See, e.g.*, Ctr. for Sustainable Econ. v. Jewell, 779 F.3d 588, 605-12 (D.C. Cir. 2015) (upholding an interpretation of the Outer Continental Shelf Lands Act in opening new areas for leasing); Desert Citizens Against Pollution v. EPA, 699 F.3d 524, 525 (D.C. Cir. 2012) (rejecting challenges to the EPA's CAA mercury emission rule for gold mines); La. Envtl. Action Network v. EPA, 172 F.3d 65, 69-70 (D.C. Cir. 1999) (rejecting a challenge to a variance governing the treatment of hazardous waste landfills).

[356] *See, e.g.*, Oceana, Inc. v. Locke, 670 F.3d 1238, 1240-43 (D.C. Cir. 2011) (finding that a fishery management plan was impermissibly vague where a statute directed the FWS to "establish" a standardized methodology); Sierra Club v. EPA, 356 F.3d 296, 301-04 (D.C. Cir. 2004) (part II of op. by Garland, J., vacating the EPA's conditional approval of ozone control plans).

[357] *See* Appalachian Power Co. v. EPA, 135 F.3d 791, 820-22 (D.C. Cir. 1998) (per curiam; section by Garland, J.) ("[W]hether a retrofitted cell burner can properly be classified as a wall-fired boiler turns upon [statutory language]. Neither party contends that this question can be resolved under *Chevron*'s step one ... and we therefore proceed to *Chevron*'s step two.... Because EPA has not adequately justified its treatment of retrofitted cell burners as wall-fired boilers, we vacate and remand....").

[358] 5 U.S.C. §706.

[359] 42 U.S.C. §7607(d)(9).

[360] *See, e.g.*, UARG v. EPA, 744 F.3d 741, 748-50 (D.C. Cir. 2014) (Garland, J.) (upholding the EPA's new source performance standards for particulate matter emissions from steam generating units against an industry challenge); Coal. of Battery Recyclers Ass'n v. EPA, 604 F.3d 613 (D.C. Cir. 2010) (panel upholding air standards for lead); Catawba Cty. v.

EPA, 571 F.3d 20, 25 (D.C. Cir. 2009) (per curiam) (finding that the EPA "satisfied—indeed, quite often surpassed—its basic obligation of reasoned decisionmaking" for 224 of 225 area classifications for fine particulate matter pollution); *Sierra Club*, 356 F.3d at 301-10 (part III of opinion by Garland, J.) (denying claims that EPA's technical adjustments to models underlying its approvals of ozone control plans were arbitrary, capricious, or not in accordance with law); Allied Local & Reg'l Mfrs. Caucus v. EPA, 215 F.3d 61, 73-81 (D.C. Cir. 2000) (rejecting challenges to the reasonableness of a rule limiting the volatile organic compounds in architectural coatings); Grand Canyon Air Tour Coal. v. FAA, 154 F.3d 455, 459-60 (D.C. Cir. 1998) (Garland, J.) ("Three of the four petitioners ... essentially argue that the FAA's rule [to reduce aircraft noise from sightseeing tours in a national park] does 'too much, too soon.' [One] charges that the rule does 'too little, too late.' We ... uphold the rule ... not because we necessarily believe the rule is 'just right,' but because we defer to the agency's reasonable exercise of its judgment and technical expertise....").

[361] 682 F.3d 1032, 1036-41 (D.C. Cir. 2012). As another example, Judge Garland also joined the 2013 decision in In re *Polar Bear Litigation* upholding the FWS's rule listing the polar bear as "threatened" under the Endangered Species Act, against challenges from industry groups, states, and environmental organizations. *See generally* 709 F.3d 1 (D.C. Cir. 2013) (affirming the district court's grant of summary judgment to the FWS).

[362] 559 F.3d 512, 524 (D.C. Cir. 2009). *See also, e.g.*, Del. Dep't of Nat. Res. & Envtl. Control v. EPA, 785 F.3d 1, 10-19 (D.C. Cir. 2015) (panel holding that the EPA acted arbitrarily and capriciously when it modified CAA rules allowing backup generators to operate without emissions controls for up to 100 hours per year as part of an emergency demand-response program).

[363] *See* 42 U.S.C. §§4321 *et seq*. While National Environmental Policy Act (NEPA) claims often overlap with substantive claims relating to reasoned decisionmaking, as a recent opinion joined by Judge Garland summarized, "NEPA's mandate 'is essentially procedural.'" Grunewald v. Jarvis, 776 F.3d 893, 903 (D.C. Cir. 2015) (internal citations omitted); *see id.* at 903-07 (finding reasonable the analysis underlying an agency's NEPA determinations in reducing white-tailed deer in Rock Creek Park). For background information on NEPA, see CRS Report RL33152, *The National Environmental Policy Act (NEPA): Background and Implementation*, by Linda Luther.

[364] *See, e.g.*, *Grunewald*, 776 F.3d at 903-07; Theodore Roosevelt Conservation P'ship v. Salazar, 616 F.3d 497, 50720 (D.C. Cir. 2010) (panel finding standing for the challengers, as well as no violations of NEPA or other statutes in approval of the Atlantic Rim Natural Gas Field project); Nat'l Comm. for the New River, Inc. v. FERC, 373 F.3d 1323, 1327-34 (D.C. Cir. 2004) (rejecting challenges to a NEPA environmental impact statement based on close review of the record).

[365] 661 F.3d 1147, 1156-57 (D.C. Cir. 2011). Similarly, a per curiam decision by a panel including Judge Garland vacated a NEPA order where "there [wa]s no real dispute that [communication] towers 'may' have significant environmental impact," and, thus, applicable regulations required an environmental assessment to determine whether there was indeed an impact. Am. Bird Conservancy, Inc. v. FCC, 516 F.3d 1027, 1032-34 (D.C. Cir. 2008) (upholding challenges to an FCC order denying a petition seeking protection of migratory birds from collisions with communications towers). The dissent would have dismissed the case on ripeness grounds. *Id.* at 1035-37 (Kavanaugh, J., dissenting).

[366] *See, e.g.*, Gerber v. Norton, 294 F.3d 173 (D.C. Cir. 2002) (Garland, J.) (holding that the FWS violated the ESA because it did not allow public comment on a key component of a

developer's permit application and because the agency did not make a statutorily required finding).

[367] 16 U.S.C. §1539.

[368] 294 F.3d 173, 178-84 (D.C. Cir. 2002). The court also held that the map availability violation was not harmless, *id.*, and that the FWS had failed to make a statutorily required finding before issuing the permit. *Id.* at 184-86.

[369] 725 F.3d 255 (D.C. Cir. 2013); *id.* at 268-70 (Garland, J., dissenting).

[370] Nuclear Waste Policy Act, 42 U.S.C. §10134.

[371] In re *Aiken Cty.*, 725 F.3d at 260.

[372] *Id.* at 270 (quoting United States *ex rel.* Sierra Land & Water Co. v. Ickes, 84 F.2d 228, 232 (D.C. Cir. 1936)).

[373] *See supra* "Administrative Law."

[374] Conservation Force, Inc. v. Jewell, 733 F.3d 1200, 1202 (D.C. Cir. 2013) ("This appeal concerns the straight-horned markhor, an impressive subspecies of wild goat.... As tempting as it may be to consider an arbitrary and capricious claim in a case involving a goat [describing etymological derivation of "capricious" from Italian word for "goat" in footnote], an array of justiciability problems—mootness, ripeness, and standing—require us to decline the opportunity."); Chamber of Commerce v. EPA, 642 F.3d 192, 199-212 (D.C. Cir. 2011) (finding no jurisdiction due to standing limitations and mootness).

[375] *See, e.g.*, Del. Dep't of Nat. Res. & Envtl. Control v. EPA, 785 F.3d 1, 7-10 (D.C. Cir. 2015) (holding that Delaware lacked standing to challenge an exemption from emissions controls for backup generators in low-density areas, but finding standing for other claims and other petitioners); Swanson Grp. Mfg. v. Jewell, 790 F.3d 235, 238-46 (D.C. Cir. 2015); Commuter Rail Div. of Reg'l Transp. Auth. v. Surface Transp. Bd., 608 F.3d 24, 30-31 (D.C. Cir. 2010) (finding that an environmental group did not establish causation); North Carolina v. EPA, 587 F.3d 422, 426-29 (2009) (holding that a state did not establish redressability to challenge the EPA's removal of part of Georgia from ozone regulation coverage); Wilderness Soc'y v. Norton, 434 F.3d 584, 593-94 (2006) (finding lack of redressability); Town of Stratford v. FAA, 285 F.3d 84, 88-89 (D.C. Cir. 2002) (finding lack of prudential standing).

[376] *See, e.g.*, UARG v. EPA, 471 F.3d 1333, 1339-40 (D.C. Cir. 2006); Fund for Animals v. Norton, 322 F.3d 728, 733 38 (D.C. Cir. 2003) (Garland, J.) (holding a Mongolian agency had standing to intervene); Nat'l Parks Conserv. Ass'n v. Manson, 414 F.3d 1, 4-7 (D.C. Cir. 2005) (holding that groups had standing to challenge authorization for a power plant).

[377] *See* Sierra Club v. Jewell, 764 F.3d 1, 3-9 (D.C. Cir. 2014) (finding standing to challenge the removal of Blair Mountain Battlefield from the National Register of Historic Places, over a dissent characterizing the majority's application of the "injury" requirement as too broad); Animal Legal Def. Fund, Inc. v. Glickman, 154 F.3d 426 (D.C. Cir. 1998) (divided en banc opinion); Amfac Resorts v. Dep't of Interior (DOI), 282 F.3d 818 (D.C. Cir. 2002) (unanimous panel upholding Park Service regulation), *vacated sub nom.*, Nat'l Park Hosp. Ass'n v. DOI, 538 U.S. 803 (2003) (ruling the suit was not ripe); La. Envtl. Action Network v. EPA, 172 F.3d 65, 65 (D.C. Cir. 1999) (joining an opinion that found standing, but rejected a challenge to EPA action under RCRA, over a dissent that would not have found standing).

[378] *See supra* "Administrative Law."

[379] *See, e.g.*, Cement Kiln Recycling Coal. v. EPA, 493 F.3d 207, 215-16 (D.C. Cir. 2007) (holding challenges to a rule ripe for review); Am. Bird Conservancy, Inc. v. FCC, 516 F.3d 1027, 1035 (D.C. Cir. 2008) (Kavanaugh, J., dissenting) (arguing that the claims were not

ripe). Note that cases can often reach the merits without substantial discussion of ripeness or similar issues.

[380] *See, e.g.*, Thomas Lorenzen, as quoted by Wilhelm, *Observers*, *supra* note 346 (describing Judge Garland as a "stickler for exhaustion of administrative remedies").

[381] Conservation Force, Inc. v. Jewell, 733 F.3d 1200, 1203-07 (D.C. Cir. 2013); Devia v. NRC, 492 F.3d 421 (D.C. Cir. 2007) (Garland, J.) ("Because it is speculative whether the project will ever be able to proceed, we find the petitioners' challenge unripe and direct that the case be held in abeyance."); *Cement Kiln Recycling Coal.*, 493 F.3d at 226-28 (rejecting the argument that the Human Health Risk Assessment Protocol was a legislative rule and holding that it was not a final requirement over which the court had jurisdiction).

[382] *See, e.g.*, White Stallion Energy Ctr., LLC v. EPA, 748 F.3d 1222, 1256-58 (D.C. Cir. 2014) (per curiam) (finding one energy company to lack standing under the "zone of interests" test); *cf. id.* at 1266-73 (Kavanaugh, J., dissenting in part) (explaining concerns with "zone of interests" precedent); Nat'l Ass'n of Home Builders v. Army Corps of Eng'rs, 417 F.3d 1272 (D.C. Cir. 2006) (finding no "substantial probability" that the appellants fell within NEPA's "zone of interest"); Atl. States Legal Found., Inc. v. EPA, 325 F.3d 281, 283-85 (D.C. Cir. 2003) (sua sponte rejecting the petitions as unripe).

[383] 744 F.3d 741, 747 (D.C. Cir. 2014). *See also, e.g.*, Vt. Dep't of Pub. Serv. v. United States, 684 F.3d 149 (D.C. Cir. 2012) ("conclud[ing] the petitioners waived their [objection to license renewal for the Vermont Yankee facility] because they repeatedly failed to present it directly to the [agency] and thereby failed to exhaust their administrative remedies").

[384] *See, e.g.*, Ctr. for Sustainable Econ. v. Jewell, 779 F.3d 588, 599-600 (D.C. Cir. 2015) (holding that certain claims were not ripe because the obligation to comply fully with NEPA does not mature until leases are issued); Wy. Outdoor Council v. Forest Serv., 165 F.3d 43, 47-51 (D.C. Cir. 1999) (dismissing a NEPA claim brought before any oil and gas leases had been issued).

[385] Am. Trucking Ass'ns, Inc. v. EPA, 175 F.3d 1027 (D.C. Cir. 1999).

[386] Am. Trucking Ass'ns, Inc. v. EPA, 195 F.3d 4, 16-17 (D.C. Cir. 1999) (denying of reh'ing en banc) (Tatel, J., dissenting from denial of reh'ing en banc).

[387] 531 U.S. 457, 472-76 (2001).

[388] 323 F.3d 1062, 1064-80 (D.C. Cir. 2003) (interpreting, *inter alia*, United States v. Lopez, 514 U.S. 549 (1995)); U.S. CONST. art. I, §8, cl. 3. Then Judge John Roberts dissented from a denial of en banc rehearing of the case on the grounds that the interpretation of the Commerce Clause, while in line with D.C. Circuit precedent, was too broad. Rancho Viejo, LLC v. Norton, 334 F.3d 1158, 1160 (D.C. Cir. 2003) (Roberts, J., dissenting from denial of reh'ing en banc). *See infra* "Federalism."

[389] 790 F.3d 138, 165, 174-84 (D.C. Cir. 2015). As previously noted, *supra* note 349, the court also rejected various other challenges. *See generally* 790 F.3d at 150-86.

[390] See CRS Legal Sidebar WSLG1489, *UPDATED: Circuit Court Denies Stay of Clean Power Plan; States Ask Supreme Court to Step In (Part 2)*, by Alexandra M. Wyatt.

[391] For more information on the Clean Power Plan litigation, see CRS Report R44341, *EPA's Clean Power Plan for Existing Power Plants: Frequently Asked Questions*, by James E. McCarthy et al., at 35-40 (discussing judicial review).

[392] In his writings prior to being appointed to the D.C. Circuit, Judge Garland supported the application of federalism principles—at least in some circumstances—in arguing for more narrow applications of antitrust laws to preempt state and local economic regulations. *See* Garland, *Antitrust and State Action*, *supra* note 87, at 502.

[393] *See* Miss. Comm'n on Envtl. Quality v. EPA, 790 F.3d 138 (D.C. Cir. 2015); Barbour v. WMATA, 374 F.3d 1161 (D.C. Cir. 2004); Rancho Viejo, LLC v. Norton, 323 F.3d 1062 (D.C. Cir. 2003); Watters v. WMATA, 295 F.3d 36 (D.C. Cir. 2002); Allied Local & Reg'l Mfrs. Caucus v. EPA, 215 F.3d 61 (2000).

[394] *See* U.S. CONST. amend. X.

[395] *Id.* at art. I, §8, cl. 1.

[396] *Id.* at art. I, §8, cl. 3.

[397] *Id.* at amend. XI.

[398] *See* New York v. United States, 505 U.S. 144, 177 (1992).

[399] *See* Printz v. United States, 521 U.S. 898, 919 (1997).

[400] U.S. CONST. amend. X. ("The powers not delegated to the United States by the Constitution, nor prohibited by it to the States, are reserved to the States respectively, or to the people.").

[401] Miss. Comm'n on Envtl. Quality v. EPA, 790 F.3d 138, 174-75 (D.C. Cir. 2015) (per curiam opinion joined by Garland, C.J., Henderson & Srinivasan, JJ.) (internal citations and quotations omitted).

[402] *See, e.g., id.* at 176-80; Barbour v. WMATA, 374 F.3d 1161, 1164-70 (D.C. Cir. 2004).

[403] *Miss. Comm'n*, 790 F.3d at 174-80.

[404] South Dakota v. Dole, 483 U.S. 203, 207-08 (1987).

[405] 567 U.S. __, 132 S. Ct. 2566 (2012).

[406] *Miss. Comm'n*, 790 F.3d at 176-77 (citing *NFIB*, 132 S. Ct. at 2604).

[407] *Id.* at 178 (citing *NFIB*, 132 S. Ct. at 2604-05).

[408] *Id.* at 179.

[409] Barbour v. WMATA, 374 F.3d 1161, 1168 (D.C. Cir. 2004). Under 42 U.S.C. §2000d-7, federal funds are conditioned on a state's willingness to subject itself to damages lawsuits for discriminating against employees on the basis of disability.

[410] *Barbour*, 374 F.3d at 1168 (internal citations and quotations omitted). *Dole* established that conditions on federal grants are invalid if "unrelated" to the federal interest in the program. South Dakota v. Dole, 483 U.S. 203, 207-08 (1987). *See also* New York v. United States, 505 U.S. 144, 167 (1992) ("Such conditions must (among other requirements) bear some relationship to the purpose of the federal spending....").

[411] *Barbour*, 374 F.3d at 1168.

[412] In dissent, Judge Sentelle stressed that a robust interpretation of *Dole*'s nexus requirement is a vital restraint on Congress's spending power and "essential to maintain some semblance of the Framer's original framework of a federal government of limited and enumerated regulatory power." *Id.* at 1172 (Sentelle, J., dissenting). Judge Sentelle found "no reasonably close relationship" between the federal grant of transportation funds and subjecting WMATA to lawsuits for disability discrimination in employment. *Id.* He further observed that "[t]he core of our disagreement is whether Congress's disapproval of disability discrimination is enough of a connection between the transportation funds and the condition imposed here." *Id.* at 1172 n.1.

[413] *Id.* at 1168-69 (citing Lau v. Nichols, 414 U.S. 563, 569 (1974) and Grove City College v. Bell, 465 U.S. 555, 575 (1984)).

[414] While acknowledging that the federal funds in question were not directly "tied" to disability related issues, the majority opinion in *Barbour* relied on *Sabri v. United States*, 541 U.S. 600 (2004), wherein the Supreme Court held that Congress could, under the Spending Clause, criminalize the bribery of state officials who receive federal funds even if federal funds are not directly implicated by a given bribe, in concluding that no direct connection is needed between the grant and the condition imposed. *Barbour*, 374 F.3d at 1170. Instead,

Judge Garland concluded that the "connection between the congressional goal ... and the congressional means" at issue in *Barbour* was "close enough to be sustained." *Id.* at 1168.

[415] *Id.* at 1170.

[416] *See* Miss. Comm'n on Envtl. Quality v. EPA, 790 F.3d 138 (D.C. Cir. 2015); Rancho Viejo, LLC v. Norton, 323 F.3d 1062 (D.C. Cir. 2003); Allied Local & Reg'l Mfrs. Caucus v. EPA, 215 F.3d 61 (2000).

[417] United States v. Lopez, 514 U.S. 549 (1995) (holding that provisions of the Gun-Free School Zones Act were beyond Congress's power under the Commerce Clause).

[418] United States v. Morrison, 529 U.S. 598 (2000) (holding that certain provisions of the Violence Against Women Act were beyond Congress's power under the Commerce Clause).

[419] *Lopez*, 514 U.S. at 558-59.

[420] *Rancho Viejo*, 323 F.3d at 1069-70 (citing *Lopez*, 514 U.S. at 561).

[421] *Allied Local*, 215 F.3d at 61.

[422] *Id.* at 83.

[423] *Id.* at 81-83.

[424] Rancho Viejo, LLC v. Norton, 323 F.3d 1062, 1062 (D.C. Cir. 2003).

[425] *Id.* at 1065.

[426] *Id.* at 1071.

[427] *Id.* at 1072.

[428] *Id.* ("That regulated activity is Rancho Viejo's planned commercial development, not the arroyo toad that it threatens.").

[429] *Id.* at 1079.

[430] Gibbs v. Babbitt, 214 F.3d 483 (4th Cir. 2000).

[431] Rancho Viejo, LLC v. Norton, 323 F.3d 1062, 1079 (D.C. Cir. 2003) (quoting *Gibbs*, 214 F.3d at 500).

[432] Miss. Comm'n on Envtl. Quality v. EPA, 790 F.3d 138, 182 (D.C. Cir. 2015) (emphasis added).

[433] *Id.* at 181.

[434] Rancho Viejo, LLC v. Norton, 334 F.3d 1158 (D.C. Cir. 2003) (denying reh'ing en banc).

[435] *Id.* at 1159 (Sentelle, J., dissenting from denial of reh'ing en banc).

[436] *Id.* at 1158-59 (Sentelle, J., dissenting). Judge Sentelle also appears to have disagreed with Judge Garland's views of the scope of Congress's power under the Commerce Clause in dissenting from the D.C. Circuit's denial of en banc review in *Navegar, Inc. v. United States*, 200 F.3d 868 (D.C. Cir. 2000). Whereas Judge Garland voted to deny en banc review of a panel decision holding that the Violent Crime Control and Law Enforcement Act of 1994 was within Congress's power under the Commerce Clause, Judge Sentelle concluded that the decision "perpetuate[d] an approach to Commerce Clause jurisprudence hopelessly out of date under contemporary Supreme Court interpretations of the Constitution." *Rancho Viejo*, 334 F.3d at 869 (Sentelle, J., dissenting from denial of reh'ing en banc).

[437] *Rancho Viejo*, 334 F.3d at 1160 (Roberts, J., dissenting from denial of reh'ing en banc) (emphasis in original).

[438] *Id.* (quoting GDF Realty Invs., Ltd. v. Norton, 326 F.3d 622, 634-35 (5th Cir. 2003)). Judge Roberts's dissent from rehearing was premised on the idea that *Lopez* and *Morrison* were facial challenges to a federal statute, which, under *United States v. Salerno,* 481 U.S 739 (1987), meant that the Court in striking down these laws was of the view that there were no circumstances in which the laws could be constitutionally applied. 334 F.3d at 1160

(Roberts, J., dissenting). On this basis, Judge Roberts concluded that the appropriate focus could not be on whether the challenged regulation substantially affects interstate commerce; otherwise, "if the defendant in *Lopez* possessed the firearm because he was part of an interstate ring," there would be a circumstance where the law in *Lopez could* be applied constitutionally. *Id.*

Although the future Chief Justice felt Judge Garland's approach was inconsistent with Supreme Court precedent, Judge Roberts himself differed in tone and approach from Judge Sentelle in his dissent, suggesting that Judge Garland had "faithfully applied" D.C. Circuit precedent as established in *National Association of Home Builders (NAHB) v. Babbitt*, 130 F.3d 1041 (D.C. Cir. 1997). *Rancho Viejo*, 334 F.3d at 1160 (Roberts, J., dissenting). Judge Roberts further noted, however, that he viewed en banc review as "appropriate" in this case because the panel's approach in *NAHB* "conflicts with the opinion of a sister circuit—a fact confirmed by that circuit's quotation from the *NAHB* dissent. Such review would also afford the opportunity to consider alternative grounds for sustaining application of the Act that may be more consistent with Supreme Court precedent." *Id.* In particular, Judge Roberts suggested that the law in question in *Rancho Viejo* could be sustained on alternate grounds; namely, that a species that resides wholly within one state can have a substantial effect on interstate commerce. *Id.*

439 *See, e.g.*, Seminole Tribe of Fla. v. Florida, 517 U.S. 44, 54 (1996).

440 Watters v. WMATA, 295 F.3d 36, 40 (D.C. Cir. 2002) (holding that a provision that made WMATA liable "for its contracts and for its torts and those of its ... agents" fell "far short of a clear and unequivocal waiver of WMATA's immunity against attorney's charging liens.").

441 Barbour v. WMATA, 374 F.3d 1161, 1164 (D.C. Cir. 2004).

442 *Id.* at 1166-67.

443 *See* Garcia v. S.U.N.Y. Health Scis. Ctr., 280 F.3d 98 (2d Cir. 2001).

444 *See* CRS Scalia report, *supra* note 9, at 22-24 (noting that "Justice Scalia viewed federalism ... to be 'one of the Constitution's structural protections of liberty'") (quoting Printz v. United States, 521 U.S. 898, 921 (1997) (Scalia, J.)).

445 *See, e.g.*, Levitan v. Ashcroft, 281 F.3d 1313, 1315 (D.C. Cir. 2002) (Edwards, J., joined by Garland & Henderson, JJ.) (reversing the district court's decision, which had granted summary judgment to uphold a prison regulation prohibiting inmates' consumption of wine as a religious sacrament under the Free Exercise Clause and remanding the case for further consideration); Henderson v. Kennedy, 253 F.3d 12, 13-19 (D.C. Cir. 2001) (Randolph, J., Garland & Henderson, JJ.) (affirming the district court's decision, which had granted summary judgment upholding a generally applicable restriction limiting commercial transactions, including the sale of religious items, on the National Mall under constitutional and statutory religious freedom claims), *reh'g denied*, 265 F.3d 1072 (D.C. Cir. 2001), *cert. denied*, 535 U.S. 986 (2002).

446 772 F.3d 229 (D.C. Cir. 2014), *reh'g en banc denied*, 808 F.3d 1 (D.C. Cir. 2015), *cert. granted*, --- U.S. ---, 136 S. Ct. 446 (2015).

447 *Priests for Life*, 772 F.3d at 237. For further discussion of the requirement and related litigation, see CRS Report R44422, *Nonprofit Challenges to the Contraceptive Coverage Requirement: The Meaning of Substantial Burdens on Religious Exercise Under the Religious Freedom Restoration Act*, by Cynthia Brown.

448 *See* Priests for Life v. UHHS, 808 F.3d 1 (D.C. 2015) (denying reh'ing en banc).

449 *Id.*

[450] *See supra* "Predicting Nominees' Future Decisions on the Court" (discussing the value of interpreting a judge's votes to grant or deny a rehearing en banc).

[451] In addition to *Priests for Life*, the Court has consolidated six other cases for its review, each raising similar claims. *See* Zubik v. Burwell, No. 14-1418, 577 U.S. __, 136 S. Ct. 444 (2015).

[452] See CRS Legal Sidebar WSLG1534, *Supreme Court, Seemingly Divided at Oral Arguments, Requests Potential Compromises in Contraceptive Coverage Challenges*, by Cynthia Brown.

[453] Nonetheless, Judge Garland's previous role in considering the case at the D.C. Circuit could result in him electing to recuse himself from the Court's reconsideration of the cases. Supreme Court Justices are not formally subject to a codeof judicial conduct that governs recusal. *See* Admin. Office of the U.S. Courts, *Code of Conduct for United States Judges*, http://www.uscourts.gov/judges-judgeships/code-conduct-united-states-judges (last visited April 13, 2016); *see also* Letter from John Roberts, Chief Justice, U.S. Supreme Court, to Patrick J. Leahy, Chairman, U.S. Senate Committee on the Judiciary (February 17, 2012) (copy on file with CRS Legislative Attorney Cynthia Brown). Federal law generally requires federal judges to recuse themselves in proceedings in which their impartiality may be questioned, among other reasons. *See* 28 U.S.C. §455. While this disqualification statute applies to Supreme Court Justices, it lacks an enforcement mechanism at that stage of litigation, meaning that there is no process by which Justices may be forced to recuse themselves. *See* CRS Legal Sidebar WSLG600, *Judicial Ethics and the U.S. Supreme Court*, by Cynthia Brown.

[454] *See* FEC v. Nat'l Right to Work Comm'n, 459 U.S. 197 (1983) (noting exclusive jurisdiction in the D.C. district court under Section 309(a)(8)(A) of the Federal Election Campaign Act (FECA) of 1971 (codified, as amended, in 52 U.S.C. §30109(a)(8)(A)).

[455] On matters outside the context of First Amendment law, but touching on election law more broadly, it is notable that Judge Garland was a member of a three-judge panel of the U.S. District Court for the District of Columbia which issued an unsigned opinion that, among other things, denied preclearance under the Voting Rights Act (VRA), 52 U.S.C. §10304; 28 C.F.R. §51.10, to proposed changes in Florida voting law. *See* Florida v. United States, 885 F. Supp. 2d 299, 357 (D.D.C. 2012) (per curiam). For further discussion on preclearance and the VRA, see CRS Report R42482, *Congressional Redistricting and the Voting Rights Act: A Legal Overview*, by L. Paige Whitaker.

[456] 793 F.3d 1 (D.C. Cir. 2015) (en banc), *cert. denied sub nom.*, Miller v. FEC, 136 S. Ct. 895 (2016).

[457] 52 U.S.C. §30119(a); 11 C.F.R. §115.1(b). This FECA prohibition applies at any time between the earlier of when the request for proposals is sent out or contract negotiations commence, and the termination of negotiations or the completion of contract performance, whichever is later. *See id.* The term "contract" includes "[a] sole source, negotiated, or advertised procurement." 11 C.F.R. §115.1(c)(1).

[458] Under FECA, a traditional political action committee or PAC (also known as a "separate segregated fund"), as opposed to a super PAC, is permitted to make contributions to political parties and candidates, and is subject to contribution limits. 52 U.S.C. §§30116(a)(2); 30118(b)(2)(C).

[459] *See Wagner*, 793 F.3d at 3-4 ("In short, the plaintiffs challenge § 30119 only insofar as it bans campaign contributions by individual contractors to candidates, parties, or traditional PACs that make contributions to candidates and parties.").

[460] Id. at 21-26. For further discussion, see CRS Legal Sidebar WSLG1335, *D.C. Circuit Upholds Ban on Campaign Contributions by Federal Contractors*, by L. Paige Whitaker.

[461] 793 F.3d 1, 6 (D.C. Cir. 2015) (citing FEC v. Beaumont, 539 U.S. 146, 161-63 (2003); Citizens United v. FEC, 558 U.S. 310, 359 (2010) ("But the reason for applying strict scrutiny [in *Citizens United*] was not that the case involved a ban, but that it involved independent expenditures rather than contributions.").

[462] 793 F.3d at 14 (quoting *Beaumont*, 539 U.S. at 162 n.9 (2003)).

[463] *See, e.g.*, McCutcheon v. FEC, --- U.S. ---, 134 S. Ct. 1434, 1459 (2014) (observing that, instead of the law that the Court held unconstitutional, Congress has "numerous alternative approaches available" to accomplish the same goals); Davis v. FEC, 554 U.S. 724, 742 (2008) (cautioning that it is "a dangerous business for Congress to use the election laws to influence the voters' choices"). *See also* Citizens United v. FEC, 558 U.S. 310, 460 (2010) (Stevens, J., concurring in part and dissenting in part) (characterizing the majority as not "show[ing] any deference to a coordinate branch of Government" and being "dismissive of Congress").

[464] 582 F.3d 1 (D.C. Cir. 2009).

[465] *See id.* at 22.

[466] *Id.* at 18. Judge Garland has exhibited similar sympathies for Congress's broader interests with respect to campaign finance regulation in cases outside of the context of the First Amendment. For instance, in *Shays v. FEC*, 528 F.3d 914 (D.C. Cir. 2008), Judge Garland joined a unanimous court in requiring the FEC to rewrite more stringent campaign finance regulations. Addressing one regulation, the court found it insufficient to further Congress's goal of prohibiting unregulated "soft money" from being used in connection with federal elections. *Id.* at 925.

[467] Although generally regulated as political committees under federal campaign finance law, super PACs, which are also known as independent expenditure-only committees, are not subject to contribution limits. For further discussion, see CRS Report R43719, *Campaign Finance: Constitutionality of Limits on Contributions and Expenditures*, by L. Paige Whitaker, at 8.

[468] 599 F.3d 686 (D.C. Cir. 2010), *cert. denied sub nom.*, Keating v. FEC, 562 U.S. 1003 (2010).

[469] *See id.* at 696.

[470] *See id.* (citing *Citizens United*, 558 U.S. at 310).

[471] *See id.* at 689.

[472] *Id.* at 693.

[473] *See, e.g.*, Richard L. Hasen, *Garland Is No Sure Bet on Overturning* Citizens United, DAILY J. (March 21, 2016), http://electionlawblog.org/wp-content/uploads/hasen-garland-citizens.pdf ("We should not read too much into Garland's vote in the *SpeechNow v. Federal Election Commission* (2010) case, which established Super PACs. That unanimous ruling was essentially compelled by the Supreme Court's *Citizens United* decision.").

[474] 682 F.3d 72 (D.C. Cir. 2012).

[475] *See id.* at 76-77.

[476] 152 F.3d 974 (D.C. Cir. 1998).

[477] *See id.* at 998.

[478] *Id.* at 997-98.

[479] For examples of Judge Garland's written opinions on free speech, *see, e.g.*, Mpoy v. Rhee, 758 F.3d 285, 287 (D.C. Cir. 2014) (Garland, J.) (affirming the dismissal of a First Amendment retaliation lawsuit brought by a District of Columbia special education teacher); Lee v. U.S. Dep't of Justice (DOJ), 428 F.3d 299, 302 (D.C. Cir. 2005) (en banc)

(Garland, J., dissenting from denial of reh'ing en banc) (contending, in the context of a Privacy Act lawsuit, that the First Amendment requires balancing the public interest in protecting a reporter's sources against the private need for civil discovery); Initiative & Referendum Inst. v. U.S. Postal Serv., 417 F.3d 1299, 1302 (D.C. Cir. 2005) (Garland, J.) (reversing a district court order upholding a regulation banning certain solicitations on Postal Service property); Schoenbohm v. FCC, 204 F.3d 243, 249 (D.C. Cir. 2000) (Garland, J.) (rejecting a First Amendment challenge to an FCC decision not to renew a radio station operator's license). Outside of cases interpreting the Free Speech Clause of the First Amendment, Judge Garland upheld, against a First Amendment Petition Clause challenge, a provision in an appropriations act barring the Federal Transit Administration from enforcing certain regulations related to charter bus service. *See* Am. Bus Ass'n v. Rogoff, 649 F.3d 734, 736-37 (D.C. Cir. 2011).

For examples of free speech cases that Judge Garland participated in while on the D.C. Circuit, *see, e.g.*, Navab-Safavi v. Glassman, 637 F.3d 311, 313 (D.C. Cir. 2011) (Sentelle, C.J., joined by Garland & Williams, JJ.); Thompson v. District of Columbia, 428 F.3d 283 (D.C. Cir. 2005) (Tatel, J., joined by Edwards & Garland, JJ.); Trans Union, LLC v. FTC, 295 F.3d 42, 53 (D.C. Cir. 2002) (Henderson, J., joined by Edwards & Garland, JJ.); Toolasprashad v. Bureau of Prisons, 286 F.3d 576, 584 (D.C. Cir. 2002) (Tatel, J., joined by Garland & Silberman, JJ.); Americable Int'l v. Dep't of Navy, 129 F.3d 1271, 1275 (D.C. Cir. 1997) (Henderson, J., joined by Garland & Wald, JJ.).

For an example of Judge Garland's scholarship that touched upon freedom-of-speech principles prior to his tenure on the D.C. Circuit, see Garland, *Antitrust and State Action*, *supra* note 87, at 516-18.

480 *See, e.g.*, Jeffrey Rosen, *The Nomination of Merrick Garland Is a Victory for Judicial Restraint*, THE ATLANTIC, (March 17, 2016), *available at* http://www.theatlantic.com/politics/archive/2016/03/why-merrick-garland-is-a-judgesjudge/474246/ (citing the ruling in *IRI* as evidence that Garland is a "robust defender ... of the First Amendment rights of speech and petition").

481 *See Initiative & Referendum Inst.*, 417 F.3d at 1302.

482 *Id.* at 1312. The *IRI* court ultimately remanded the case—which involved a facial challenge to the Postal Service regulation—for a determination as to whether the regulation abridged a substantial amount of protected free speech in public forums. *Id.* at 1318.

483 *Id.* at 1307-08.

484 Initiative & Referendum Inst. v. USPS, 417 F.3d 1299, 1307-08 (D.C. Cir. 2005) (quoting Am. Library Ass'n v. Reno, 33 F.3d 78, 88 (D.C. Cir. 1994)).

485 *See id.* at 1306-07 (concluding that the regulation in question, while being content neutral and serving a significant interest, was not narrowly tailored and did not preserve ample alternative channels of communication).

486 Commercial speech is "speech that *proposes* a commercial transaction." Board of Trs. of the State Univ. of New York v. Fox, 492 U.S. 469, 482 (1989) (emphasis in original). For more information on the commercial speech doctrine, see CRS Report 95-815, *Freedom of Speech and Press: Exceptions to the First Amendment*, by Kathleen Ann Ruane, at 14-17.

487 *See, e.g.*, Sorrell v. IMS Health Inc., 564 U.S. 552, 557 (2011) (6-3 decision) (striking down a Vermont law restricting the sale, disclosure, and use of pharmacy records that reveal the prescribing practices of individual doctors for marketing purposes); Thompson v. W. States Med. Ctr., 535 U.S. 357, 360 (2002) (5-4 decision) (striking down a federal restriction on the advertising or promotion of compounded drugs).

[488] *See, e.g.*, POM Wonderful v. FTC, 777 F.3d 478, 500 (D.C. Cir. 2015) ("[I]nsofar as the FTC imposed liability on petitioners for the nineteen ads found to be deceptive by the administrative law judge, the Commission sanctioned petitioners for misleading speech unprotected by the First Amendment.").

[489] *See, e.g.,* Trans Union, LLC v. FTC, 295 F.3d 42, 53 (D.C. Cir. 2002) (holding that the government's interest in "protecting the privacy of consumer credit information" is a substantial one that justifies the regulation of commercial speech).

[490] Am. Meat Inst. v. USDA, 760 F.3d 18, 20 (D.C. Cir. 2014) (en banc) (holding that a rational basis standard of review for commercial disclosure requirements of "purely factual and uncontroversial information" could be applied to requirements beyond those intended to remedy consumer deception).

[491] *Id.* at 23 ("But here we think several aspects of the government's interest in country-of-origin labeling for food combine to make the interest substantial: the context and long history of country-of-origin disclosures to enable consumers to choose American-made products; the demonstrated consumer interest in extending country-of-origin labeling to food products; and the individual health concerns and market impacts that can arise in the event of a food-borne illness outbreak.").

[492] Timothy Noah & Brian Mahoney, *How Liberal is Merrick Garland?*, POLITICO (March 16, 2016), http://www.politico.com/story/2016/03/supreme-court-merrick-garland-220904 ("Invoking First Amendment rights has become a common vehicle for conservatives to challenge agency regulations, but [Judge] Garland has shown little receptivity to that argument.").

[493] For more information on the public employee speech doctrine, see Ruane, *supra* note 486, at 30-36.

[494] *See* Garcetti v. Ceballos, 547 U. S. 410, 421 (2006) (holding that statements made by public employees pursuant to their official duties receive no First Amendment protection); *but see* Lane v. Franks, --- U.S. ---, 134 S. Ct. 2369, 2378 (2014) (holding that the First Amendment "protects a public employee who provides truthful sworn testimony, compelled by subpoena, outside the scope of his ordinary job responsibilities").

[495] *See, e.g.*, Navab-Safavi v. Glassman, 637 F.3d 311, 313 (D.C. Cir. 2011) (affirming the district court's denial of qualified immunity on a public employee's First Amendment claim); LeFande v. District of Columbia, 613 F.3d 1155, 1161 (D.C. Cir. 2010) (holding that a First Amendment retaliation lawsuit was improperly dismissed because the underlying speech touched on matters of public concern); Thompson v. District of Columbia, 428 F.3d 283, 284 (D.C. Cir. 2005) (reversing the dismissal of a claim that the D.C. Lottery Control Board fired a public employee because he engaged in activity protected by the First Amendment); *but see* Baumann v. District of Columbia, 795 F.3d 209, 219 (D.C. Cir. 2015) (affirming the dismissal of a public employee's First Amendment retaliation claim on the grounds that the employee was disclosing confidential information that could jeopardize the work of his employer).

[496] 758 F.3d 285, 295 (D.C. Cir. 2014).

[497] *Id.* at 294.

[498] The existence and extent of journalists' privilege to refuse to divulge confidential sources has long been debated. In *Branzburg v. Hayes*, 408 U.S. 665 (1972), a majority of the Supreme Court held that there is no journalists' privilege under the First Amendment in grand jury investigations. However, Justice Powell, who had joined the majority opinion, also wrote a concurring opinion in which he found that journalists do have a qualified privilege to refuse to testify in criminal cases under certain circumstances. *Id.* at 710 (Powell, J., concurring).

Furthermore, *Branzburg* dealt with a criminal investigation. M ost circuit courts of appeals have limited *Branzburg* to its context (i.e., criminal proceedings, or, even more specifically, grand jury investigations) and have held that a qual ified testimonial privilege does exist for journalists in the context of private civil litigation. *See e.g.*, Gonzales v. Nat'l Broad. Co., 194 F.3d 29 (2d Cir. 1999); Si l kwood v. Kerr-M cGee Corp., 563 F.2d 433, 438 (10th Cir. 1977); Zerel l i v. Smith, 656 F.2d 705, 712 (D.C. Cir. 1981).

499 428 F.3d 299, 302 (D.C. Cir. 2005) (Garland, J, dissenting from denial of reh'ing en banc).

500 *Id.* The appellate panel had upheld a number of contempt orders agai nst journalists who refused to divulge confidential sources of information on the investigation into whether Wen Ho Lee was a spy for the Chinese government in the context of Lee's private civil suit for damages.

501 Lee v. DOJ, 413 F.3d 53, 61 (D.C. Cir. 2005) (affirming contempt orders against four of the journalists, and reversing the contempt order against one journalist); *see also id.* at 56-57 (concluding that the privilege had been overcome because the information sought went to the heart of the matter, and the plaintiff had exhausted all other reasonable sources of the information that were not the journal ists).

502 *Lee*, 428 F.3d at 302.

503 *Id.*

504 *Id.*

505 *Id.* (quoting New York Times Co. v. United States, 403 U.S. 713, 717 (1971) (Black, J., concurring)).

506 *See* 484 F.3d 573 (D.C. Cir. 2007) (en banc).

507 *See id.* at 581 (Sentelle, J., dissenting). Judge Sentelle's dissent garnered a majority of the D.C. Circuit for the proposition that the First Amendment prohibits the punishment of a publisher who discloses information obtained lawfully from a source who obtained the underlying information unlawfully. *Id.* However, Judge Thomas Griffith disagreed on the question of whether the publisher did indeed obtain the underlying information lawfully. *Id.* at 581 (Griffith, J., concurring) ("I believe it is worth noting that a majority of the members of the Court—those who join Part I of Judge Sentelle's dissent—would have found his actions protected by the First Amendment. Nonetheless, because Representative McDermott cannot here wield the First Amendment shield that he voluntarily relinquished as a member of the Ethics Committee, I join Judge Randolph's opinion in concluding that his disclosure of the tape recording was not protected by the First Amendment.").

508 *See id.* at 578 (noting gag orders with respect to grand jury proceedings and several federal laws that criminalize the publication of information lawfully obtained).

509 *See, e.g.*, Mark Joseph Stern, *Supreme Court Breakfast Table*, SLATE (March, 16, 2016), http://www.slate.com/ blogs/browbeat/2016/04/06/what_s_fact_and_what_s_fiction_in_the_people_v_oj_simpson_finale.html ("He takes a fairly broad view of the First Amendment without swinging toward free speech absolutism and typically sides with transparency over the government's efforts to maintain internal secrecy."); James R. Copland, *Merrick Garland Is a 'Qualified' Supreme Court Nominee—But He Doesn't Pass Obama's Test*, FORBES (March 16, 2016), http://www.forbes.com/sites/realspin/2016/03/16/merrick-garland-supreme-court-nominee-obama/#17fc58922d6a ("In First Amendment free speech cases, Judge Garland has tended to take a broad view—except when it comes to campaign-finance regulations.").

510 *See generally* CRS Scalia report, *supra* note 9, at 30-32.

511 *In re* Charges of Judicial Misconduct, 769 F.3d 762, 780 (D.C. Cir. 2014). Judge Garland has, on occasion, applied or examined foreign law in circumstances that have not involved

matters of constitutional interpretation, including in litigation concerning the recognition of foreign judgment or arbitration awards, as well as cases where the D.C. Circuit applied the District of Columbia's choice-of-law rules in civil litigation involving activities occurring abroad. *See, e.g.*, Oveissi v. Islamic Republic of Iran, 573 F.3d 835 (D.C. Cir. 2009) (applying District of Columbia choice-of-law rules and concluding that French rather than U.S. law governed the plaintiff's claims under the Foreign Sovereign Immunities Act); TermoRio S.A. E.S.P. v. Electranta S.P., 487 F.3d 928 (D.C. Cir. 2007) (declining to enforce an arbitration award that had been issued in Colombia, when the award had been lawfully nullified by Colombia's highest administrative court).

512 *See* Al-Bihani v. Obama, 619 F.3d 1 (D.C. 2010) (denying reh'ing en banc) (joining an opinion by Judge Sentelle which stated that "[w]e decline to en banc this case to determine the role of international law-of-war principles in interpreting the [2001 statutory authorization to use military force against those responsible for the September 11, 2001, terrorist attacks] because, as the various opinions issued in the case indicate, the panel's discussion of that question is not necessary to the disposition of the merits"); Saleh v. Titan Corp., 580 F.3d 1, 35 n.30 (D.C. Cir. 2009) (Garland, J., dissenting) (dissenting from a panel opinion that dismissed claims brought by Iraqi nationals against military contractors for abuse inflicted at the Abu Ghraib detention facility, but only expressing clear disagreement with the majority's conclusion that federal law preempted petitioners' state tort claims, and not the majority's conclusion that the alleged torture by private actors was not a violation of the law of nations actionable under the Alien Tort Statute (ATS); "because I conclude that we should permit the state-law claims to go forward at this stage, and because the plaintiffs do not contend that their [ATS] claims would provide them with different relief ... I do not address the latter.").

513 *See, e.g.*, Roeder v. Islamic Republic of Iran (*Roeder II*), 646 F.3d 56 (D.C. Cir. 2011) (2008 amendments to the Foreign Sovereign Immunities Act did not preclude the continued effect of the Algiers Accords, an executive agreement between the United States and Iran that had settled claims relating to the 1979-1981 Iran hostage crisis); Fund for Animals, Inc. v. Kempthorne, 472 F.3d 872 (D.C. Cir. 2006) (Migratory Bird Treaty Reform Act superseded requirements established by earlier bird treaties and their implementing legislation); Roeder v. Islamic Republic of Iran (*Roeder I*), 333 F.3d 228 (D.C. Cir. 2003) (2002 amendments to the Foreign Sovereign Immunities Act did not abrogate the earlier Algiers Accords); Kappus v. Comm'r of Internal Revenue, 337 F.3d 1053 (D.C. Cir. 2003) (Garland, J.) (provisions of the Internal Revenue Code superseded conflicting provisions in an earlier United States-Canada Tax Treaty).

514 Whitney v. Robinson, 120 U.S. 190, 194 (1888) ("[I]f there be any conflict between the stipulations of the treaty and the requirements of the law, the latter must control.").

515 *See Kempthorne*, 472 F.3d at 878-79 (discussing the relationship between the two canons). While both canons derive from Supreme Court opinions concerning the relationship between federal statutes and ratified treaties, *see, e.g.*, Whitney v. Robertson, 120 U.S. 190, 194 (1888) and Cook v. United States, 288 U.S. 102, 120 (1933), courts including the D.C. Circuit have applied the canon of abrogation to avoid nullifying provisions of international legal compacts taking the form of executive agreements rather than treaties. *See, e.g.*, *Roeder II*, 646 F.3d at 61-62 (concerning an executive agreement settling claims with Iran); *Roeder I*, 333 F.3d at 237 ("[N]either a treaty nor an executive agreement will be considered abrogated or modified by a later statute unless such purpose on the part of Congress has been clearly expressed.") (internal quotations omitted).

516 *See Kempthorne*, 472 F.3d at 879; *Kappus*, 337 F.3d at 1057-60.

[517] *Roeder II*, 646 F.3d at 59-50; *Roeder I*, 333 F.3d at 238 (panel opinion holding the Algiers Accords were not abrogated by general language in amendments to the Foreign Sovereign Immunities Act; "Congress (or the President acting alone) may abrogate an executive agreement, but legislation must be clear to ensure that Congress—and the President—have considered the consequences.").

[518] 724 F.3d 230 (D.C. Cir. 2013) (Brown, J., joined by Garland, J.).

[519] *Id.* at 232.

[520] *Id.* at 234.

[521] *Id.* Writing in dissent, Judge Sentelle criticized the majority for looking beyond the clear text of the statute for evidence of "ambiguity" that would warrant interpreting the law in a manner that would not supersede the earlier agreements. He argued that no Supreme Court decision required that a superseding statute offer a clear statement of its intent to abrogate an agreement, and that the majority's recognition of such a requirement "elevates treaties above statutes by making it more difficult for Congress to abrogate prior treaties than prior statutes." *Id.* at 240 (Sentelle, J., dissenting).

[522] *See generally* CRS Scalia report, *supra* note 9, at 30-32.

[523] *See* Hartford Fire Ins. Co. v. California, 509 U.S. 764, 814-15 (1993) (Scalia, J., dissenting) (approvingly citing Chief Justice John Marshall's statement in *Murray v. Schooner Charming Betsy*, 6 U.S. (2 Cranch) 64 (1804), that "an act of congress ought never to be construed to violate the law of nations if any other possible construction remains").

[524] *See Hartford Fire Ins. Co.*, 509 U.S. at 814-15 (1993) (Scalia, J., dissenting) (arguing that an antitrust statute should be construed consistently with international principles concerning respect for foreign sovereignty); Hoffmann-La Roche Ltd. v. Empagran S.A., 542 U.S. 155, 176 (2004) (Scalia, J., concurring) (concurring in judgment because the majority's construction of the relevant statute was "consistent with the principle that statutes should be read in accord with the customary deference to the application of foreign countries' laws within their own territories").

[525] For example, Justice Scalia joined a number of Supreme Court opinions which recognized that the Vienna Convention on Consular Relations, Apr. 24, 1963, 21 U.S.T. 77, 596 U.N.T.S. 261, and related protocols, along with judgments issued by the International Court of Justice instructing U.S. authorities to reconsider the capital sentences issued to foreign nationals who were not properly notified of their ability to contact consular officials upon arrest, did not carve out an exception to later-in-time federal and state procedural default rules that denied reconsideration of many of these criminal sentences. *See* Medellin v. Texas, 552 U.S. 491 (2008); Sanchez-Llamas v. Oregon, 548 U.S. 331 (2006); Breard v. Greene, 523 U.S. 371 (1998) (per curiam). These cases may be distinguishable because they involved matters where the requirements of the earlier *international agreements* were arguably perceived to be ambiguous, rather than the later-in-time federal and state statutes. *See Medellin*, 552 U.S. at 552-53 (declining to interpret a protocol to the Vienna Convention on Consular Relations as rendering a judgment by the International Court of Justice into enforceable U.S. law; "[n]othing in the text, background, negotiating and drafting history, or practice among signatory nations suggests" the underlying agreement was intended to give domestic effect to International Court of Justice judgements); *Sanchez-Llamas*, 548 U.S. at 337 (expressly declining to "resolve the question whether the Vienna Convention grants ... enforceable rights" relating to consular notification to foreign nationals).

[526] *See supra* "Statutory Interpretation."

[527] See CRS Legal Sidebar WSLG1519, *Merrick B. Garland: Selected Primary Material*, by Emily E. Roberts and Eva M. Tarnay.

[528] *See, e.g.*, Chris Eger, *Merrick Garland Termed "Most Anti-Gun Nominee in Recent History,"* GUNS.COM (March 17, 2016), http://www.guns.com/2016/03/17/merrick-garland-termed-most-anti-gun-nominee-in-recent-history/ (quoting a commentator of the view that "a basic analysis of Merrick Garland's judicial record shows that he does not respect our fundamental, individual right to keep and bear arms for self-defense"); Nina Totenberg, *Why Merrick Garland's Judicial Record Slips Through Critics' Fingers*, NAT'L PUB. RADIO (March 27, 2016), http://www.npr.org/2016/03/27/472051889/a-look-at-garlands-judicial-record-reveals-few-hot-buttons (quoting a commentator to the effect that "[t]he evidence that is being cited for the accusation that Judge Garland has some bias against Second Amendment rights is from thin to nonexistent").

[529] 2007 U.S. App. LEXIS 11029 (D.C. Cir. May 8, 2007) (per curiam) (order denying en banc review).

[530] 478 F.3d 370 (D.C. Cir. 2007).

[531] *See* 2007 U.S. App. LEXIS 11029, at *4.

[532] *See id.*; *see also supra* "Predicting Nominees' Future Decisions on the Court" (discussing the difficulties of inferring a nominee's views from votes on procedural matters, particularly where the nominee did not author an opinion).

[533] District of Columbia v. Heller, 552 U.S. 1035 (2007).

[534] District of Columbia v. Heller, 554 U.S. 570 (2008).

[535] Seegars v. Ashcroft, 396 F.3d 1248 (D.C. Cir. 2005), *reh'g denied sub nom.*, Seegars v. Gonzales, 413 F.3d 1 (D.C. Cir. 2005), *cert. denied*, 2006 U.S. LEXIS 1049 (January 23, 2006). The D.C. Circuit panel had dismissed this case for lack of justiciability.

[536] 216 F.3d 122 (D.C. Cir. 2000) (Tatel, J., majority opinion), *cert. denied*, 533 U.S. 928 (2001). Since FY2004, Congress has included provisions in the Commerce, Justice, Science, and Related Agencies appropriations act that require the Federal Bureau of Investigation to destroy within 24 hours the background check records on persons who are eligible to receive firearms. This provision was crafted in response to the rule that was at issue in the *NRA* decision. *See, e.g.*, P.L. 108-199, §617(a)(2), 118 Stat. 95 (January 23, 2004); P.L. 112-55, §511(2), 125 Stat. 632 (November 18, 2011) (including futurity language ("hereafter") in this appropriations provision); *but see* 3 FEDERAL APPROPRIATIONS LAW at 2-34-35 (3d. ed. 2004) (noting that "use of the word hereafter may not guarantee that an appropriation act provision will be found to constitute permanent law.").

[537] 216 F.3d at 132, 137. A dissent, however, opined that Congress did not authorize, and in fact prohibited, DOJ from taking such action. *Id.* at 141 (Sentelle, J., dissenting).

[538] For an overview of the functionalist and formalist lines of separation of powers analysis, see generally John F. Manning, *Separation of Powers as Ordinary Interpretation*, 124 HARV. L. REV. 1939 (2011).

[539] *See* U.S. CONST. art. 1, §7, cl. 1 ("All Bills for raising Revenue shall originate in the House of Representatives; but the Senate may propose or concur with Amendments as on other Bills.").

[540] Sissel v. HHS, 760 F.3d 1 (D.C. Cir. 2014). The plaintiff asserted that the Affordable Care Act (ACA) is unconstitutional as a revenue-raising measure that was introduced in the Senate. To resolve what it viewed as a dispute involving the separation of powers between the House of Representatives and the Senate, the panel held unanimously that the ACA does not fall under the Origination Clause because "the paramount aim of the ACA is 'to increase the number of Americans covered by health insurance and decrease the cost of health care,' ... not to raise revenue by means of the shared responsibility payment.'" *Id.* at 8 (citing NFIB v. Sebelius, --- U.S. ---, 132 S. Ct. 2566, 2580 (2012)).

[541] Sissel v. HHS, 799 F.3d 1035, 1049 (D.C. Cir. 2015) (Kavanaugh, J., joined by Henderson, Brown, & Griffith, JJ., dissenting from denial of reh'ing en banc).

[542] *Id.* at 1036 (Rogers, J., joined by Pillard & Wilkins, JJ., concurring in the denial of reh'ing en banc).

[543] The concurrence is essentially a defense of the original panel's opinion, written by its authors, against points raised by the dissent.

[544] *Sissel*, 799 F.3d at 1049 (Kavanaugh, J., dissenting from denial of reh'ing en banc) ("The panel opinion sets a constitutional precedent that is too important to let linger and metastasize. Although no doubt viewed by some today as a trivial or anachronistic annoyance, the Origination Clause was an integral part of the Framers' blueprint for protecting the people from excessive federal taxation.... By newly exempting a substantial swath of tax legislation from the Origination Clause, the panel opinion degrades the House's origination authority in a way contrary to the Constitution's text and history, and contrary to congressional practice.").

[545] Sissel v. HHS, 136 S. Ct. 925 (2016).

[546] Zivotofsky v. Sec'y of State, 571 F.3d 1227 (D.C. Cir. 2009), *reh'g en banc denied*, 610 F.3d 84 (D.C. Cir. 2010). Judge Edwards filed a statement objecting to the denial of en banc review on the basis that the courts have a responsibility to decide the constitutionality of statutes that are alleged to impinge on presidential powers. 610 F.3d at 85 (Edwards, J., statement on denial of reh'ing en banc) ("[T]he court has effectively conflated the distinction between cases involving justiciable separation of powers issues and nonjusticiable political questions....").

[547] Zivotofsky v. Clinton, --- U.S. ---, 132 S. Ct. 1421 (2013). For more information and analysis of the *Zivotofsky* cases, see CRS Report R43834, *The Political Question Doctrine: Justiciability and the Separation of Powers*, by Jared P. Cole; CRS Report R43773, *Zivotofsky v. Kerry: The Jerusalem Passport Case and Its Potential Implications for Congress's Foreign Affairs Powers*, by Jennifer K. Elsea.

[548] 725 F.3d 255, 268 (D.C. Cir. 2013) (Garland, C.J., dissenting). For more information about the Yucca Mountain litigation, see CRS Report R44151, *Yucca Mountain: Legal Developments Relating to the Designated Nuclear Waste Repository*, by Todd Garvey and Alexandra M. Wyatt.

[549] *In re Aiken Cty.*, 725 F.3d. at 259.

[550] *Id.* at 257 (Kavanaugh, J., majority opinion). The statute at issue was the Nuclear Waste Policy Act, which provides that the NRC "shall consider" the Yucca Mountain license and "shall issue a final decision approving or disapproving" the application within three years of its submission. 42 U.S.C. §10134(d).

[551] *Id.* at 268-69 (Garland, C.J., dissenting).

[552] *Id.* (citing United States *ex rel.* Sierra Land & Water Co. v. Ickes, 84 F.2d 228, 232 (D.C. Cir. 1936)).

[553] *Id.* at 269-70. Judge Garland suggested it might be the court rather than the Commission that was overstepping its constitutional authority. *Id.* at 270 ("[W]e are not in a position—nor do we have any basis—to second-guess [the NRC's] conclusion [that progress on the application was impossible given the available funds].").

[554] 5 U.S.C. §552.

[555] Judicial Watch, Inc. v. U.S. Secret Serv., 726 F.3d 208 (D.C. Cir. 2013).

[556] *Id.* at 226 (Garland, C.J., opinion for the court).

[557] For an overview of detainee cases at the D.C. Circuit, see CRS Report R41156, *Judicial Activity Concerning Enemy Combatant Detainees: Major Court Rulings*, by Jennifer K. Elsea and Michael John Garcia.

[558] 321 F.3d 1134 (D.C. Cir. 2003).

[559] *Id.* at 1139 ("Judicial proceedings would engender a 'conflict between judicial and military opinion' and 'would diminish the prestige of' any field commander as he was called 'to account in his own civil courts' and would 'divert his efforts and attention from the military offensive abroad to the legal defensive at home.'") (citing Johnson v. Eisentrager, 339 U.S. 763, 779 (1950)).

[560] 542 U.S. 466 (2004) (holding that the habeas statute, 28 U.S.C. §2241, extends to Guantanamo Bay, Cuba).

[561] Congress first passed the Detainee Treatment Act, P.L. 109-148, Title X, 119 Stat. 2739-2745 (December 30, 2005); P.L. 109-163, Title XIV, 119 Stat. 3474-80 (January 6, 2006). After the Supreme Court interpreted the habeas-stripping language inapplicable to pending cases, Hamdan v. Rumsfeld, 548 U.S. 557 (2006), Congress enacted a new measure as part of the Military Commissions Act of 2006, P.L. 109-366, 102 Stat. 2600 (October 17, 2006).

[562] Boumediene v. Bush, 553 U.S. 723, 764 (2008). Judge Garland did not participate in this case or the *Hamdan* case when they were considered by the D.C. Circuit.

[563] Al Odah v. United States, 611 F.3d 8 (D.C. Cir. 2010), *cert. denied*, 131 S. Ct. 1812 (2011).

[564] Hatim v. Obama, 760 F.3d 54, 57-58 (D.C. Cir. 2014) (Griffith, J., majority opinion) (relying on Aamer v. Obama, 742 F.3d 1023 (D.C. Cir. 2014)).

[565] *Id.* at 59.

[566] 532 F.3d 834 (D.C. Cir. 2008).

[567] *Id.* at 836 (Garland, J., opinion for the court) (directing the government to release the detainee, transfer him, or "expeditiously convene a new Combatant Status Review Tribunal to consider evidence submitted in a manner consistent with this opinion"). The detainee, an ethnic Uighur who had conceded that he attended a training camp in Afghanistan run by a Chinese dissident group, argued that the tribunal based its determination on insufficient evidence to demonstrate his affiliation with an "associated force" as the government defined the term. *Id.*

[568] Bismullah v. Gates, 503 F.3d 137 (D.C. Cir. 2007) (holding that the record on review of CSRT decisions must include all information reasonably available to the government), *reh'g en banc denied*, 514 F.3d 1291 (D.C. Cir. 2008). The circuit split 5-5 in denying a rehearing to the government, which had urged the court to order narrowly circumscribed review of CSRT determinations considering only information that had been presented to the tribunal. All 10 circuit judges wrote or joined opinions explaining why they would grant or deny rehearing. Judge Garland alone wrote separately to concur in the denial but take no position on the merits, explaining the case ought to move forward so that the Supreme Court could take it into consideration in its then pending *Boumediene* decision. 514 F.3d at 1299 (Garland, J., concurring in the denial of reh'ing en banc).

[569] *Parhat*, 532 F.3d at 846-47 (Garland, J., opinion for the court) ("The documents repeatedly describe [] activities and relationships [among asserted enemy forces] as having 'reportedly' occurred, as being 'said to' or 'reported to' have happened, and as things that 'may' be true or are 'suspected of' having taken place. But in virtually every instance, the documents do not say who 'reported' or 'said' or 'suspected' those things. Nor do they provide any of the underlying reporting upon which the documents' bottom-line assertions are founded, nor any assessment of the reliability of that reporting.").

[570] The Detainee Treatment Act permitted a limited review by the D.C. Circuit of "whether the status determination of the [CSRT] ... was consistent with the standards and procedures specified by the Secretary of Defense for [CSRTs] (including the requirement that the conclusion of the Tribunal be supported by a preponderance of the evidence and allowing a rebuttable presumption in favor the Government's evidence); and ... to the extent the Constitution and laws of the United States are applicable, whether the use of such standards and procedures to make the determination is consistent with the Constitution and laws of the United States." 10 U.S.C. §801 note. The Supreme Court held that this limited review was an inadequate substitute for habeas corpus review. Boumediene v. Bush, 553 U.S. 723, 787-93 (2008).

[571] When *Bismullah* returned to the D.C. Circuit after *Boumediene*, the appellate court implied that, despite its determination that the Detainee Treatment Act review process was no longer available, the circuit court's ruling in *Parhat* remained in force. Bismullah v. Gates, 551 F.3d 1068, 1075 (D.C. Cir. 2009); *see also* Bensayah v. Obama, 610 F.3d 718, 725-26 (D.C. Cir. 2010) ("In *Parhat* we made clear that the reliability of evidence can be determined not only by looking at the evidence alone but, alternatively, by considering 'sufficient additional information ... permit[ting the fact finder] to assess its reliability.'").

[572] *See, e.g.*, Khan v. Obama, 655 F.3d 20, 27 (D.C. Cir. 2011) (Garland, J.) (finding Army intelligence collectors' declarations added sufficient indicia of reliability to meet the *Parhat* test); Al Alwi v. Obama, 653 F.3d 11, 20 (D.C. Cir. 2011) (Garland, J.) (detainees' own statements may be deemed reliable without corroboration if other indicia of reliability exist, such as the failure of the detainee to retract statements, the consistency of the statements, and the supporting evidence from which relevant inferences may be drawn); Alsabri v. Obama, 684 F.3d 1298, 1308 (D.C. Cir. 2012) (Garland, J., opinion for the court) (confirming that it is proper for the district court to afford the government an opportunity to supplement evidence with sufficient additional information to permit the fact finder to assess the reliability of a document that, by itself, lacked sufficient indicia of reliability); Obaydullah v. Obama, 688 F.3d 784, 792 (D.C. Cir. 2012) (per curiam) (affirming the district court's finding that the government's evidence was reliable despite minor discrepancies between the intelligence report and corroborating information).

[573] *See, e.g.*, Awad v. Obama, 608 F.3d 1, 7 (D.C. Cir. 2010) (Sentelle, C.J.) ("[T]he fact that the district court generally relied on items of evidence that contained hearsay is of no consequence. To show error in the court's reliance on hearsay evidence, the habeas petitioner must establish not that it is hearsay, but that it is unreliable hearsay.").

[574] Al Bahlul v. United States, 767 F.3d 1 (D.C. Cir. 2014) (en banc), *overruling* Hamdan v. United States, 696 F.3d 1238 (D.C. Cir. 2012).

[575] P.L. 109-366, 102 Stat. 2600 (October 17, 2006).

[576] 10 U.S.C. §950p (2006) (declaring the MCA "codif[ies] offenses that have traditionally been triable by military commissions," and that "because the provisions ... codify offenses that have traditionally been triable under the law of war or otherwise triable by military commission, this subchapter does not preclude trial for offenses that occurred before the date of the enactment...."). When Congress replaced this statute with the Military Commission Act of 2009, P.L. 111-84, div. A, Title XVIII, it included substantially the same language. 10 U.S.C. §950p(d).

[577] *Al Bahlul*, 767 F.3d at 16 (citing Ass'n of Am. R.R.s v. Dep't of Transp., 721 F.3d 666, 673 n.7 (D.C. Cir. 2013)).

[578] U.S. CONST. art. I, §9, cl. 3 ("No Bill of Attainder or ex post facto Law shall be passed.").

[579] *Al Bahlul*, 767 F.3d at 18. The government had taken the position that the Clause applies, while the judges on the court took different views. Judge Garland would have found the Clause applicable. *Id.* at 18 n.9.

[580] *Id.* at 31. The questions to be addressed included (1) whether Congress exceeded its Article I, §8, authority by defining crimes triable by military commission to include conduct that does not violate the international law of war, and (2) whether Congress violated Article III by vesting the executive branch with authority to try crimes that are not violations of the international law of war.

[581] *Id.* at 35 (Rogers, J., concurring in the judgment in part and dissenting in part) ("Every extension of military jurisdiction is an encroachment on the jurisdiction of the civil courts....") (quoting Reid v. Covert, 354 U.S. 1, 21 (1957)).

[582] Al Bahlul v. United States, 792 F.3d 1 (D.C. Cir. 2015).

[583] For more information about the Al Bahlul case, see CRS Legal Sidebar WSLG1309, *Al Qaeda Propagandist's Remaining Military Commission Conviction Voided*, by Jennifer K. Elsea.

[584] *See supra* notes 38-41 and accompanying text.

[585] *See* Griswold v. Connecticut, 381 U.S. 479, 484 (1965).

[586] *See* Planned Parenthood v. Casey, 505 U.S. 833, 851 (1992).

[587] *See* Loving v. Virginia, 388 U.S. 1, 12 (1967).

[588] *See, e.g.*, Charlotte Alter, *Nobody Knows Where Merrick Garland Stands on Abortion Rights* (March 17, 2016), http://time.com/4261844/merrick-garland-the-abortion-rights-sphinx/ ("Yet nobody seems to know what Judge Garland thinks about abortion."); Laura Bassett, *Merrick Garland's Abortion Stance Is a Big Question Mark* (March 16, 2016), http://www.huffingtonpost.com/entry/merrick-garland-abortion-rights_us_56e9a58be4b065e2e3d8378d ("The ninth Supreme Court justice could determine the fate of reproductive rights for millions of American women—but Merrick Garland, President Barack Obama's nominee to fill the vacancy on the court, has not specified where he stands on abortion or whether he would uphold the decision made in the landmark abortion rights case Roe v. Wade.").

[589] 495 F.3d 695, 697 (D.C. Cir. 2007).

[590] The *Lochner* era refers to the 1908 case of *Lochner v. New York*, 198 U.S. 45 (1908), and its progeny in the early 20th century, where the Court struck down state economic regulations on substantive due process grounds.

[591] Garland, *Antitrust and State Action*, *supra* note 87, at 499-500, 507-09 (criticizing a limitation on the state action doctrine in antitrust law and comparing it to the *Lochner* era).

[592] Ass'n of Bituminous Contrs. v. Apfel, 156 F.3d 1246, 1255 (D.C. Cir. 1998).

[593] *Id.*

[594] *See* CRS Scalia report, *supra* note 9, at 37-39.

[595] *See* 448 F.3d 392, 403 (D.C. Cir. 2006) (Silberman, J., concurring).

[596] *See* 235 F.3d 637, 651 (D.C. Cir. 2001) ("[A]n individual can assert a substantive due process right to protection by the District of Columbia from third-party violence when District of Columbia officials affirmatively act to increase or create the danger that ultimately results in the individual's harm.").

[597] Deshaney v. Winnebago Cty. Dep't of Social Servs., 489 U.S. 189, 196 (1989).

[598] 188 F.3d 531, 534 (D.C. Cir. 1999).

[599] *Id.* at 552 (Wald & Garland, JJ., concurring in part and concurring in result).

[600] *Id.* at 538 (part II-A).

[601] Michael H. v. Gerald D., 491 U.S. 110, 127 n.6 (1988) (Scalia, J., joined by Rehnquist, C.J.).

[602] 188 F.3d at 538.

[603] *Id.* at 552 (Wald and Garland, JJ., concurring in part and concurring in result).

[604] *See* CRS Scalia report, *supra* note 9, at 39-41. The Takings Clause limits government action by providing that private property shall not be "taken for public use" without "just compensation." *See* U.S. Const. amend. V.

[605] In one of the few cases that CRS identified which raised takings claims in which he participated, Judge Garland joined an opinion rejecting a facial takings challenge to an FCC rule that forbid landlords from restricting tenants' installation or use of certain over-the-air reception devices on property leased to the tenants. Bldg. Owners & Managers Assoc. Int'l v. FCC, 254 F.3d 89, 91, 97-100 (D.C. Cir. 2001).

[606] *See* 28 U.S.C. §§1346(a)(2), 1491(a)(1). The $10,000 amount specified here would encompass most claims for just compensation against the federal government.

[607] For example, the D.C. Circuit has exercised jurisdiction over a facial takings challenge to a federal agency rule. *E.g., Bldg. Owners & Managers Assoc. Int'l*, 254 F.3d at 97-100; *see generally* Nat'l Mining Ass'n v. Kempthorne, 512 F.3d 702, 711 (D.C. Cir. 2008) ("[T]he Claims Court is not a proper venue if a statute creates an identifiable class of cases in which application of the statute will necessarily constitute a taking.") (internal citations and quotations omitted).

[608] The CFC has exclusive jurisdiction over such claims "by default." In other words, no federal law vests another federal court with jurisdiction over these claims. Robert Meltz, *The Impact of* Eastern Enterprises *and Possible Legislation on the Jurisdiction and Remedies of the U.S. Court of Federal Claims*, 51 ALA. L. REV. 1161, 1161 (2000).

[609] 28 U.S.C. §1295(a)(3).

[610] *See* Chicago, Burlington & Quincy R.R. Co. v. City of Chicago, 166 U.S. 226, 234-35 (1897).

[611] *See, e.g.*, Tate v. District of Columbia, 627 F.3d 904, 909 (D.C. Cir. 2010); Roth v. King, 449 F.3d 1272, 1283 (D.C. Cir. 2006).

In: Judge Merrick Garland
Editor: Collin Weber
ISBN: 978-1-63485-991-2

Chapter 2

MAJORITY, CONCURRING, AND DISSENTING OPINIONS AUTHORED BY JUDGE MERRICK GARLAND*

R. Chuck Mason

SUMMARY

On March 16, 2016, President Obama nominated Judge Merrick Garland of the U.S. Court of Appeals for the District of Columbia Circuit (D.C. Circuit) to fill the vacancy on the Supreme Court left by the death of Justice Antonin Scalia on February 13, 2016. Judge Garland was appointed to the D.C. Circuit in April 1997, and since February 2013 has served as the circuit court's Chief Judge, an administrative position that rotates among the active judges on the circuit. To assist Members and committees of Congress and their staff in their ongoing research into Judge Garland's approach to the law, CRS attorneys have prepared tabular listings of cases in which Judge Garland authored an opinion. These opinions are categorized into two tables: one table identifying opinions authored by Judge Garland on behalf of the reviewing court, and the other table identifying opinions authored by Judge Garland that concur with or dissent from the majority opinion.

While this report identifies and briefly describes judicial opinions authored by Judge Garland during his tenure on the federal court, it does not analyze the implications of his judicial opinions or suggest how he

* This is an edited, reformatted and augmented version of a Congressional Research Service, Publication No. R44484, dated May 2, 2016.

might approach legal issues if appointed to the Supreme Court. Those matters are discussed in *Judge Merrick Garland: His Jurisprudence and Potential Impact on the Supreme Court*, coordinated by Andrew Nolan, Kate M. Manuel, and Brandon J. Murrill.

INTRODUCTION

On March 16, 2016, President Obama nominated Judge Merrick Garland of the U.S. Court of Appeals for the District of Columbia Circuit (D.C. Circuit) to fill the vacancy on the Supreme Court left by the death of Justice Antonin Scalia on February 13, 2016. Judge Garland was appointed to the D.C. Circuit in April 1997, and since February 2013 has served as the circuit court's Chief Judge, an administrative position that rotates among the active judges on the circuit.[1] During his nearly two decades on the bench, Judge Garland has served on three-judge or en banc D.C. Circuit panels that have made rulings in well over 1,000 cases.[2] He has also served on a few panel decisions at the district court level.[3] Cases considered by Judge Garland have concerned a wide range of legal topics ranging from rulemaking by federal administrative agencies, to criminal law and procedure, to the review of legal challenges arising under the local laws of the District of Columbia.

To assist Members and committees of Congress and their staff in their ongoing research into Judge Garland's approach to the law, this report identifies and briefly summarizes each of the more than 350 cases in which Judge Garland has authored a majority, concurring, or dissenting opinion. Arguably, these written opinions provide the greatest insight into Judge Garland's judicial approach, as a judge's vote in a case or decision to join an opinion authored by a colleague may be based upon a number of considerations and may not necessarily represent full agreement with a joined opinion.[4] This report does not address instances when Judge Garland sat on a reviewing judicial panel but did not author an opinion. Accordingly, instances where Judge Garland was part of a panel that issued a per curiam opinion, which did not credit a particular judge as the author, are omitted from this report. The report also does not address subsequent legal proceedings that may have occurred after a cited decision was issued.[5]

The opinions listed in this report are categorized into two tables: one table identifying opinions authored by Judge Garland on behalf of the reviewing court, and the other table identifying opinions authored by Judge Garland separate from the majority opinion. Cases are listed in reverse chronological order by date of decision. In each case, the key ruling or rulings of the case are succinctly described. Judicial opinions discussed in this report are categorized using the following 19 legal subject areas:

- Administrative law
- Civil liability (e.g., tort preemption, arbitration, class actions, statutory right to sue)
- Civil rights
- Criminal law/procedure
- D.C. local government
- Election law
- Environmental law
- Energy
- Federalism
- Federal courts (e.g., standing to sue, civil procedure)
- First Amendment (e.g., freedom of speech, freedom of the press)
- Government information (e.g., claims concerning the Freedom of Information Act)
- Health care (e.g., Medicare or Medicaid reimbursement)
- International law
- Labor law
- National security
- Separation of powers
- Tax law
- Transportation

Where appropriate, multiple subject areas are identified as relevant to a particular case. The list above is not an exhaustive accounting of all possible subject areas addressed by the cases below, but focuses on those legal topics that have most frequently arisen in cases adjudicated by Judge Garland. Moreover, the fact that a case is categorized under a particular legal subject area does not necessarily mean that some observers might not deem other categories to be pertinent. For example, several cases concerning the disposition of challenges brought by wartime detainees held at the U.S. Naval Station at Guantanamo Bay, Cuba, are categorized solely under the legal subject area of "National security," though some observers may believe that such cases also could be deemed to fall under the "Separation of powers" category (because they arguably concern judicial review of executive discretion in wartime matters) or the "Administrative law" category (because such cases often involve review of determinations made through an administrative process employed by the U.S. military to assess whether a person is properly detained as an enemy belligerent). Accordingly, while the categorizations employed by this report may provide a helpful guide to readers in locating decisions dealing with particular topics, they do not necessarily reflect the full range of legal issues raised by a judicial opinion.

METHODOLOGY

The cases included in this report were compiled utilizing the following methodology:

- The majority opinions were found by searching the District of Columbia Circuit—U.S. Court of Appeals database on Lexis for *OpinionBy(Garland).*[6]
- The concurring opinions were found by searching the District of Columbia Circuit—U.S. Court of Appeals database on Lexis for *ConcurBy(Garland).*[7]
- The dissenting opinions were found by searching the District of Columbia Circuit—U.S. Court of Appeals database on Lexis for *DissentBy(Garland).*[8]
- Concurring or dissenting opinions issued in cases where Judge Garland wrote the majority opinion were found by searching the District of Columbia Circuit—U.S. Court of Appeals database on Lexis for *OpinionBy(Garland),*[9] and limiting those results by searching for *Judges(concur! or dissent!).*[10]
- District court opinions in which Judge Garland is credited as an author were found by searching the District of Columbia Circuit—U.S. District Court Cases database on Lexis for *Judges(Garland).*[11]

Not all results from these searches ultimately proved to be relevant, such as when the D.C. Circuit declined a petition for en banc rehearing in a one-sentence decision joined by all of the reviewing judges.[12] That decision and similar rulings are not discussed in this report. Ultimately, this methodology resulted in the identification of 355 instances in which Judge Garland is credited as an author of a judicial opinion in cases either before the D.C. Circuit (354 cases) or the U.S. District Court for the District of Columbia (a single case).

Table 1. Majority Opinions Authored by Judge Garland

Case Name	Citation	Year	Role	Subject	Holding
Fed. Election Comm'n (FEC)v. Craig for U.S. Senate	No. 14-5297, 2016 U.S. App. LEXIS 4094	2016	Authored Majority	Election law	*Affirmed:* A former U.S. Senator's conversion of campaign funds for his legal defense violated the Federal Election Campaign Act.
Minter v. District of Columbia	809 F.3d 66	2015	Authored Majority	Labor law	*Motion Denied:* District court summary judgment in favor of the District of Columbia was affirmed; former city employee had challenged her firing under the Americans with Disabilities Act (ADA) and the Rehabilitation Act.
United States v. Law	806 F.3d 1103	2015	Authored Majority	Criminal law/procedure	*Affirmed:* The district court did not err in sentencing a drug offender; the sentence was substantively reasonable and it did not violate the Eighth Amendment.
Spurlino Materials, LLC v. Nat'l Labor Relations Bd. (NLRB)	805 F.3d 1131	2015	Authored Majority	Labor law	*Petition for review Denied; cross-application for enforcement of order Granted:* Substantial evidence supported a NLRB ruling that an employer engaged in an unfair labor practice.

Table 1. (Continued)

Case Name	Citation	Year	Role	Subject	Holding
Pac. Coast Supply, LLC v. NLRB	801 F.3d 321	2015	Authored Majority	Labor law	*Petition for review Denied; cross-application for enforcement of order Granted:* Substantial evidence supported a NLRB order that determined employer violated the National Labor Relations Act (NLRA) when it unilaterally withdrew recognition from a union; and NLRB did not wrongly bar employer from supporting its position with post-withdrawal evidence.
Cause of Action v. Fed. Trade Comm'n (FTC)	799 F.3d 1108	2015	Authored Majority	Government information	*Reversed and Remanded:* District court applied incorrect analysis in rejecting nonprofit's application for waiver of two Freedom of Information Act (FOIA) request fees; a third application was not moot.
Intercollegiate Broad. Sys. v. Copyright Royalty Bd. & Librarian of Cong.	796 F.3d 111	2015	Authored Majority	Separation of powers	*Affirmed:* Properly appointed Copyright Royalty Board's de novo review of prior decision by improperly appointed officials did not violate the Appointments Clause; and Board's decision setting a fee was not arbitrary and capricious.

Table 1. (Continued)

Case Name	Citation	Year	Role	Subject	Holding
					should affect the defendant's sentence and for further factual development regarding defendant's ineffective assistance of counsel claims.
Harris v. D.C. Water & Sewer Auth.	791 F.3d 65	2015	Authored Majority	Labor law& Civil rights	*Reversed:* The court reversed the district court's dismissal of plaintiff's retaliation suit under Title VII of the Civil Rights Act of 1964, because plaintiff alleged facts that made the claim plausible.
United States v. Sanders	778 F.3d 1042	2015	Authored Majority	Criminal law/procedure	*Affirmed:* Conviction was affirmed because, among other things, the district court did not err in instructing defendant regarding his rights; and any assumed error in jury instructions did not prejudice the defendant.
Robinson v. Wash. Metro. Area Transit Auth.(WMATA)	774 F.3d 33	2014	Authored Majority	Civil liability	*Affirmed:* Under the common law of the District of Columbia, there was insufficient evidence for a reasonable jury to hold a bus company liable for a passenger's injuries.

Case Name	Citation	Year	Role	Subject	*Holding*
United States v. Schmuckler	792 F.3d 158	2015	Authored Majority	Criminal law/procedure	*Affirmed in part and Vacated and Remanded in part:* The court vacated one count of a conviction because of insufficient evidence, but denied request for remand to the district court to inquire into jury selection.
Wagner v. FEC	793 F.3d 1	2015	Authored Majority	Election law & First Amendment	*Ordered by en banc Court of Appeals:* A federal statute that prohibited individuals and companies, who at the time were performing or negotiating contracts with the federal government, from contributing to a federal political campaign did not violate the First Amendment or equal protection requirements of the Fifth Amendment.
United States v. Kaufman	791 F.3d 86	2015	Authored Majority	Criminal law/procedure	*Affirmed:* The sentence imposed by the district court for embezzlement conviction was within the range of the U.S. Sentencing Guidelines, reasonable, and thoroughly explained.
United States v. Gray-Burriss	791 F.3d 50	2015	Authored Majority	Criminal law/procedure	*Affirmed in part and Remanded in part:* Lower court erred in excluding evidence; D.C. Circuit remanded for reconsideration of whether this evidence

Case Name	Citation	Year	Role	Subject	*Holding*
Metz v. Bae Sys. Tech. Solutions & Servs.	774 F.3d 18	2014	Authored Majority	Federal courts	*Affirmed:* The court affirmed the lower court's denial of the plaintiff's motion to certify question of whether District of Columbia law recognizes cause of action for tortuous interference with at-will employment against a third party former employer who procured the plaintiff's discharge from his new employer.
United States v. Williams	773 F.3d 98	2014	Authored Majority	Criminal law/procedure	*Affirmed:* Evidence was seized in compliance with the Fourth Amendment; the prosecutor's plain error did not affect the outcome of the case; and sentencing guidelines were properly followed.
Daniel v. Fulwood	766 F.3d 57	2014	Authored Majority	Criminal law/procedure	*Reversed and Remanded:* The prisoners plausibly alleged that retroactive application of federal parole guidelines constituted significant risk of prolonging their incarceration.
United States v. Verrusio	762 F.3d 1	2014	Authored Majority	Criminal law/procedure	*Affirmed:* A congressional aide's indictment did not omit a necessary charge, there was sufficient evidence to support the conviction, and the lower court's exclusion of evidence was not prejudicial.

Table 1. (Continued)

Case Name	Citation	Year	Role	Subject	Holding
Schnitzler v. United States	761 F.3d 33	2014	Authored Majority	Federal courts	*Reversed and Remanded:* Prisoner had standing and his claim that the federal government violated his constitutional rights by refusing to allow him to renounce his U.S. citizenship was not moot.
United States v. Baxter	761 F.3d 17	2014	Authored Majority	Criminal law/procedure	*Affirmed:* The court granted motion for certificates of appealability on two of three claims, but affirmed dismissal of defendant's motion to vacate convictions.
Vill. of Barrington v. Surface Transp. Bd.	758 F.3d 326	2014	Authored Majority	Administrative law	*Petition Denied:* The D.C. Circuit lacked jurisdiction to consider a petition to review a Surface Transportation Board (STB) acquisition decision; STB did not abuse its discretion by refusing to reopen the proceeding.
Mpoy v. Rhee	758 F.3d 285	2014	Authored Majority	First Amendment	*Affirmed:* Public school officials were protected from a wrongful termination suit by qualified immunity, and a fired teacher's speech was not protected by the First Amendment.

Case Name	Citation	Year	Role	Subject	Holding
Mittleman v. Postal Regulatory Comm'n	757 F.3d 300	2014	Authored Majority	Administrative law& Federal courts	*Ordered:* Petitions to review the Postal Service Commission's decision to close certain post offices were either non reviewable or moot.
All. for Safe, Efficient & Competitive Truck Transp. v. Fed. Motor Carrier Safety Admin.	755 F.3d 946	2014	Authored Majority	Administrative law & Transportation	*Dismissed:* Challenges to the agency's Safety Measurement System and explanatory Power Point presentations posted on the agency's website were time-barred.
Util. Air Regulatory Grp. v. Envtl. Prot. Agency (EPA)	744 F.3d 741	2014	Authored Majority	Administrative law	*Denied:* Petition for review of challenges to final regulations concerning new source performance standards for steam-generating units was denied because the EPA's rule was not arbitrary and capricious and certain challenges were not properly before the court. *Concurring (Kavanaugh, J.):* Exhaustion/finality rule described in the majority opinion most likely should not be considered jurisdictional in light of recent Supreme Court rulings.

Table 1. (Continued)

Case Name	Citation	Year	Role	Subject	Holding
Blanca Tel. Co. v. Fed. Commc'n Comm. (FCC)	743 F.3d 860	2014	Authored Majority	Administrative law	*Petition Denied:* FCC's order, declining to waive deadline requirements or liability for tardy compliance with respect to requirements for digital wireless service providers to offer telephone handsets compatible with hearing aids, was not arbitrary and capricious.
McKinley v. Fed. Hous. Fin. Agency	739 F.3d 707	2014	Authored Majority	Government information	*Affirmed:* District court's determination that plaintiff was not eligible under FOIA to be awarded legal costs was not an abuse of discretion.
United States v. Cross	766 F.3d 1	2013	Authored Majority	Criminal law/procedure	*Affirmed:* Criminal conviction was affirmed because any errors made in jury instructions or by the prosecutor were harmless.
Judicial Watch, Inc.v. U.S. Secret Serv.	726 F.3d 208	2013	Authored Majority	Government information& Separation of powers	*Reversed in part, Affirmed in part, and Remanded:* White House Access Control Systems records that would disclose information concerning visitors to the

Case Name	Citation	Year	Role	Subject	Holding
					Office of the President were not agency records under the Freedom of Information Act (FOIA); records that would disclose visitors to offices in the White House Complex covered by FOIA were agency records.
Conservation Force, Inc. v. Jewell	733 F.3d 1200	2013	Authored Majority	Administrative law	*Remanded with instructions to Dismiss complaint and Vacate order:* Challenges to Fish and Wildlife Service actions were non-justiciable.
United States v. Swangin	726 F.3d 205	2013	Authored Majority	Criminal law/procedure	*Affirmed:* Fair Sentencing Act's new mandatory minimum sentence for a criminal offense did not apply retroactively to defendant who was sentenced before its enactment.
Gentiva Healthcare Corp. v. Sebelius	723 F.3d 292	2013	Authored Majority	Administrative law& Health care	*Affirmed:* D.C. Circuit affirmed lower court's judgment that the Department of Health and Human Services' (HHS's)interpretation of ambiguous statute was reasonable and entitled to deference under *Chevron U.S.A., Inc. v. Natural Resources Defense Council*,467 U.S. 837 (1984).

Table 1. (Continued)

Case Name	Citation	Year	Role	Subject	Holding
Lacson v. U.S.Dep't of Homeland Sec.	726 F.3d 170	2013	Authored Majority	Administrative law	*Affirmed in part, set aside in part:* Substantial evidence supported most of the Transportation Security Administration's (TSA's) order terminating employee for disclosing Safety Sensitive Information.
Taylor v. Huerta	723 F.3d 210	2013	Authored Majority	Administrative law	*Petition Denied:* Federal Aviation Administration's (FAA's) decision to revoke pilot and medical certificates was not arbitrary and capricious and revocation process afforded plaintiff due process.
United States v. Caso	723 F.3d 215	2013	Authored Majority	Criminal law/procedure	*Reversed:* Reversed the lower court's denial of motion to vacate criminal conviction and sentence because plaintiff was innocent of convicted offense and was not compelled to prove innocence on a "less serious" (per sentencing guidelines) offense for which he was not charged.

Case Name	Citation	Year	Role	Subject	Holding
Luan v. United States	722 F.3d 388	2013	Authored Majority	Criminal law/procedure	*Affirmed:* Application for a restraining order complied with procedural due process and federal statutory forfeiture protections.
Sibert-Dean v. WMATA	721 F.3d 699	2013	Authored Majority	Federal courts	*Affirmed:* Error in jury instructions was harmless.
Millard Refrigerated Servs. v. Sec'y of Labor	718 F.3d 892	2013	Authored Majority	Administrative law	*Denied:* Petition for review of challenges to findings of fact and citations issued by the Occupational Safety and Health Administration (OSHA), relating to the escape of anhydrous ammonia from one of the petitioner's storage facilities, was denied.
United States v. Legg	713 F.3d 1129	2013	Authored Majority	Criminal law/procedure	*Affirmed:* Supervised release conditions imposed by the lower court restricting use of Internet and computer access were affirmed.
United States v. Davis	711 F.3d 174	2013	Authored Majority	Criminal law/procedure	*Affirmed:* Defendant's supervised release term did not begin until the day that defendant was sentenced.
Am. Civil Liberties Union (ACLU) v. Cent. Intelligence Agency (CIA)	710 F.3d 422	2013	Authored Majority	Government information	*Reversed and remanded:* The CIA's decision to neither confirm nor deny the existence of documents requested under FOIA, pertaining to the use of unmanned

Table 1. (Continued)

Case Name	Citation	Year	Role	Subject	Holding
					aerial vehicles to engage in targeted killing, was unjustified; court remanded for further consideration of whether other FOIA exemptions might apply.
United States v. Blackson	709 F.3d 36	2013	Authored Majority	Criminal law/procedure	*Affirmed:* District court understood its resentencing authority on remand and did not commit error in applying its authority.
United States v. Purvis	706 F.3d 520	2013	Authored Majority	Criminal law/procedure	*Affirmed:* Lower court's judgment was affirmed because jury instructions were not plainly erroneous.
United States v. Gaskins	690 F.3d 569	2012	Authored Majority	Criminal law/procedure	*Reversed and remanded:* There was insufficient evidence for a reasonable juror to find that the government proved, beyond a reasonable doubt that the defendant had knowingly entered into a conspiracy with the specific intent to further an unlawful objective of drug distribution.

Case Name	Citation	Year	Role	Subject	Holding
Miller v. Clinton	687 F.3d 1332	2012	Authored Majority	Civil rights	*Reversed and remanded:* District court's order dismissing Age Discrimination in Employment Act (ADEA) claim was reversed and remanded for further consideration. *Dissenting (Kavanaugh, J.):* An existing statutory exception to ADEA allowed the State Department to negotiate employment contracts with mandatory retirement at age 65 for employees working abroad.
Taylor v. Reilly	685 F.3d 1110	2012	Authored Majority	Civil liability	*Affirmed:* Application of Parole Commission regulations did not violate a clearly established constitutional right that a reasonable official at the time of the hearing would have known, so parole board officials were entitled to qualified immunity. *Concurring (Kavanaugh, J.):* While the court did not address the argument that the parole officials were entitled to absolute immunity for their decision to deny parole to the appellant, such an argument would fail under Supreme Court precedents.

Table 1. (Continued)

Case Name	Citation	Year	Role	Subject	Holding
Newport Aeronautical Sales v. Dep't of the Air Force	684 F.3d 160	2012	Authored Majority	Government information	*Affirmed:* Exemption 3of FOIA applies to all technical data with a military or space application covered by 10 U.S.C. §130(a).
Burke v. Air Serv. Int'l, Inc.	685 F.3d 1102	2012	Authored Majority	Federal courts	*Affirmed:* Under the *Erie* doctrine regarding choice of law, D.C. Circuit was required to apply District of Columbia's expert testimony requirement for proof of the standard of care in a suit for negligence.
Nat'l Ass'n of Home Builders v. EPA	682 F.3d 1032	2012	Authored Majority	Administrative law	*Denied petition for review:* EPA's amendment to a rule eliminating an opt-out provision to that rule was not arbitrary and capricious.
United States v. Rubio	677 F.3d 1257	2012	Authored Majority	Criminal law/ procedure	*Affirmed:* Guilty plea could not be vacated based on defendant's claim of not understanding her plea where defendant was provided with a translation of the plea deal and a translator.

Case Name	Citation	Year	Role	Subject	Holding
Alsabri v. Obama	684 F.3d 1298	2012	Authored Majority	National security	*Affirmed:* Lower court did not commit a clear error in finding sufficient evidence that foreign national held at U.S. Naval Station at Guantanamo Bay, Cuba, was lawfully detained as an enemy belligerent on account of being part of the Taliban or Al Qaeda.
Salazar v. Dist. of Columbia	671 F.3d 1258	2012	Authored Majority	Federal courts	*Appeal Dismissed:* Lower court decision was not an appealable "order refusing to dissolve an injunction" because another issue remained unresolved.
Monmouth Care Ctr. v. NLRB	672 F.3d 1085	2012	Authored Majority	Labor law	*Denied petition for review:* NLRB's decision concerning employer's failure to meet with union was upheld because there was substantial evidence supporting NLRB's finding that there was no bargaining impasse or bad faith on the part of the union that would excuse employer's failure to bargain.
Nat'l Auto. Dealers Ass'n v. FTC	670 F.3d 268	2012	Authored Majority	Administrative law& Federal courts	*Denied petition for review:* A judicial appeal of FTC rulemaking under the Fair Credit Reporting Act must first be heard in federal district court.

Table 1. (Continued)

Case Name	Citation	Year	Role	Subject	Holding
Braintree Elec. Light Dep't v. Fed. Energy Regulatory Comm'n. (FERC)	667 F.3d 1284	2012	Authored Majority	Administrative law	*Agency order Affirmed:* FERC's interpretation of a settlement agreement within its jurisdiction was entitled to deference.
McGrath v. Clinton	666 F.3d 1377	2012	Authored Majority	Civil rights & Labor law	*Affirmed:* Evidence offered no reasonable grounds for a juror to conclude that an employee's termination was due to unlawful retaliation.
Holistic Candlers & Consumers Ass'n v. Food & Drug Admin. (FDA)	664 F.3d 940	2012	Authored Majority	Administrative law	*Affirmed:* Warning letters issued by the FDA did not constitute final agency action subject to judicial review under the Administrative Procedure Act.
PSEG Energy Res. & Trade, LLC v. FERC	665 F.3d 203	2011	Authored Majority	Administrative law	*Petition for review Granted and Remanded to agency for further consideration:* Because a FERC order was based on a finding that the statute was clear but the agency subsequently agreed that the statute was ambiguous, and FERC failed to address legitimate objections to the order, reconsideration by the agency was warranted.

Case Name	Citation	Year	Role	Subject	Holding
Wayne view Care Ctr. v. NLRB	664 F.3d 341	2011	Authored Majority	Labor law	*Denied petition for review and granted cross-application for enforcement:* Substantial evidence supported NLRB's finding that a lawful impasse in collective bargaining negotiations had not been reached.
ACLU v. U.S. Dep't of Justice (DOJ)	655 F.3d 1	2011	Authored Majority	Government information	*Affirmed in part and Remanded in part:* A list of case names, docket numbers, and courts where the DOJ had used cell phone location data in criminal prosecutions did not fall under any exemption to FOIA; however, remand was appropriate for further factual development as to other material.
Khanv. Obama	655 F.3d 20	2011	Authored Majority	National security	*Affirmed:* Sufficient evidence existed to find that the petitioner, a detainee held at Guantanamo as an enemy belligerent, was lawfully held on account of membership in Al Qaeda or the Taliban; denial of petition for habeas corpus upheld.
Katz v. Sec. & Exch. Comm'n. (SEC)	647 F.3d 1156	2011	Authored Majority	Administrative law	*Denied petition for review:* SEC's decision sustaining a New York Stock Exchange disciplinary action against the petitioner was reasonable and supported by substantial evidence.

Table 1. (Continued)

Case Name	Citation	Year	Role	Subject	Holding
Jones v. Astrue	647 F.3d 350	2011	Authored Majority	Administrative law	*Reversed and Remanded:* The failure of an administrative law judge to explain his rejection of treating physician's testimony violated the treating physician rule, and newly available evidence should have been admitted because there was good cause for failure to initially incorporate the evidence.
Spectrum Health—Kent Cmty. Campus v. NLRB	647 F.3d 341	2011	Authored Majority	Labor law	*Denied petition for review:* NLRB properly interpreted a collective bargaining agreement to have taken effect less than three years prior, triggering the conclusive presumption that the union had the support of a majority of employees.
Bally's Park Place v. NLRB	646 F.3d 929	2011	Authored Majority	Labor law	*Denied petition for review and granted cross-application for enforcement:* Substantial evidence supported NLRB decision finding that company committed an unfair labor practice.

Case Name	Citation	Year	Role	Subject	Holding
United States v. Salahmand	651 F.3d 21	2011	Authored Majority	Criminal law/ procedure	*Affirmed:* Lower court correctly interpreted the U.S. Sentencing Guidelines.
Al Alwi v. Obama	653 F.3d 11	2011	Authored Majority	National security	*Affirmed:* Sufficient evidence existed to find that the petitioner was a member of Al Qaeda or the Taliban; denial of petition for habeas corpus upheld.
United States v. Stubblefield	643 F.3d 291	2011	Authored Majority	Criminal law/ procedure	*Affirmed:* Defendant's trial did not violate the Speedy Trial Act and any error that may have been committed by the lower court was harmless.
United States v. Jones	642 F.3d 1151	2011	Authored Majority	Criminal law/ procedure	*Affirmed in part and Remanded in part:* It was not an abuse of discretion for the district court to deny defendant's motion to withdraw his guilty plea. The D.C. Circuit remanded for a hearing regarding ineffective assistance of counsel claim.
Am. Bus. Ass'n v. Rogoff	649 F.3d 734	2011	Authored Majority	Administrative law& First Amendment	*Reversed:* Appropriations restriction on agency's ability to enforce a rule did not violate petitioners' right to petition the government or Fifth Amendment right to equal protection under the law.

Table 1. (Continued)

Case Name	Citation	Year	Role	Subject	Holding
Dickson v. Nat'l Transp. Safety Bd. (NTSB)	639 F.3d 539	2011	Authored Majority	Administrative law	*Denied petition for review:* NTSB's denial of an application because the applicant was not medically qualified was not arbitrary and capricious and was supported by substantial evidence.
Chamber of Commerce of U.S.v. EPA	642 F.3d 192	2011	Authored Majority	Administrative law & Federal courts	*Dismissed:* The court lacked jurisdiction to hear challenge to the EPA's decision granting California a waiver from preemption under the Clean Air Act because plaintiffs did not have standing and the petition was moot.
Peterson v. Archstone Cmtys., LLC	637 F.3d 416	2011	Authored Majority	Federal courts	*Vacated and Remanded:* Lower court had not sufficiently justified its decision to dismiss the plaintiff's claim based on alleged violation of the ADEA.
In re Zdravkovich	634 F.3d 574	2011	Authored Majority	Federal courts	*Order:* Attorney was disbarred for misappropriation of client trust funds.
Figueroa v. Dist, of Columbia Metro. Police Dep't	633 F.3d 1129	2011	Authored Majority	Administrative law & Labor Law	*Affirmed in part and Reversed and Remanded in part:* The court remanded for consideration of claims alleging violations of the Fair Labor Standards Act (FLSA) that the district court erroneously interpreted to be time-barred.

Case Name	Citation	Year	Role	Subject	*Holding*
Calhoun v. Johnson	632 F.3d 1259	2011	Authored Majority	Civil rights& Labor law	*Affirmed in part and Reversed in part:* An employee's claim of discrimination based on her race was remanded for trial where a reasonable jury could find that she was not only reasonably qualified but was substantially more qualified than the person ultimately selected for the position.
Little v. King	768 F. Supp.2d 56	2011	Authored Majority (as part of federal district court panel)	Election law & Federal courts	*Dismissed in part, Remainder of case Transferred:* The plaintiff brought suit under the Voting Rights Act, arguing that the act required federal pre-approval of an Alabama law that, among other things, mandated the disclosure of campaign contributions to state judges. The court dismissed the U.S. Attorney General (AG) as a defendant because the plaintiff did not state a claim against, or seek relief, from the AG. The court transferred the remainder of the plaintiff's claims to the Middle District of Alabama as this was consistent with the convenience of the parties and witnesses and in the interest of justice.

Table 1. (Continued)

Case Name	Citation	Year	Role	Subject	Holding
Payne v. Salazar	619 F.3d 56	2010	Authored Majority	Administrative law & Labor law	*Affirmed in part and Reversed in part:* Employee was not required to appeal claim that she had won before an administrative law judge to obtain review of the claim that she had lost in that same administrative case.
Sigmund v. Starwood Urban Retail VI, LLC	617 F.3d 512	2010	Authored Majority	Civil liability	*Affirmed:* In a civil negligence action, an intervening criminal act was not foreseeable, precluding third-party liability.
TNA Merch. Projects, Inc. v. FERC	616 F.3d 588	2010	Authored Majority	Administrative law	*Vacated and Remanded:* FERC had not properly addressed in its order petitioner's argument that its filed rate could not be a "changed rate" under the statute.
United States v. Tepper	616 F.3d 583	2010	Authored Majority	Criminal law/ procedure	*Affirmed:* Defendant's sentence could not be reduced because Sentencing Commission had not reduced sentences for the crime on which his sentence was based.

Case Name	Citation	Year	Role	Subject	Holding
Phillips v. Fulwood	616 F.3d 577	2010	Authored Majority	Criminal law/ procedure	*Affirmed:* Because there was no significant risk that application of the 2000 U.S. Sentencing Guidelines rather than the 1987 Guidelines would have elongated defendant's sentence, dismissal was affirmed.
United States v. Project on Gov't Oversight	616 F.3d 544	2010	Authored Majority	Criminal law/ procedure	*Reversed:* Contrary to the district court's finding, intent is a required element for violations of 18 U.S.C. §209(a), concerning unauthorized compensation of a government employee by a non-government entity. *Concurring in judgment and Concurring in part in the opinion (Edwards, J.):* The judge could not concur in the majority's disposition of the government's cross-appeal challenging the district court's civil penalty determination. The majority's construction of the ambiguous civil penalty provision was only marginally better than the government's interpretation.

Table 1. (Continued)

Case Name	Citation	Year	Role	Subject	Holding
United States v. Shabban	612 F.3d 693	2010	Authored Majority	Criminal law/ procedure	*Affirmed in part and Remanded in part:* There was sufficient evidence of defendant's guilt that a reasonable juror could have been persuaded, but because the trial record did not conclusively show whether the defendant had a viable claim for ineffective assistance of counsel, the case was remanded for an evidentiary hearing on that issue.
Mogenhan v. Napolitano	613 F.3d 1162	2010	Authored Majority	Labor law	*Reversed in part and Affirmed in part:* The court reversed the lower court's grant of summary judgment because there was sufficient evidence that a reasonable juror could have found that employer's retaliatory actions would have dissuaded an employee from engaging in protected activity, but it affirmed the grant of summary judgment for the employer on a failure-to-accommodate claim.

Table 1. (Continued)

Case Name	Citation	Year	Role	Subject	Holding
					but erred in application of D.C. choice-of-law rules when it applied California and British law, rather than French law, in dismissing the plaintiff's intentional infliction of emotional distress and wrongful death claims.
Se.Ala. Med. Ctr. v. Sebelius	572 F.3d 912	2009	Authored Majority	Administrative law& Health care	*Affirmed in part, Reversed and Remanded in part*: HHS properly included certain types of costs in its reimbursement payments to hospitals under Medicare statute and implementing regulations, but it failed to provide a reasonable explanation regarding its treatment of certain postage costs in its calculations.
Robinson-Reeder v. Am. Council on Educ.	571 F.3d 1333	2009	Authored Majority	Civil rights & Federal courts	*Dismissed:* D.C. Circuit lacked jurisdiction to hear plaintiff's claims against her employer under Title VII of the 1964 Civil Rights Act, as the district court had not entered a final judgment in the case.

Case Name	Citation	Year	Role	Subject	Holding
Nat'l Ass'n of Mfrs. v. Taylor	582 F.3d 1	2009	Authored Majority	Election law & First Amendment	*Affirmed:* Lobbying disclosure statute satisfied strict scrutiny and was upheld.
Malik v. District of Columbia	574 F.3d 781	2009	Authored Majority	Civil rights & Federal courts	*Reversed and Remanded:* The provision of the Prison Litigation Reform Act requiring prisoners to exhaust their administrative remedies before filing suit is inapplicable in instances where "there [is] no administrative process to exhaust."
Abington Crest Nursing & Rehab. Ctr. v. Sebelius	575 F.3d 717	2009	Authored Majority	Administrative law& Health care	*Affirmed:* Skilled nursing facilities were properly denied reimbursement from the Secretary of HHS for certain bad debt costs pursuant to the Medicare statute and accompanying regulations.
Lucas v. Duncan	574 F.3d 772	2009	Authored Majority	Federal courts	*Vacated*: Statements made by attorney in pleadings filed on behalf of client did not warrant imposition of sanctions under Rule 11 of the Federal Rules of Civil Procedure.
Oveissi v. Islamic Republic of Iran	573 F.3d. 835	2009	Authored Majority	Federal courts& International law	*Reversed and Remanded*: The lower court correctly determined that it had jurisdiction over the plaintiff's suit under the terrorism exception of the Foreign Sovereign Immunities Act(FSIA),

Table 1. (Continued)

Case Name	Citation	Year	Role	Subject	Holding
Kersey v. WMATA	586 F.3d 13	2009	Authored Majority	Civil rights	*Affirmed: WMATA's reliance on binding settlement agreement to deny employee a promotion when the statute of limitations to challenge that agreement had passed was not a pretext for discrimination and retaliation in violation of the Rehabilitation Act.*
Skinner v. DOJ	584 F.3d 1093	2009	Authored Majority	Government information	*Affirmed and Affirmed on alternate grounds: The court affirmed district court's dismissal of plaintiff's Privacy Act amendment claim because records were exempt. The court also affirmed dismissal of plaintiff's claim for damages under the Privacy Act because that they were not cognizable unless plaintiff first secured relief via a writ of habeas corpus.*
Rempfer v. Sharfstein	583 F.3d 860	2009	Authored Majority	Administrative Law & Federal courts	*Affirmed: The FDA's finding of vaccine effectiveness was not arbitrary and capricious; and plaintiffs lacked standing to challenge the subjection of military members to mandatory immunization by the Department of Defense.*

Case Name	Citation	Year	Role	Subject	Holding
United States v. Battle	613 F.3d 258	2010	Authored Majority	Criminal law/ procedure	*Affirmed in part and Remanded in part:* Evidence was sufficient to support the defendant's convictions, but two of the convictions merged and to uphold both would violate the Due Process Clause of the Constitution. One of the convictions was, therefore, remanded to district court to be vacated.
United States v. Coughlin	610 F.3d 89	2010	Authored Majority	Criminal law/ procedure	*Reversed in part, Affirmed in part, and Remanded: Defendant was acquitted of committing a number of counts of mail fraud, but the jury could not reach a decision on other mail fraud counts as well as counts of false claim and theft of public funds. Double jeopardy attached to the undecided counts of mail fraud, but not to the false claim and theft of public funds counts.*
United States v. Motley	587 F.3d 1153	2009	Authored Majority	Criminal law/ procedure	*Affirmed: The government's refusal to file a motion authorizing the court to sentence defendant to a length of time less than the mandatory minimum sentence was not irrational or a violation of due process where the motion the government did file complied with the plea deal signed by the defendant.*

Case Name	Citation	Year	Role	Subject	Holding
United States v. Blalock	571 F.3d 1282	2009	Authored Majority	Criminal law/procedure	*Affirmed:* Appellant was properly subject to an enhanced sentence under the U.S. Sentencing Guidelines for possessing a firearm in connection with another felony offense.
Guard Publ'gCo. v. NLRB	571 F.3d 53	2009	Authored Majority	Labor law	*Petition Denied in part and Granted in part, and Remanded:* NLRB correctly determined that a company committed unfair labor practices when it disciplined employees for engaging in certain activities related to their union participation, but the Board erred in holding that the company acted lawfully when it disciplined one of the employees for using company email to solicit on behalf of the union.
Novak v. Capital Mgmt. & Dev. Corp.	570 F.3d 305	2009	Authored Majority	Civil liability& D.C. local government	*Affirmed:* A reasonable jury could find that a nightclub owed an injured patron a duty of care, and the evidence presented could establish foreseeability of this injury.
Horning v. SEC	570 F.3d 337	2009	Authored Majority	Administrative law	*Affirmed:* SEC's order to sanction president and director of an investment company pursuant to Securities Exchange Act was not arbitrary and capricious.

Table 1. (Continued)

Case Name	Citation	Year	Role	Subject	Holding
Entergy Servs., Inc.v. FERC	568 F.3d 978	2009	Authored Majority	Administrative law& Energy	*Petition Denied:* FERC's order regarding a contract dispute over a public utility holding company's billing rates was not arbitrary and capricious.
United States v. Berkeley	567 F.3d 703	2009	Authored Majority	Criminal law/procedure	*Affirmed:* The denial of a criminal defendant's motion to withdraw his guilty plea was not an abuse of discretion, and the calculation of his sentence was not erroneous.
United States v. Jones	567 F.3d 712	2009	Authored Majority	Criminal law/procedure	*Affirmed and Remanded:* The appellant was not entitled to a new trial, as the district court did not err in failing to suppress the appellant's statements at the time of arrest, and it was not clear that that the government presented in admissible evidence to the jury. However, the case was remanded to give the appellant an opportunity to request a reduced sentence.
Dean Transp. v. NLRB	551 F.3d 1055	2009	Authored Majority	Labor law	*Petition denied and cross-application for enforcement of order Granted*: NLRB properly determined that a transportation company's refusal to recognize and

Case Name	Citation	Year	Role	Subject	Holding
					bargain with the union representing employees of a school district facility (and instead bargaining with the union representing bus drivers at other facilities) violated the NLRA.
Montgomery v. Chao	546 F.3d 703	2008	Authored Majority	Civil rights	*Affirmed:* Pension Benefit Guaranty Corporation's (PBGC's) decisions not to promote or appoint employee to certain positions did not constitute unlawful discrimination or retaliation in violation of Title VII of the Civil Rights Act of 1964.
Feemster v. BSA Ltd. P'ship	548 F.3d 1063	2008	Authored Majority	D.C. local government	*Affirmed in part, Reversed in part*: Property owner unlawfully refused to accept tenants' federal vouchers as payment for rent in violation of federal housing statutes and the District of Columbia Human Rights Act.
Ass'n of Civilian Technicians v. Fed. Labor Relations Auth.	534 F.3d 772	2008	Authored Majority	Administrative law& Labor law	*Petition Denied:* Federal Labor Relations Authority's decision to reject a disputed contract provision as a violation of the Federal Services Labor-Management Relations Act was entitled to judicial deference.

Table 1. (Continued)

Case Name	Citation	Year	Role	Subject	Holding
Steele v. Schafer	535 F.3d 689	2008	Authored Majority	Civil rights	*Reversed and Remanded*: Lower court wrongly dismissed employee's claims against her former employer for creating a hostile work environment and unlawfully retaliating against her in violation of Title VII of the Civil Rights Act of 1964.
Klamath Water Users Ass'n v. FERC	534 F.3d 735	2008	Authored Majority	Energy& Federal courts	*Dismissed*: Water users association lacked standing to challenge a FERC order because it failed to demonstrate that a favorable decision by the court would redress its injury.
Pac. Gas & Elec. Co. v. FERC	533 F.3d 820	2008	Authored Majority	Energy& Federal courts	*Petition Dismissed*: Court lacked jurisdiction to hear case, as company's petition for review of certain FERC orders was an impermissible collateral attack on orders issued in earlier years.
Public Citizen v. Rubber Mfrs. Ass'n	533 F.3d 810	2008	Authored Majority	Government information	*Affirmed:* A provision of the Transportation Recall Enhancement, Accountability, and Documentation Act limiting the disclosure of certain early warning reporting data did not exempt the data from disclosure under FOIA.

Case Name	Citation	Year	Role	Subject	Holding
United States v. Andrews	532 F.3d 900	2008	Authored Majority	Criminal law/Procedure	*Affirmed:* The government did not violate the defendant's rights by failing to produce certain exculpatory evidence prior to trial, and no error was committed under the U.S. Sentencing Guidelines and the Constitution's Ex Post Facto Clause by calculating defendant's sentence based on the 2006 Sentencing Guidelines Manual, rather than on an earlier version. *Concurring (Rogers, J.,):* The defendant failed to show plain error with respect to prosecution's failure to produce certain exculpatory evidence and calculation of the defendant's sentence. With respect to the defendant's ex post facto challenge to her sentence, there was no need for the court to address the timing of the termination of the conspiracy.
United States v. Cassell	530 F.3d 1009	2008	Authored Majority	Criminal law/Procedure	*Affirmed*: Because the district court properly treated the defendant's possession of a particular type of firearm as a sentencing factor, his counsel did not err in failing to request a jury instruction on the issue.

Table 1. (Continued)

Case Name	Citation	Year	Role	Subject	Holding
Aliron Int'l v. Cherokee Nation Indus.	531 F.3d 863	2008	Authored Majority	Civil liability	*Affirmed*: Subcontractor was compelled to arbitrate its claims against the primary contractor in a breach of contract dispute.
In re Core Commc'ns, Inc.	531 F.3d 849	2008	Authored Majority	Administrative law	*Writ of mandamus Granted:* FCC was directed to respond to a remand order in an earlier case and explain the legal basis for certain rules applying to payment for dial-up Internet connections. *Concurring (Griffith, J.):* The circumstances surrounding the majority's decision called into question the wisdom of the open-ended remand without vacatur; future panels should consider alternatives to this approach.
Parhat v. Gates	532 F.3d 834	2008	Authored Majority	National security	*Petition Granted and motion Denied:* A Combatant Status Review Tribunal's determination that a detainee at the U.S. Naval Station at Guantanamo Bay, Cuba, was an "enemy combatant" was not supported by sufficient evidence and in a manner allowing a reviewing court to assess its reliability;

Case Name	Citation	Year	Role	Subject	Holding
					the D.C. Circuit also denied without prejudice the government's motion to designate certain unclassified material in the tribunal record as "protected information."
Muir v. Navy Fed. Credit Union	529 F.3d 1100	2008	Authored Majority	Civil liability	*Affirmed in part, Reversed in part*: With respect to credit union's use of funds deposited by plaintiff to satisfy a debt owed by the plaintiff's father, the district court appropriately granted summary judgment for the credit union on the plaintiff's breach of fiduciary duty claim, and properly denied the plaintiff's request for punitive damages; however, plaintiff's claims of tortious interference with a business expectancy, tortious conversion, and certain violations of the Fair Debt Collection Practices Act should not have been dismissed by the lower court.
United States v. Johnson	519 F.3d 478	2008	Authored Majority	Criminal law/procedure	*Affirmed:* District court did not err in denying defendant's motion to suppress certain gun and drug evidence, admitting evidence of a prior firearms conviction at trial, denying a motion for judgment of acquittal based on the drugs at issue, and not granting defendant a new trial.

Table 1. (Continued)

Case Name	Citation	Year	Role	Subject	Holding
United States v. Pettiford	517 F.3d 584	2008	Authored Majority	Criminal law/procedure	*Affirmed:* District court did not err in admitting evidence of a prior drug offense at trial, in denying defendant's motion for a new trial, and in denying defendant's motion for a judgment of acquittal on the basis of insufficient evidence to establish that the drug defendant possessed was crack cocaine.
United States v. Branham	515 F.3d 1268	2008	Authored Majority	Criminal law/procedure	*Conviction Affirmed; Remanded*: The evidence against the criminal defendant was sufficient to support his conviction, and the district court properly admitted expert testimony against defendant; the case was remanded for resentencing in light of the mandatory application of the U.S. Sentencing Guidelines at the defendant's original sentencing.
Kassem v. Wash. Hosp. Ctr.	513 F.3d 251	2008	Authored Majority	Civil liability, D.C. local government & Labor law	*Affirmed in part and Reversed in part*: The lower court correctly dismissed the appellant's wrongful discharge claim against his former employer, but improperly dismissed the claim of intentional infliction of emotional distress.

Case Name	Citation	Year	Role	Subject	Holding
United States v. Ginyard	511 F.3d 203	2008	Authored Majority	Criminal law/procedure	*Affirmed in part and dismissed in part:* One defendant could be retried on certain lesser-included offenses without violating the Double Jeopardy Clause; the court lacked jurisdiction to hear the other defendant's challenge based on an aiding and abetting theory.
Segar v. Mukasey	508 F.3d 16	2007	Authored Majority	Civil rights & Labor law	*Interim injunction Vacated and Remanded:* A consent decree governing the promotion of special agents to positions in the Drug Enforcement Administration's (DEA's) Senior Executive Service (SES) was not ambiguous or invalid; it restricted the Administrator of the DEA from promoting an agent who was not on the list of best-qualified candidates to an SES position, but provided the Administrator with the discretion to choose which candidate to promote from that list.
Kleiman & Hochberg v. U.S.Dep't of Agric.(USDA)	497 F.3d 681	2007	Authored Majority	Administrative law & Civil liability	*Petition Denied:* Secretary of Agriculture's revocation of wholesale produce merchant's license to do business under the Perishable

Table 1. (Continued)

Case Name	Citation	Year	Role	Subject	Holding
					Agricultural Commodities Act, which triggered certain employment restrictions on the company's president, was not arbitrary or unreasonable.
United States v. Bowman	496 F.3d 685	2007	Authored Majority	Criminal law/procedure	*Affirmed in part, Remanded in part:* The district court did not err in denying defendant's motion to dismiss his indictment; there was insufficient evidence to evaluate the constitutionality of the road block where defendant was arrested, so the case was remanded to lower court for an evidentiary hearing.
United States v. Edwards	496 F.3d 677	2007	Authored Majority	Criminal law/procedure	*Affirmed:* District court's application of the U.S. Sentencing Guidelines was proper for defendant convicted of bribery and extortion.
Holland v. Williams Mt. Coal Co.	496 F.3d 670	2007	Authored Majority	Labor law	*Reversed and Remanded*: District court relied on improper grounds in awarding attorney's fees to a mining company following a lawsuit over the company's liability for retired miner's health benefits.

Case Name	Citation	Year	Role	Subject	Holding
United States v. Curry	494 F.3d 1124	2007	Authored Majority	Criminal law/procedure	*Affirmed:* District court did not abuse its discretion in denying defendant's request to withdraw his guilty plea or hold an evidentiary hearing.
Owner-Operator Indep. Drivers Ass'n v. Fed. Motor Carrier Safety Admin.	494 F.3d 188	2007	Authored Majority	Administrative law& Transportation	*Petition Granted in part and Denied in part:* The Federal Motor Carrier Safety Administration did not act arbitrarily or capriciously with respect to certain aspects of regulations relating to the hours of commercial motor vehicle operators, but the agency violated the Administrative Procedure Act when it failed to provide certain information and neglected to give interested parties an opportunity to comment on the regulations.
Cement Kiln Recycling Coal.v. EPA	493 F.3d 207	2007	Authored Majority	Administrative law& Environmental law	*Petition Denied in part and Dismissed in part*: An EPA rule reasonably prescribed requirements relating to a permitting process for facilities that burn hazardous waste as fuel, as required by the Resource Conservation and Recovery Act, and a related guidance document was a non-binding statement of EPA policy that was outside the scope of the court's jurisdiction.

Table 1. (Continued)

Case Name	Citation	Year	Role	Subject	Holding
Muldrow v. Re-Direct, Inc.	493 F.3d 160	2007	Authored Majority	Civil liability	*Affirmed:* The defendant not entitled to a new trial, as the district court correctly excluded certain testimony as inadmissible hearsay, permitted the plaintiff's juvenile justice expert testimony, and properly instructed the jury regarding the standard for finding plaintiff's son contributorily negligent.
Devia v. Nuclear Regulatory Comm'n (NRC)	492 F.3d 421	2007	Authored Majority	Energy & Federal courts	*Case held in abeyance*: Because the petitioners' challenge to the NRC decision to issue a license allowing for the construction and operation of a nuclear waste facility was unripe, the case was held in abeyance.
Cambridge Holdings Grp., Inc. v. Fed. Ins. Co.	489 F.3d 1356	2007	Authored Majority	Federal courts	*Dismissed:* Corporation's appeal of its breach of contract claim against insurance company dismissed because it was untimely.
United States v. Bentley	489 F.3d 360	2007	Authored Majority	Criminal law/procedure	*Affirmed*: An incident involving several items accidentally sent to the jury room during the course of the jury's deliberations constituted harmless error and did not have a "substantial and injurious effect or influence" on the jury's verdict.

Case Name	Citation	Year	Role	Subject	*Holding*
In re Sealed Case No. 05-3030	488 F.3d 1011	2007	Authored Majority	Criminal law/procedure	*Affirmed:* Counsel's failure to correctly advise defendant regarding U.S. Sentencing Guidelines was not prejudicial; lower court's denial of defendant's motion to vacate his sentence was appropriate.
Mueller v. Winter	485 F.3d 1191	2007	Authored Majority	Government information & Labor law	*Affirmed:* Lower court properly rejected a challenge under the Privacy Act and the Administrative Procedure Act to the Navy's refusal to remove a lieutenant's allegedly erroneous fitness report from his personnel record, as well as the lieutenant's request to convene a special selection board under 10 U.S.C. §628.
United States v. Bras	483 F.3d 103	2007	Authored Majority	Criminal law/procedure	*Affirmed:* Lower court committed no error in calculating criminal defendant's sentence.
Carpenters & Millwrights, Local Union 2471 v. NLRB	481 F.3d 804	2007	Authored Majority	Labor law	*Vacated and Remanded in part:* NLRB failed to cite sufficient evidence to reverse administrative law judge's decision and failed to explain why it disregarded contrary evidence.

Table 1. (Continued)

Case Name	Citation	Year	Role	Subject	Holding
Czekalski v. Peters	475 F.3d 360	2007	Authored Majority	Civil rights& Labor law	*Reversed:* The court found that there were genuine issues of material fact as to whether federal agency discriminated against employee on basis of her gender in violation of Title VII of the Civil Rights Act of 1964.
Flying Food Group, Inc. v. NLRB	471 F.3d 178	2006	Authored Majority	Labor law& Administrative law	*Petition Denied and cross-petition for enforcement Granted: The* NLRB did not err procedurally in reaching its decision; and the statute barred judicial consideration of petitioner's substantive argument because the company did not seek prior Board reconsideration of the issue.
United States v. Adewani	467 F.3d 1340	2006	Authored Majority	Criminal law/procedure	*Affirmed:* The lower court committed no legal error in calculating criminal defendant's sentence, and the record contained sufficient evidence to support his conviction.
Davis v. DOJ	460 F.3d 92	2006	Authored Majority	Government information	*Affirmed in part, Reversed in part, and Remanded:* Because the FBI did not make a "reasonable effort to ascertain" whether two subjects were dead,

Case Name	Citation	Year	Role	Subject	Holding
					the agency may not have reasonably responded to the FOIA request; but the district court's denial of attorney's fees was correct.
Conseil Alain Aboudaram, S.A. v. De Groote	460 F.3d 46	2006	Authored Majority	Federal courts	*Affirmed:* The court upheld the lower court's decision in all respects regarding a contract dispute between a lender and a borrower.
Charter Commc'ns, Inc. v. FCC	460 F.3d 31	2006	Authored Majority	Administrative law	*Petition Denied:* FCC's order refusing to rescind a rule restricting cable television operators from providing certain set-top devices was not arbitrary or capricious.
United States v. West	458 F.3d 1	2006	Authored Majority	Criminal law/procedure	*Affirmed:* The district court did not abuse its discretion in determining how to conduct the voir dire or in its denial of the defendant's motion to dismiss evidence because of a purported Fourth Amendment violation.
Alpharma, Inc. v. Leavitt	460 F.3d 1	2006	Authored Majority	Administrative law	*Judgment Set Aside and Remanded:* The FDA's response to an earlier remand to explain its approval of new animal drug applications raised new questions which prevented the court from concluding that the decision was the product of reasoned decisionmaking.

Table 1. (Continued)

Case Name	Citation	Year	Role	Subject	Holding
					Concurring in part and Dissenting in part (Williams, J.): The FDA's response to remand was insufficient, and the agency should have been compelled to explain how its use of single-dose study satisfied relevant standards.
Soc'y of Lloyd's v. Siemon-Netto	457 F.3d 94	2006	Authored Majority	Civil liability, D.C. local government& International law	*Affirmed:* Money judgment obtained in England for nonpayment of reinsurance premiums is enforceable against residents of the District of Columbia under the District's Uniform Foreign Money Judgments Recognition Act.
Trudeau v. FTC	456 F.3d 178	2006	Authored Majority	Administrative law, Federal court, &First Amendment	*Affirmed:* The district court erroneously dismissed the plaintiff's complaint against FTC for lack of subject-matter jurisdiction; but the allegations were nevertheless insufficient to state a claim upon which relief could be granted.
Kurke v. Oscar Gruss & Son, Inc.	454 F.3d 350	2006	Authored Majority	Civil liability	*Affirmed:* The arbitration award reached by an arbitration panel against a securities firm and firm executive was not made in manifest disregard of the law.

Case Name	Citation	Year	Role	Subject	Holding
United States v. Project on Gov't Oversight	454 F.3d 306	2006	Authored Majority	Criminal law/procedure	*Reversed and Remanded:* Genuine issues of material fact existed regarding whether a non-profit political organization made a contribution, in violation of criminal statute, to the salary of a Department of the Interior economist as compensation for his services as a government employee.
Sec'y of Labor v. Twentymile Coal Co.	456 F.3d 151	2006	Authored Majority	Administrative law & Labor law	*Petition Granted, order Vacated:* The Secretary of Labor had prosecutorial discretion to cite an owner-operator of a mine for safety violations committed by its contractor; and the Federal Mine Safety and Health Review Commission generally lacked authority to review the Secretary's decisions.
In re Core Commc'ns, Inc.	455 F.3d 267	2006	Authored Majority	Administrative law	*Petitions Denied:* FCC's decisions regarding forbearance of its rules governing telecommunications traffic bound for Internet service providers were not arbitrary or capricious.
Consumer Fed'n of Am. v. USDA	455 F.3d 283	2006	Authored Majority	Government information	*Affirmed in part, Reversed in part:* Electronic appointment calendars of the five most senior USDA officials were "agency records" subject to production

Table 1. (Continued)

Case Name	Citation	Year	Role	Subject	Holding
					under FOIA, but an assistant administrator's appointment calendar was not covered. *Concurring (Henderson):* The majority should not have relied so heavily on earlier D.C. Circuit jurisprudence in reaching decision, as subsequent Supreme Court precedent called earlier circuit rulings into question; moreover, there were key differences between the facts of an earlier D.C. Circuit case and the present one.
United States v. Mejia	448 F.3d 436	2006	Authored Majority	Criminal law/procedure	*Affirmed in part and Remanded in part*: Criminal defendants' conviction for conspiracy to distribute cocaine with intent that it be unlawfully imported into the United States upheld; however, one of the defendant's sentence was instructed to be vacated and remanded for resentencing consistent with *United States v.*

Case Name	Citation	Year	Role	Subject	*Holding*
					Booker, 543 U.S. 220 (2005), and the other defendant was entitled to an evidentiary hearing regarding his claim that his attorney had provided ineffective assistance of counsel.
Boivin v. U.S. Airways, Inc.	446 F.3d 148	2006	Authored Majority	Administrative law & Labor law	*Vacated in part and Remanded in part:* Court dismissed claims against the PBGC regarding alleged errors in calculating benefits due to retired airline pilots under the Employment Retirement Income Security Act and corporate retirement income plan because the retirees had not yet exhausted their administrative remedies.
Messina v. Krakower	439 F.3d 755	2006	Authored Majority	Federal courts& First Amendment	*Affirmed:* The lower court committed no error when it found that the defendants (attorney and his law firm) were protected by the judicial proceedings privilege regarding content in a letter attorney wrote that contained allegedly defamatory matter about the plaintiff.
Washburn v. Lavoie	437 F.3d 84	2006	Authored Majority	Civil liability & First Amendment	*Affirmed:* The lower court committed no error in finding that defendants were protected by their qualified privilege of self-defense from liability for defamation and false-light invasion of privacy claims brought by a neighbor.

Table 1. (Continued)

Case Name	Citation	Year	Role	Subject	Holding
United States v. Fonseca	435 F.3d 369	2006	Authored Majority	Criminal law/procedure	*Affirmed:* The district court neither violated the Speedy Trial Act nor abused its discretion in limiting cross-examination of a government witness by the criminal defendant, who was convicted of unlawful possession of a firearm and ammunition.
Ceridian Corp. v. NLRB	435 F.3d 352	2006	Authored Majority	Labor law	*Petition Denied; cross-petition Granted:* The NLRB's conclusion that company unlawfully interfered with employees' choice of representatives for collective bargaining purposes was reasonable and supported by substantial evidence.
In re Zambrano	433 F.3d 886	2006	Authored Majority	Criminal law/procedure	*Application Denied:* Pro se defendant's request for leave to file a second motion to vacate his criminal sentence, on the assertion that the sentence is unconstitutional under *United States v. Booker,* was denied because the Supreme Court had not made *Booker* retroactive to cases on collateral review.

Case Name	Citation	Year	Role	Subject	Holding
United States v. Simpson	430 F.3d 1177	2005	Authored Majority	Criminal law/procedure	*Affirmed:* The lower court committed no constitutional *Booker* error in calculating sentence for criminal defendant who reentered the United States unlawfully after having been deported following conviction for distributing a large amount of marijuana. *Concurring (Silberman, J.):* Although the court correctly rested its decision on alternative grounds, it should have first considered whether, as the government contended, the appellant waived his right to appeal his sentence on *Booker* grounds.
Initiative & Referendum Inst. v. U.S.Postal Serv.	417 F.3d 1299	2005	Authored Majority	First Amendment	*Reversed and Remanded:* Postal Service regulation wholly prohibiting the solicitation of signatures outside postal buildings did not withstand First Amendment scrutiny as a valid "time, place, and manner" regulation of speech, as the rule was "neither... narrowly tailored nor ensure[d] ample alternative channels of communication.

Table 1. (Continued)

Case Name	Citation	Year	Role	Subject	Holding
					”The D.C. Circuit remanded the case—which involved a facial challenge to the Postal Service regulation—for a determination as to whether the regulation abridged a substantial amount of protected free speech in public forums.
Edmonds v. Fed. Bureau of Investigation	417 F.3d 1319	2005	Authored Majority	Government information	*Reversed and Remanded:* A former FBI employee substantially prevailed on her FOIA claim by obtaining court-ordered, expedited processing of her FOIA request to obtain records related to the FBI's decision to terminate her, and thus was eligible for attorney fees; remanded to the lower court to consider whether she was entitled to such fees.
PPL Wallingford Energy LLC v. FERC	419 F.3d 1194	2005	Authored Majority	Energy	*Vacated and Remanded:* FERC's order rejecting wholesale electricity seller's agreement to provide power to an independent system operator was arbitrary and capricious.

Case Name	Citation	Year	Role	Subject	Holding
Crawford v. FCC	417 F.3d 1289	2005	Authored Majority	Administrative law	*Petition for review Dismissed in part and Denied in part:* The court dismissed a petition for review of FCC's dismissal of two proposals to amend the Commission's Table of Allotments for FM radio channels; as to the first proposal, the petition was moot; the second was denied on the merits because the petitioner received adequate notice that one of his proposals could be precluded by another applicant's earlier-filed submission.
Mwani v.Bin Laden	417 F.3d 1	2005	Authored Majority	Federal courts	*Affirmed in part and Reversed in part:* Lower court properly dismissed Kenyan plaintiffs' claims against Afghanistan (relating to the 1998 bombing of an American embassy in Kenya) for lack of subject-matter jurisdiction under the FSIA; however, the court erred in concluding that it lacked personal jurisdiction to adjudicate their claims (under the Alien Tort Statute) against Osama bin Laden and Al Qaeda.

Table 1. (Continued)

Case Name	Citation	Year	Role	Subject	Holding
S.Co. Servs., Inc. v. FERC	416 F.3d 39	2005	Authored Majority	Administrative law& Energy	*One order Vacated as moot and the other order Vacated and Remanded:* Petition for review of FERC order rejecting an agreement to roll over transmission service was moot because the agreement had expired; however, FERC's order rejecting a similar agreement was arbitrary and capricious.
Sec'y of Labor v. Spartan Mining Co.	415 F.3d 82	2005	Authored Majority	Administrative law & Labor law	*Petition Granted; Vacated and Remanded:* Secretary of Labor's interpretation of Labor Department regulations regarding hazardous conditions in coal mines was not plainly erroneous or inconsistent with the regulations; thus, the court vacated a Federal Mine Safety and Health Review Commission's decision that adopted a conflicting interpretation.
Heartland Reg'l Med. Ctr. v. Leavitt	415 F.3d 24	2005	Authored Majority	Health care	*Affirmed:* Hospital was not entitled to "sole community hospital" status under the Medicare statute and to reimbursement in accordance with such status.

Case Name	Citation	Year	Role	Subject	Holding
ITT Indus. v. NLRB	413 F.3d 64	2005	Authored Majority	Administrative law & Labor law	*Petition Denied and application for enforcement Granted:* In finding that an employer committed an unfair labor practice due to its restrictions on offsite employees' union organization efforts, the NLRB's interpretation of an ambiguous provision of the NLRA was reasonable.
Edison Elec. Inst. v.OSHA	411 F.3d 272	2005	Authored Majority	Administrative law, Federal courts& Labor law	*Petition Dismissed:* The court lacked jurisdiction over petition challenging a compliance directive issued by OSHA because the directive did not promulgate a new occupational safety or health standard.
Minn. Christian Broads., Inc. v. FCC	411 F.3d 283	2005	Authored Majority	Administrative law	*Affirmed:* FCC's denial of a new entrant bidding credit to the winner of a FCC auction to construct a new FM radio station was based on a reasonable interpretation of its own regulations.
United States v. Dykes	406 F.3d 717	2005	Authored Majority	Criminal law/procedure	*Affirmed:* The lower court committed no constitutional error in denying criminal defendant's motion to suppress drugs and firearm found on his person in the course of his brief detention by police officers who had reason to suspect criminal

Table 1. (Continued)

Case Name	Citation	Year	Role	Subject	Holding
					activity was occurring; there was sufficient evidence to support the defendant's conviction for possession of marijuana.
Rooney v. Sec'y of the Army	405 F.3d 1029	2005	Authored Majority	Federal courts	*Decision Vacated:* The lower court lacked jurisdiction over serviceman's declaratory judgment action regarding the validity of his initial discharge from the Army and the Army's subsequent effort to revoke it, as the action must be treated as a habeas petition that can only be filed in the federal court with jurisdiction over the Army based where he was located.
Columbia Gas Transmission Corp. v. FERC	404 F.3d 459	2005	Authored Majority	Energy	*Petition Granted; orders Vacated:* FERC exceeded its jurisdiction in ordering petitioner, a gas pipeline company, to install and pay for meters on certain natural gas wells.
Robertson v. Am. Airlines, Inc.	401 F.3d 499	2005	Authored Majority	Civil liability& International law	*Affirmed:* Airline passenger's claims against American Airlines for injuries she sustained during a flight were barred by an international civil aviation agreement's statute of limitations;

Case Name	Citation	Year	Role	Subject	*Holding*
					lower court was correct that her flight qualified as "international transportation" within the meaning of the Warsaw Convention.
U.S.Telecom Ass'n v. FCC	400 F.3d 29	2005	Authored Majority	Administrative law	*Petitions for review Granted in part and Denied in part; Remanded:* FCC failed to follow notice-and-comment requirements of the Administrative Procedure Act in issuing an order establishing conditions under which wire line telecommunications carriers must transfer telephone numbers to wireless carriers, and also failed to comply with requirements under the Regulatory Flexibilities Act to prepare a final regulatory flexibility analysis regarding the order's impact on small entities.
United States v. Coumaris	399 F.3d 343	2005	Authored Majority	Criminal law/procedure	*Conviction Affirmed, Remanded for resentencing:* The lower court did not abuse its discretion in its rulings regarding the admissibility of evidence against criminal defendant; sentence vacated and remanded for resentencing in conformity with the Supreme Court's

Table 1. (Continued)

Case Name	Citation	Year	Role	Subject	Holding
					decision in *United States v. Booker*, which had been issued during the defendant's appeal.
United States v. Hewlett	395 F.3d 458	2005	Authored Majority	Criminal law/procedure	*Affirmed:* The criminal defendant's arrest was lawful, and therefore the lower court was correct in denying his motion to suppress evidence (firearm and ammunition) seized incident to that arrest.
Haynes v. Williams	392 F.3d 478	2004	Authored Majority	Labor law	*Affirmed:* The evidence failed to raise a genuine issue of fact that a former budget analyst for the D.C. government had a disability withint he meaning of the ADA, and thus the court affirmed the dismissal of his lawsuit against the District and its Mayor for alleged discrimination. *Concurring (Williams, J.):* The judge wrote separately to question the premise, assumed by all parties and not ruled upon by the court, that sleeping is a "major life activity" for purposes of the ADA.

Case Name	Citation	Year	Role	Subject	Holding
Boca Airport, Inc. v. FAA	389 F.3d 185	2004	Authored Majority	Administrative law & Transportation	*Petition Denied:* Petitioner(a fixed-base operator that offers fueling, maintenance, and storage to aviators at public airports) had no federally enforceable right to compel the Boca Raton Airport Authority to construct, develop, and operate the last parcel of undeveloped aviation land at the Boca Raton airport. In addition, there was nothing arbitrary, capricious, or otherwise unlawful in FAA's conclusion that the Airport Authority's lease with a third party to develop the land was in compliance with federal requirements.
United States v. Edwards	388 F.3d 896	2004	Authored Majority	Criminal law/procedure	*Affirmed:* The lower court made no error in admitting police officer's redirect testimony over criminal defendant's relevance objection. In addition, the testimony's probative value was not substantially outweighed by any danger of unfair prejudice.
Bucheit v. Palestinian Liberation Org.	388 F.3d 346	2004	Authored Majority	Federal courts	*Affirmed:* The calculation of the valuation of converted property may be based in part on offers to buy the property. The district court did not abuse its discretion when it denied recovery of pre-judgment interest.

Table 1. (Continued)

Case Name	Citation	Year	Role	Subject	Holding
Egan v. U.S. Agency for Int'l Dev.	381 F.3d 1	2004	Authored Majority	Administrative law	*Affirmed:* Grievances contesting the Foreign Service Grievance Board's dismissal of an employee that were brought after the employee left the U.S. Agency for International Development were untimely under the Foreign Service Act.
In re Sealed Case (Medical Records)No. 03-7021	381 F.3d 1205	2004	Authored Majority	Federal courts	*Vacated and Remanded:* Medical records were not required to be produced without first determining whether any were subject to the federal psychotherapist privilege and without weighing the probative value of non-privileged records against intruding into a patient's legitimate privacy interests.
United States v. Eli	379 F.3d 1016	2004	Authored Majority	Criminal law/procedure	*Affirmed:* Defendant who did in fact distribute crack cocaine did not suffer prejudice because of his counsel's alleged failure to argue that the substance he distributed was only a form of cocaine, rather than crack cocaine.

Case Name	Citation	Year	Role	Subject	Holding
United States v. McLendon	378 F.3d 1109	2004	Authored Majority	Criminal law/procedure	*Affirmed:* The district court did not abuse its discretion in denying defendant's motion for a mistrial due to a government witness possibly having given improper testimony, so long as the witness's testimony was not unfairly prejudicial per se and the impact of the allegedly improper evidence was minimal when compared with the strength of the admissible evidence.
JMM Corp. v. District of Columbia	378 F.3d 1117	2004	Authored Majority	Federal courts	*Affirmed*: In a case involving zoning regulations, the District of Columbia was entitled to the benefit of the abstention doctrine recognized in *Younger v. Harris*,401 U.S. 37 (1971),which provides that, except in extraordinary circumstances, a federal court should not enjoin a pending state proceeding that is judicial in nature and involves important state interests.
SEC v. Bilzerian	378 F.3d 1100	2004	Authored Majority	Federal courts	*Affirmed:* Among other things, the court held that the district court had jurisdiction over a Florida resident for collection on the principal and interest on a loan owed to the receivership estate.

Table 1. (Continued)

Case Name	Citation	Year	Role	Subject	Holding
					The receivership estate was created to satisfy a judgment for federal securities law violations.
United States v. Riley	376 F.3d 1160	2004	Authored Majority	Criminal law/procedure	*Set aside and Remanded:* The United States appealed a lower federal court's decision granting a defendant a downward departure in his sentence for a felony conviction. The court held that the departure was improper. *Concurring in part and Dissenting in part (Rogers, J.):* The case should have been remanded to allow the lower court to make detailed findings in support of its decision to depart from the U.S. Sentencing Guidelines
Advanced Commc'ns Corp. v. FCC	376 F.3d 1153	2004	Authored Majority	Administrative law	*Affirmed:* FCC did not abuse its discretion in declining to reopen a case when it decided that the "new evidence" was insufficient to reopen the proceedings.

Case Name	Citation	Year	Role	Subject	Holding
Kilburn v. Socialist People's Libyan Arab Jamahiriya	376 F.3d 1123	2004	Authored Majority	Civil liability, Federal courts& International law	*Affirmed in part. Court Declined Jurisdiction over remaining claims:* The terrorism exception of the FSIA stripped Libya of its defense of sovereign immunity in its motion to dismiss a case brought for wrongful death.
Summers v. Howard Univ.	374 F.3d 1188	2004	Authored Majority	Federal courts	*Affirmed:* Magistrate judge did not abuse his discretion in denying motion to vacate a consent decree, and there was no clear error in magistrate's adoption of special master's calculations of fees and damages.
Barbour v. WMATA	374 F.3d 1161	2004	Authored Majority	Civil liability, Federalism& Transportation	*Affirmed:* Sovereign immunity did not protect WMATA from suit under the Rehabilitation Act of 1973 because it waived its immunity when it accepted federal transportation funds. Congress had power under the Spending Clause to condition the receipt of federal funds on such a waiver of immunity. *Dissenting (Sentelle, J.):*Congress lacks the power under the Spending Clause or the Fourteenth Amendment to subject

Table 1. (Continued)

Case Name	Citation	Year	Role	Subject	Holding
					states, or entities like WMATA treated as states for purposes of immunity, to suits for money damages for disability discrimination without a reasonably close nexus between the grant of funds and the imposed condition.
Francis v. Rodman Local Union 201 Pension Fund	367 F.3d 937	2004	Authored Majority	Labor law	*Affirmed:* An employee was entitled to pension benefits only for the time he actually worked, rather than time that he would have worked but for the union's discrimination.
United States v. Goree	365 F.3d 1086	2004	Authored Majority	Criminal law/procedure	*Remanded:* Additional information was needed to determine whether a search was constitutional.
United States v. Thomas	361 F.3d 653	2004	Authored Majority	Criminal law/procedure	*Affirmed in part, Remanded in part:* The criminal offense of escape is a crime of violence under the U.S. Sentencing Guidelines; D.C. Circuit remanded the question of whether an erroneous reference to a defendant's arrests affected his sentence.

Case Name	Citation	Year	Role	Subject	Holding
United States v. Heard	359 F.3d 544	2004	Authored Majority	Criminal law/procedure	*Affirmed:* The lower court did not abuse its discretion in deciding on consecutive, rather than concurrent, sentences under the U.S. Sentencing Guidelines Manual.
Sierra Club v. EPA	356 F.3d 296	2004	Authored Majority	Environmental law	*Vacated in part, Remanded in part, Petitions for review otherwise Denied:* Among other things, the court held that EPA was not authorized to grant conditional approval to ozone control plans promising only to do later what the Clean Air Act required now.
Ciralsky v. CIA	355 F.3d 661	2004	Authored Majority	Federal courts	*Remanded:* The uncertainty of D.C. Circuit as to what district court would have ruled if it had known of the precise nature of a statute of limitations problem resulted in remand for further proceedings.
Singletary v. District of Columbia	351 F.3d 519	2003	Authored Majority	Administrative law & Labor law	*Affirmed in part, Reversed in part, and Remanded:* Among other things, the court held that the timeliness of the plaintiff employee's claim of a hostile work environment did not depend on whether the alleged acts by themselves were actionable.

Table 1. (Continued)

Case Name	Citation	Year	Role	Subject	Holding
Ranger Cellular v. FCC	348 F.3d 1044	2003	Authored Majority	Administrative law& Federal courts	*Affirmed in part, Dismissed in part:* Among other things, the court held that plaintiffs lacked standing to challenge FCC's licenses to provide cellular phone service.
Shamrock Foods Co. v. NLRB	346 F.3d 1130	2003	Authored Majority	Labor law	*Petition for review Denied, cross-application for enforcement Granted:* Substantial evidence supported the NLRB's finding that a violation of the NLRA had occurred when a company discharged an employee for allegedly committing misconduct by soliciting co-workers for a union.
United States v. Pettigrew	346 F.3d 1139	2003	Authored Majority	Criminal law/procedure	*Affirmed:* A defendant's claims that his conviction and sentence were unconstitutional, which the defendant did not raise at trial or on direct appeal, required showing of "cause and prejudice" to overcome procedural default.

Case Name	Citation	Year	Role	Subject	Holding
United States v. Taylor	339 F.3d 973	2003	Authored Majority	Criminal law/procedure	*Affirmed:* Adefendant who was unable to show ineffective assistance of counsel on the basis that counsel had not complied with his instructions to appeal a lower court's judgment may not have his sentence reviewed.
United States v. Hanson	339 F.3d 983	2003	Authored Majority	Criminal law/procedure	*Affirmed:* Among other things, the court held that the lower court did not abuse its discretion when it gave little weight to a defendant's belated claim of entrapment.
Info. Handling Servs., Inc. v. Def. Automated Printing Services	338 F.3d 1024	2003	Authored Majority	Federal courts	*Reversed:* A private contractor may conduct discovery related to whether it might have provided products to the government at a cost lower than the system that the agency had developed.
Mo.Public Serv.Comm'n v. FERC	337 F.3d 1066	2003	Authored Majority	Administrative law & Energy	*Vacated and Remanded:* FERC orders that departed from basing rates on cost-based principles were vacated and remanded with instructions that FERC address the question of an appropriate refund.
Kappus v. Comm'r of Internal Revenue	337 F.3d 1053	2003	Authored Majority	International law & Tax law	*Affirmed:* A provision within a federal tax statute enacted after a tax treaty superseded any preexisting treaty obligation with which it conflicted.

Table 1. (Continued)

Case Name	Citation	Year	Role	Subject	Holding
United States v. Lafayette	337 F.3d 1043	2003	Authored Majority	Criminal law/procedure	*Affirmed:* Because the same mandatory punishment would be applied under a provision of the U.S. Sentencing Guidelines, there was no reason to remand a case for resentencing in which a harmless error occurred.
Lathram v. Snow	336 F.3d 1085	2003	Authored Majority	Civil rights & Labor law	*Affirmed in part, Reversed in part, and Remanded:* Among other things, the court held that an issue of discrimination exists when an employer does not use the same application and scoring process for similar positions.
United States v. Pindell	336 F.3d 1049	2003	Authored Majority	Criminal law/procedure	*Affirmed:* The D.C. Circuit found no error in challenged decisions of the lower court, and, among other things, ruled that the execution of a search warrant that included the phrase "evidence of a violation of 18 U.S.C. §242"at the end of a list of specific items to be seized did not violate the Fourth Amendment's particularity requirement.

United States v. Hinds	329 F.3d 184	2003	Authored Majority	Criminal law/procedure	*Affirmed:* A provision of the U.S. Sentencing Guidelines was not applicable to a defendant's claim that his sentence should be reduced due to entrapment when he showed no hesitation in selling drugs to undercover officers.
Morgan v. Fed.l Home Loan Mortg. Corp.	328 F.3d 647	2003	Authored Majority	Civil rights & Labor law	*Affirmed:* An employee failed to show critical elements of a prima facie case for discrimination or retaliation.
United States v. Hall	326 F.3d 1295	2003	Authored Majority	Criminal law/procedure	*Affirmed:* Defendant suffered no prejudice when the wrong provision of the U.S. Sentencing Guidelines was applied because the correct provision, like the one relied upon, mandated consecutive rather than concurrent sentences.
Rancho Viejo, LLC v. Norton	323 F.3d 1062	2003	Authored Majority	Environmental law& Federalism	*Affirmed:* The court declined to invalidate a provision of the Endangered Species Act as exceeding Congress's legislative powers under the Commerce Clause.

Case Name	Citation	Year	Role	Subject	Holding
Trans. Intelligence, Inc. v. FCC	336 F.3d 1058	2003	Authored Majority	Administrative law	*Affirmed:* FCC's denial of a company's petition for reconsideration of an agency order authorizing its competitor to market a radio transmitter was neither arbitrary nor capricious.
United States v. Brown	334 F.3d 1161	2003	Authored Majority	Criminal law/procedure	*Affirmed:* The warrantless search of car was permissible based upon the totality of the circumstances; the resulting discovery of a firearm in the vehicle gave police probable cause to search the car's trunk. *Dissenting (Rogers, J.):* The failure of the government to offer evidence that the police had articulable suspicion to believe the suspect was engaged in criminal wrongdoing made the stop and frisk exception to the warrant requirement inapplicable. Additionally, even if it was a lawful stop, the search of the trunk was not limited in scope, and government failure to introduce evidence of probable cause to search the trunk made seizure of contraband contained therein unlawful.

Table 1. (Continued)

Case Name	Citation	Year	Role	Subject	Holding
Fontana v. White	334 F.3d 80	2003	Authored Majority	Federal courts	*Affirmed:* Military service obligations deriving from free undergraduate and medical school educations are to run consecutively, not concurrently.
Ark Las Vegas Rest. Corp. v. NLRB	334 F.3d 99	2003	Authored Majority	Labor law	*Order Enforced in part:* Substantial evidence supported the NLRB's findings that several actions by an employer countering union activities of employees were coercive and violated the NLRA.
Sec'y of Labor v. Excel Mining, LLC	334 F.3d 1	2003	Authored Majority	Administrative law	*Reversed:* Secretary of Labor's interpretation of the Mine Act's compliance methodology related to measuring mine dust was reasonable and therefore given deference. *Dissenting (Sentelle, J.):* The Secretary of Labor exceeded her statutory authority and therefore the reasonableness of her interpretation was irrelevant. The statute did not authorize manner of measurement utilized.

Case Name	Citation	Year	Role	Subject	Holding
United States v. Powell	334 F.3d 42	2003	Authored Majority	Criminal law/procedure	*Affirmed:* The district court did not err when it admitted into evidence a prior consistent statement by a police officer who arrested the defendant.
Public Citizen, Inc. v. HHS	332 F.3d 654	2003	Authored Majority	Health care	*Affirmed:* The court found that a Medicare beneficiary who files a complaint with a Peer Review Organization must be provided more information than a form letter that states that the organization has examined the concerns and will take appropriate action if warranted.
United States v. Johnson	331 F.3d 962	2003	Authored Majority	Criminal law/procedure	*Affirmed:* The court concluded, among other things, that alleged procedural deficiencies in the trial and sentencing of

Table 1. (Continued)

Case Name	Citation	Year	Role	Subject	Holding

Case Name	Citation	Year	Role	Subject	*Holding*
					Concurring in opinion (Ginsburg, C.J.): Supreme Court precedent requires that there be a logical stopping point to the court's rationale for upholding the constitutionality of Congress's exercise of its Commerce Clause power. Therefore, with respect to a species that is not an article in interstate commerce and does not affect interstate commerce, a take of the species can be regulated if and only if the take itself substantially affects interstate commerce.
Fund for Animals, Inc. v. Norton	322 F.3d 728	2003	Authored Majority	Federal courts	*Reversed:* A Mongolian government agency established standing and was permitted to intervene as a right in an endangered species listing because it satisfied such criteria of Federal Rules of Civil Procedure 24(a)(2) as showing an interest relating to the property or transaction that was the subject of the action.

Table 1. (Continued)

Case Name	Citation	Year	Role	Subject	Holding
Waters v. Rumsfeld	320 F.3d 265	2003	Authored Majority	Labor law	*Affirmed in part, Vacated and Remanded in part:* Public law that exempts military commissary baggers from the FLSA is constitutional. FLSA claims for monetary damages based on baggers' additional duties were remanded to the district court with instructions to transfer claims to the U.S. Court of Federal Claims.
Lee Lumber & Bldg. Material Corp. v. NLRB	310 F.3d 209	2002	Authored Majority	Labor law	*Petition for review Denied and cross-application for enforcement Granted:* NLRB's unfair labor practice decision involving an unlawful refusal to bargain, among other practices, should be enforced and would not be reviewed because it was neither arbitrary nor unsupported by substantial evidence. *Concurring (Sentelle, J.):* Because the appellant was required to make a posting admitting its own violations, the judge suggested to the parties that, in fairness, appellant should also post D.C. Circuit opinions so that employees would know

Case Name	Citation	Year	Role	Subject	Holding
					that unlawful acts of the NLRB deprived them of a right to choose a bargaining representative (or no representative) for many years.
United States v. Arrington	309 F.3d 40	2002	Authored Majority	Criminal law/ procedure	*Affirmed:* Evidence supported the defendant's conviction, and the district court did not plainly err in instructing the jury as to the elements of the offense, including instructions as to when an automobile may be considered a "deadly or dangerous weapon" for purposes of heightening criminal penalties available under 18U.S.C. §111(b).
United States v. Brooke	308 F.3d 17	2002	Authored Majority	Criminal law/ procedure	*Affirmed:* District court's refusal to depart downward from the applicable U.S. Sentencing Guidelines was not reviewable when the court did not act in violation of the law; the sentence did not result from an incorrect application of the Guidelines; and the court did not clearly err in finding facts relevant to the potential departure.

Table 1. (Continued)

Case Name	Citation	Year	Role	Subject	Holding
Sturm, Ruger & Co. v. Chao	300 F.3d 867	2002	Authored Majority	Administrative law, Federal courts & Labor law	*Affirmed:* Courts lack subject-matter jurisdiction to consider claims challenging OSHA's Data Collection Initiative. Such claims must be pursued through the administrative review process prescribed by the Occupational Safety and Health Act.
Republican Nat'l Comm.v. Taylor	299 F.3d 887	2002	Authored Majority	Election law	*Affirmed:* The court affirmed summary judgment for the Republican National Committee because an advertisement that issued a challenge to readers was true and could not be disproved.
U.S. Air Tour Ass'n v. FAA	298 F.3d 997	2002	Authored Majority	Administrative law& Transportation	*Petition for review Granted in part and Denied in part, Remanded*: FAA rule limiting the number of air tours permitted to fly over the Grand Canyon National Park was not generally arbitrary and capricious with regard to the methodology used to evaluate noise. However, other aspects of the methodology, such as the exclusion of non-tour aircraft from the methodology, were arbitrary and capricious, and required reconsideration by the agency.

Case Name	Citation	Year	Role	Subject	Holding
Trans. Intelligence, Inc. v. FCC	336 F.3d 1058	2003	Authored Majority	Administrative law	*Affirmed:* FCC's denial of a company's petition for reconsideration of an agency order authorizing its competitor to market a radio transmitter was neither arbitrary nor capricious.
United States v. Brown	334 F.3d 1161	2003	Authored Majority	Criminal law/procedure	*Affirmed:* The warrantless search of car was permissible based upon the totality of the circumstances; the resulting discovery of a firearm in the vehicle gave police probable cause to search the car's trunk. *Dissenting (Rogers, J.):* The failure of the government to offer evidence that the police had articulable suspicion to believe the suspect was engaged in criminal wrongdoing made the stop and frisk exception to the warrant requirement inapplicable. Additionally, even if it was a lawful stop, the search of the trunk was not limited in scope, and government failure to introduce evidence of probable cause to search the trunk made seizure of contraband contained therein unlawful.

Table 1. (Continued)

Case Name	Citation	Year	Role	Subject	Holding
Fontana v. White	334 F.3d 80	2003	Authored Majority	Federal courts	*Affirmed:* Military service obligations deriving from free undergraduate and medical school educations are to run consecutively, not concurrently.
Ark Las Vegas Rest. Corp. v. NLRB	334 F.3d 99	2003	Authored Majority	Labor law	*Order Enforced in part:* Substantial evidence supported the NLRB's findings that several actions by an employer countering union activities of employees were coercive and violated the NLRA.
Sec'y of Labor v. Excel Mining, LLC	334 F.3d 1	2003	Authored Majority	Administrative law	*Reversed:* Secretary of Labor's interpretation of the Mine Act's compliance methodology related to measuring mine dust was reasonable and therefore given deference. *Dissenting (Sentelle, J.):* The Secretary of Labor exceeded her statutory authority and therefore the reasonableness of her interpretation was irrelevant. The statute did not authorize manner of measurement utilized.

Case Name	Citation	Year	Role	Subject	Holding
United States v. Powell	334 F.3d 42	2003	Authored Majority	Criminal law/procedure	*Affirmed:* The district court did not err when it admitted into evidence a prior consistent statement by a police officer who arrested the defendant.
Public Citizen, Inc. v. HHS	332 F.3d 654	2003	Authored Majority	Health care	*Affirmed:* The court found that a Medicare beneficiary who files a complaint with a Peer Review Organization must be provided more information than a form letter that states that the organization has examined the concerns and will take appropriate action if warranted.
United States v. Johnson	331 F.3d 962	2003	Authored Majority	Criminal law/procedure	*Affirmed:* The court concluded, among other things, that alleged procedural deficiencies in the trial and sentencing of a criminal defendant did not rise to the level of plain error, and a downward sentence departure in the defendant's criminal sentence was not justified because improper statements by the prosecutor did not have substantial and injurious effect or influence in determining the jury's verdict.

Table 1. (Continued)

Case Name	Citation	Year	Role	Subject	Holding
United States v. Hinds	329 F.3d 184	2003	Authored Majority	Criminal law/procedure	*Affirmed:* A provision of the U.S. Sentencing Guidelines was not applicable to a defendant's claim that his sentence should be reduced due to entrapment when he showed no hesitation in selling drugs to undercover officers.
Morgan v. Fed.l Home Loan Mortg. Corp.	328 F.3d 647	2003	Authored Majority	Civil rights & Labor law	*Affirmed:* An employee failed to show critical elements of a prima facie case for discrimination or retaliation.
United States v. Hall	326 F.3d 1295	2003	Authored Majority	Criminal law/procedure	*Affirmed:* Defendant suffered no prejudice when the wrong provision of the U.S. Sentencing Guidelines was applied because the correct provision, like the one relied upon, mandated consecutive rather than concurrent sentences.
Rancho Viejo, LLC v. Norton	323 F.3d 1062	2003	Authored Majority	Environmental law& Federalism	*Affirmed:* The court declined to invalidate a provision of the Endangered Species Act as exceeding Congress's legislative powers under the Commerce Clause.

Case Name	Citation	Year	Role	Subject	*Holding*
Waterhouse v. - District of Columbia	298 F.3d 989	2002	Authored Majority	Civil rights & Labor law	*Affirmed:* Plaintiff's proffered evidence did not satisfy her burden of showing that a reasonable jury could conclude that she was terminated on account of her race.
United States v. Samuel	296 F.3d 1169	2002	Authored Majority	Criminal law/ procedure	*Affirmed:* A sentencing enhancement that resulted from defendant's commission of an offense while on release for another crime, and that did not increase the sentence above the statutory maximum for the offense of conviction, did not require submission to a jury or proof beyond a reasonable doubt.
World Wide Minerals, Ltd.v. Republic of Kazakhstan	296 F.3d 1154	2002	Authored Majority	Federal courts & International law	*Affirmed in part and Remanded in part:* Claims against Kazakhstan and its instrumentalities were dismissed because Kazakhstan did not waive its sovereign immunity; the court lacked subject-matter jurisdiction over the claims; and the act of state doctrine barred such claims. Claims against Nukem, a New York corporation, were remanded to determine whether personal jurisdiction could be established.

Table 1. (Continued)

Case Name	Citation	Year	Role	Subject	Holding
Darrell Andrews Trucking, Inc. v. Fed. Motor Carrier Safety Admin.	296 F.3d 1120	2002	Authored Majority	Administrative law& Transportation	*Remanded:* Agency's order reflected a reasonable interpretation of its regulations, and commercial motor carrier was provided fair notice of that interpretation and appropriate process before downgrade in safety rating. However, because the agency failed to address a significant challenge to the rationality of its decision, the case was remanded to the agency for further proceeding.
A.E. Staley Mfg. Co. v. Sec'y of Labor	295 F.3d 1341	2002	Authored Majority	Labor law	*Petition for review Denied:* Substantial evidence supported determination that corn refiner was plainly indifferent to its violations of the Occupational Safety and Health Act.
U.S.Telecom Ass'n v. FCC	295 F.3d 1326	2002	Authored Majority	Administrative law	*Petition for review Denied:* FCC reasonably interpreted the Telecommunications Act and reasonably applied the applicable test when it determined that the Iowa Communications Network was a common carrier.

Case Name	Citation	Year	Role	Subject	Holding
Watters v. WMATA	295 F.3d 36	2002	Authored Majority	Civil liability & Federalism	*Vacated and Remanded:* Sovereign immunity precluded claims against WMATA for breach of contract and breach of duty to enforce equitable lien.
Gerber v. Norton	294 F.3d 173	2002	Authored Majority	Environmental law	*Reversed and Remanded:* Agency violated the Endangered Species Act by issuing a permit in connection with a proposed residential development without allowing public comment on a key component of the developer's permit application, and without making a statutorily required finding that the developer's plan would minimize the negative impact on an endangered animal to the maximum extent practicable.
Ned Chartering & Trading v. Republic of Pakistan	294 F.3d 148	2002	Authored Majority	Federal courts	*Affirmed:* The district court did not abuse its discretion when it concluded that Pakistan had sufficient time to complete the discovery it needed to defend against plaintiff's summary judgment motion.
United States v. Wesley	293 F.3d 541	2002	Authored Majority	Criminal law/ procedure	*Affirmed:* Defendant's arrest and the search of his car were not conducted in violation of the U.S. Constitution.

Table 1. (Continued)

Case Name	Citation	Year	Role	Subject	Holding
Gorman v. Ameritrade Holding Corp.	293 F.3d 506	2002	Authored Majority	Federal courts	*Affirmed:* Courts in the District of Columbia may assert general jurisdiction over a defendant that conducts its business in the District over the Internet.
Power v. Barnhart	292 F.3d 781	2002	Authored Majority	Federal courts	*Affirmed:* Remedy of mandamus is inappropriate when, among other things, the party seeking relief failed to pursue an adequate alternative remedy.
Musengo v. White	286 F.3d 535	2002	Authored Majority	Administrative law	*Affirmed:* The Army Board for Correction of Military Records did not act arbitrarily or capriciously when it refused to expunge an Officer Evaluation Report.
Breen v. U.S. Dep't of Transp.	282 F.3d 839	2002	Authored Majority	Federal courts& Labor law	*Reversed and Remanded:* Summary judgment was not appropriate when there was a genuine issue of material fact with regard to the availability of a reasonable accommodation (such a san alternative work schedule) compatible with the essential functions of the position for an employee with obsessive-compulsive disorder.

Case Name	Citation	Year	Role	Subject	Holding
Arizona v. Thompson	281 F.3d 248	2002	Authored Majority	Administrative law	*Reversed and Remanded:* Agency's directive was not entitled to deference when it involved an inaccurate interpretation of a statute and was not an exercise of the agency's own judgment.
United States v. Bookhardt	277 F.3d 558	2002	Authored Majority	Criminal law/ procedure	*Reversed:* Evidence obtained during a search incident to an arrest was admissible even if the reason for the arrest was later proven to be invalid, if there was probable cause to arrest the defendant for a different offense.
Antelope Valley Bus Co., Inc. v. NLRB	275 F.3d 1089	2002	Authored Majority	Labor law	*Petition for review Denied and cross-application for enforcement Granted:* The NLRB's findings that an employer violated the NLRA by refusing to bargain with a union were consistent with precedent and supported by substantial evidence. A union representation election was not invalid when the employer provided reasonable notice of the election to its employees, even if four employees were not provided election ballots.

Table 1. (Continued)

Case Name	Citation	Year	Role	Subject	Holding
Curtin v. United Airlines, Inc.	275 F.3d 88	2001	Authored Majority	Federal courts	*Affirmed:* The district court did not abuse its discretion when it granted summary judgment for the defendant without first permitting discovery or ruling on class certification. A court is not barred from rendering an easy decision on an individual claim to avoid an unnecessary and more difficult decision on the propriety of certification.
RAG Cumberland Res. LP v. Fed. Mine Safety & Health Review Comm’n	272 F.3d 590	2001	Authored Majority	Administrative law & Labor law	*Petition for review Denied:* The Federal Mine Safety and Health Review Commission’s decision to reinstate an order to withdraw all individuals from an unsafe area in a coal mine was supported by substantial evidence.
United States v. Venable	269 F.3d 1086	2001	Authored Majority	Criminal law/procedure	*Affirmed:* Defendant’s conviction for unlawful possession of a firearm by a convicted felon will not be reversed when prosecutor’s misstatement of the government’s burden of proof, to which defense counsel did not object, was neither plain error nor prejudicial.

Case Name	Citation	Year	Role	Subject	Holding
Glob.Crossing Telecomms., Inc. v. FCC	259 F.3d 740	2001	Authored Majority	Administrative law	*Petition for review Denied and order Affirmed:* FCC decision that compensation was owed to a local exchange carrier/payphone service provider was consistent with the Telecommunications Act and was neither arbitrary nor capricious.
Gilvin v. Fire	259 F.3d 749	2001	Authored Majority	Federal courts & Labor law	*Affirmed in part and Reversed in part:* The court held that the district court's grant of summary judgment to defendants on two of plaintiff's claims was erroneous when there were genuine issues of material fact with regard to plaintiff employee's suspension and subsequent termination.
Tourus Records, Inc. v. Drug Enf't Agency	259 F.3d 731	2001	Authored Majority	Administrative law	*Affirmed:* Agency's denial of an application to proceed in forma pauperis in a forfeiture proceeding was supported by substantial evidence. Internal agency memoranda that explained the rationale for the denial confirmed that the decision was not arbitrary or capricious.

Table 1. (Continued)

Case Name	Citation	Year	Role	Subject	Holding
Pacific Bell v. NLRB	259 F.3d 719	2001	Authored Majority	Labor law	*Petition for review Denied and cross-application for enforcement Granted:* Substantial evidence supported a finding by the NLRB that an employer's refusal to bargain was not based on a good-faith reasonable doubt concerning the appropriate bargaining representative for its employees.
Students Against Genocide v. U.S. Dep't of State	257 F.3d 828	2001	Authored Majority	Government information	*Affirmed in part and Remanded in part:* Summary judgment in favor of agencies subject to FOIA request was affirmed where documents that fell within the requested group were either produced or exempt from the act's inspection requirements. Issue of attorneys' fees and costs was remanded to the district court.
Kirby Produce Co. v. USDA	256 F.3d 830	2001	Authored Majority	Administrative law	*Petition for review Granted and case Remanded:* Agency's revocation of license to operate as a merchant of perishable agricultural products was arbitrary and capricious.

Case Name	Citation	Year	Role	Subject	Holding
United States v. Webb	255 F.3d 890	2001	Authored Majority	Criminal law/ procedure	*Affirmed:* Among other things, the court held that neither *Apprendiv. New Jersey*, 530 U.S. 466 (2000), and its progeny, nor the U.S. Sentencing Guidelines, compelled a conclusion that defendant's sentence was reversible error.
CF Indus. v. Surface Transp. Bd.	255 F.3d 816	2001	Authored Majority	Administrative law	*Petitions for review Denied:* Agency's findings reflected a reasonable application of its guidelines. Agency did not abuse its discretion when it denied pipeline customer's request to amend its complaint to seek additional rate reductions.
Al-Fayed v. CIA	254 F.3d 300	2001	Authored Majority	Government information	*Affirmed:* District courts must apply de novo review to agency denials of expedited processing under FOIA.
United States v. Johnson	254 F.3d 279	2001	Authored Majority	Federal courts	*Order vacated and matter Remanded:* A 12-page "Memorandum and Order" did not satisfy Federal Rule of Civil Procedure 58, which requires a judgment to be set forth on a separate document, when the pages were stapled, a signature was included only on the twelfth page, and the document was file-stamped only once on the first page.

Table 1. (Continued)

Case Name	Citation	Year	Role	Subject	Holding
					Concurring (Henderson, J.): The judge cautioned against applying the majority's approach to applying Federal Rule of Civil Procedure 58 too broadly.
Tenet Healthsystems Healthcorp. v. Thompson	254 F.3d 238	2001	Authored Majority	Administrative law& Health care	*Reversed:* Agency's decision with regard to reimbursement for capital-related costs in providing Medicare services was supported by substantial evidence and was not arbitrary, capricious, or contrary to law.
United States v. Green	254 F.3d 167	2001	Authored Majority	Criminal law/ procedure	*Affirmed:* Erroneous jury instruction that conflated the terms "using" and "carrying" in relation to the possession of a firearm was harmless error.
Tasty Baking Co. v. NLRB	254 F.3d 114	2001	Authored Majority	Labor law	*Petition for review Denied and cross-application for enforcement of order Granted:* Findings of the NLRB concerning unfair labor practices committed by producer of baked goods were supported by substantial evidence.
United States v. Saro	252 F.3d 449	2001	Authored Majority	Criminal law/ procedure	*Dismissed:* District court was plainly correct in ruling that defendant's motion for leave to file a motion to vacate his sentence was time-barred.

Case Name	Citation	Year	Role	Subject	Holding
United States v. Young	247 F.3d 1247	2001	Authored Majority	Criminal law/ procedure	*Affirmed:* Amendment to the U.S. Sentencing Guidelines will not result in reduction of prior criminal sentence for conspiracy to manufacture and distribute phencyclidine (PCP) when the manner in which the sentence was calculated was not affected by the amendment.
Halle Enters. v. NLRB	247 F.3d 268	2001	Authored Majority	Labor law	*Petition for review Denied and cross-application for enforcement Granted:* Substantial evidence supported the NLRB's findings that the employer's offer of reinstatement to its wrongly terminated employees was conditional. Consequently, the offer did not toll the employees' entitlement to back pay.
United States v. Greenfield	244 F.3d 158	2001	Authored Majority	Criminal law/ procedure	*Affirmed:* District court's refusal to depart downward from the sentence required by the U.S. Sentencing Guidelines was not based on a misunderstanding or misapplication of the Guidelines. A departure from the Guidelines was not appropriate when the defendant's evidence did not demonstrate that his mental capacity was significantly reduced.

Table 1. (Continued)

Case Name	Citation	Year	Role	Subject	Holding
Gray v. Poole	243 F.3d 572	2001	Authored Majority	Civil rights	*Affirmed:* Attorneys for the District of Columbia were absolutely immune from damages under 42 U.S.C. §1983 for their conduct in initiating and prosecuting civil child neglect actions.
United States v. McCoy	242 F.3d 399	2001	Authored Majority	Criminal law/ procedure	*Conviction Affirmed and Remanded for resentencing:* Ambiguity existed in the lower court record as to the legal standard utilized in application of the U.S. Sentencing Guidelines.
Dynaquest Corp. v. U.S.Postal Serv.	242 F.3d 1070	2001	Authored Majority	Federal courts	*Affirmed:* Doctrine of res judicata prohibited D.C. Circuit jurisdiction.
Sloan v. U.S. Dep't of Housing & Urban Dev. (HUD)	236 F.3d 756	2001	Authored Majority	Federal courts	*Affirmed:* HUD suspension of plaintiffs from government contracting work was discretionary act that was not subject to challenge under the Federal Tort Claims Act.
United States v. Gbemisola	225 F.3d 753	2000	Authored Majority	Criminal law/ procedure	*Affirmed:* Evidence obtained from the government's use of a mobile tracking device was admissible in criminal proceeding because, even in the absence of a valid warrant, the defendant had no reasonable expectation of privacy in activities he conducted within the view of government agents.

Case Name	Citation	Year	Role	Subject	*Holding*
Cone v. Caldera	223 F.3d 789	2000	Authored Majority	Administrative law	*Reversed:* The decision not to amend military officer's rating was not arbitrary and capricious.
United Food and Commercial Workers Int'l Union Local 400 v. NLRB	222 F.3d 1030	2000	Authored Majority	Labor law	*Petition Granted and Remanded:* Factual findings by the NLRB concerning alleged unfair labor practices were not supported by evidence.
Transitional Hosps. Corp. of La. v. Shalala	222 F.3d 1019	2000	Authored Majority	Administrative law& Health care	*Reversed and Remanded with instructions:* Congress left to HHS some discretion to determine how a hospital could qualify as a "long term care facility." Remand to the agency was appropriate so that the Secretary could determine how to exercise this authority.
Voss v. SEC	222 F.3d 994	2000	Authored Majority	Administrative law	*Affirmed:* SEC's order sanctioning petitioners for their involvement in securities violations was reasonable and supported by substantial evidence.
First Am. Disc. Corp. v. Commodity Futures Trading Comm'n	222 F.3d 1008	2000	Authored Majority	Administrative law	*Petition Denied:* The Commodity Futures Trading Commission's interpretation of a regulation was not plainly erroneous or inconsistent with the regulation.

Table 1. (Continued)

Case Name	Citation	Year	Role	Subject	Holding
					Concurring in judgment (Randolph, J.): The judge concurred in the court's opinion except the portion holding that the Commission's failure to give notice of an alteration in a proposed rule amounted to harmless error.
Daskalea v. District of Columbia	227 F.3d 433	2000	Authored Majority	Civil rights & D.C. local government	*Affirmed in part and Reversed in part:* The court upheld a jury's award of compensatory damages to a woman that had been a prisoner in a D.C. jail. However, the court held that D.C. law barred punitive damages awards against the District.
Hi-Tech Furnace Sys. v. FCC	224 F.3d 781	2000	Authored Majority	Administrative law	*Petition Denied:* FCC did not abuse its discretion when determining that revisions to tariffs were just and reasonable.
Nat. Res. Def. Council v. NRC	216 F.3d 1180	2000	Authored Majority	Administrative law	*Petition Denied:* The court declined to find that an NRC regulation's definition of "meetings" under the Sunshine Act, which adopted Supreme Court text verbatim, was inconsistent with the text and legislative history of the authorizing statute.

Case Name	Citation	Year	Role	Subject	Holding
United States v. Johnson	216 F.3d 1162	2000	Authored Majority	Criminal law/procedure	*Affirmed:* Evidence sustained the petitioner's criminal conviction, and erroneous jury instruction was harmless error.
United States v. Evans	216 F.3d 80	2000	Authored Majority	Criminal law/procedure	*Affirmed:* Among other things, the court concluded that even though inadmissible hearsay testimony was admitted, the error was harmless.
Sparrow v. United Air Lines, Inc.	216 F.3d 1111	2000	Authored Majority	Civil rights	*Reversed and Remanded:* The plaintiff was not required to set out a prima facie case in initial pleading for racial discrimination claim.
Allied Local & Reg'l Mfrs. Caucus v. EPA	215 F.3d 61	2000	Authored Majority	Administrative law & Federalism	*Petitions Denied:* Among other things, the court determined that Congress did not exceed its authority under the Commerce Clause in directing the EPA to promulgate regulations under the Clean Air Act. The court held that the regulations were not arbitrary and capricious, and the EPA's promulgation of the regulations did not exceed its statutory authority.
Contemporary Media, Inc. v. FCC	214 F.3d 187	2000	Authored Majority	Administrative law	*Affirmed:* FCC's character policy was rational and the revocation of licenses did not implicate the Excessive Fines Clause of the Eighth Amendment.

Table 1. (Continued)

Case Name	Citation	Year	Role	Subject	Holding
El-Hadad v. United Arab Emirates	216 F.3d 29	2000	Authored Majority	Federal courts	*Affirmed in part, Reversed in part, and Remanded:* Factual questions as to what constitutes "commercial activity" under the FSIA had to be resolved before the court could consider the merits of the plaintiff's claims.
Mohave Elec. Coop., Inc. v. NLRB	206 F.3d 1183	2000	Authored Majority	Administrative law & Labor law	*Petition for Review Denied and enforcement Granted:* Among other holdings, the court upheld the NLRB's determination that an employee was unlawfully discharged because the Board's findings were supported by substantial evidence and the Board did not act arbitrarily or otherwise err in applying established law.
Lomak Petroleum, Inc. v. FERC	206 F.3d 1193	2000	Authored Majority	Energy	*Petition Denied:* FERC's decision to disclaim regulatory jurisdiction over a natural gas facility was not arbitrary or capricious; the affected gas producer was not deprived of due process.
Borgo v. Goldin	204 F.3d 251	2000	Authored Majority	Civil rights & Federal courts	*Reversed and Remanded:* Factual questions concerning an employer's motivation in terminating an employee should be resolved by a jury and not by the district court.

Case Name	Citation	Year	Role	Subject	*Holding*
Schoenbohm v. FCC	204 F.3d 243	2000	Authored Majority	Administrative law & Federal courts	*Affirmed in part and Dismissed in part:* Review of FCC's decision to deny application renewal was not arbitrary, capricious, an abuse of discretion, or otherwise not in accordance with law. The court lacked jurisdiction to review the agency's rejection of the appellant's petition for reconsideration of the decision.
McGill v. Munoz	203 F.3d 843	2000	Authored Majority	Civil liability & Civil rights	*Reversed and Remanded:* Failure to offer evidence sufficient to support discrimination claim requires reversal of district court's decision denying employer's post-trial motion for judgment as a matter of law.
Fort Sumter Tours, Inc. v. Babbitt	202 F.3d 349	2000	Authored Majority	Administrative law	*Vacated and Remanded with instructions to Dismiss in part and Affirmed in part:* The court held, among other things, that it lacked jurisdiction over a claim pertaining to a non reviewable settlement decision of the National Park Service.

Table 1. (Continued)

Case Name	Citation	Year	Role	Subject	Holding
Panhandle E. Pipe Line Co. v. FERC	196 F.3d 1273	1999	Authored Majority	Administrative law & Energy	*Petition Granted and Remanded:* When FERC's orders concerning petitioner's proposed tariffs and criteria for the future construction of pipeline interconnections apparently represented a change of policy, the agency was required to provide an explanation of its reasoning.
Trunkline LNG Co. v. FERC	194 F.3d 68	1999	Authored Majority	Administrative law & Energy	*Orders Affirmed and petition for review Denied:* Review of FERC's conditions on approval of a liquefied natural gas project determined FERC did not act arbitrarily or capriciously.
Telecom*USA, Inc. v. United States	192 F.3d 1068	1999	Authored Majority	Administrative law & Tax law	*Affirmed:* Revenue rulings interpreting the Tax Reform Act were entitled to some degree of deference. For this reason, among others, the district court's decision rejecting the taxpayer's refund claims was affirmed.
Garvey v. NTSB	190 F.3d 571	1999	Authored Majority	Administrative law & Transportation	*Petition Granted; Reversed and Remanded:* NTSB was required to defer to FAA's reasonable interpretation of its own regulations.

Case Name	Citation	Year	Role	Subject	Holding
In re United Mine WorkersInt'l Union	190 F.3d 545	1999	Authored Majority	Federal courts & Labor law	*Order accordingly:* Failure to conclude rulemaking by the Department of Labor's Mine Safety and Health Administration violated timetable established by law; while writ of mandamus was not appropriate here, D.C. Circuit retained jurisdiction and required agency to file status reports until it discharged its responsibilities under the Mine Act.
Novecon Ltd. v. Bulgarian-American Enter. Fund	190 F.3d 556	1999	Authored Majority	First Amendment	*Affirmed:* Among other things, the court held that an agreement to negotiate did not constitute an agreement to contract, and that D.C. law recognized a qualified privilege of self-defense to libel or defamation.
United States v. Christian	187 F.3d 663	1999	Authored Majority	Criminal law/procedure	*Affirmed:* The search of the defendant was part of a valid investigatory stop and weapons search recognized as permissible under *Terry v. Ohio*, 392 U.S. 1 (1968), and the ultimate seizure of a weapon did not violate the Fourth Amendment.
United States v. Gloster	185 F.3d 910	1999	Authored Majority	Criminal law/procedure	*Affirmed:* Among other things, the court found that the evidence supporting the appellant's weapons conviction was properly admitted.

Table 1. (Continued)

Case Name	Citation	Year	Role	Subject	*Holding*
United States v. Weathers	186 F.3d 948	1999	Authored Majority	Criminal law/procedure	*Remanded:* Defendant waived multiplicity (double jeopardy) claim by failing to raise it before trial. Ineffective assistance of counsel claim must be resolved in district court where defense counsel's decisions could have involved a reasoned tactical choice.
United States v. Clark	184 F.3d 858	1999	Authored Majority	Criminal law/procedure	*Affirmed in part and Remanded with instructions in part:* Among other things, the court held that the defendant had been convicted of two charges for a single offense, which required vacating one conviction and resentencing.
In re Sealed Case No. 99-3096	185 F.3d 887	1999	Authored Majority	Criminal law/procedure	*Reversed and Remanded:* The district court had an obligation to conduct an evidentiary hearing to resolve existence of potentially exculpatory or impeachable evidence covered by *Brady v. Maryland*, 373 U.S. 83 (1963), and determine whether such information was material.

Case Name	Citation	Year	Role	Subject	*Holding*
United Seniors Ass'n v. Shalala	182 F.3d 965	1999	Authored Majority	Administrative law	*Affirmed:* The court was bound under the *Chevron* doctrine to defer to Secretary of HHS's reasonable interpretation of statute.
Pioneer Hotel, Inc. v. NLRB	182 F.3d 939	1999	Authored Majority	Labor law	*Enforcement Granted in part and Denied in part:* Evidentiary record did not support some of the NLRB's findings that an employer had committed unfair labor practices.
In re Sealed Case No. 97-3112	181 F.3d 128	1999	Authored Majority	Criminal law/procedure	*Affirmed:* Absent a motion by the government, the district court may not grant a downward departure from the U.S. Sentencing Guidelines on the basis of the defendant's alleged substantial assistance. *Concurring (Edwards, C.J. and Tatel, J.):* Courts should exercise caution before concluding that the Sentencing Commission has limited district judges' traditional sentencing discretion. *Concurring (Sentelle, J.):* Canons of construction clearly dictated the result in this case, and thus the majority's more detailed analysis was unnecessary.

Table 1. (Continued)

Case Name	Citation	Year	Role	Subject	*Holding*
					Concurring (Henderson, J.): The process leading up to the en banc affirmance of the district court disregarded the established procedure of the D.C. Circuit and the principle of stare decisis.
Anderson v. Zubieta	180 F.3d 329	1999	Authored Majority	Civil rights	*Reversed and Remanded:* Plaintiffs' wage discrimination claims were timely and established prima facie case.
United States v. Bridges	175 F.3d 1062	1999	Authored Majority	Criminal law/procedure	*Affirmed:* District court was not required to conduct a step-by-step analysis when the sentencing of a criminal defendant departed upwardly from the U.S. Sentencing Guidelines based on criminal history.
Davenport v. Int'l Bhd. of Teamsters	166 F.3d 356	1999	Authored Majority	Labor law	*Affirmed and Remanded:* Among other things, the court determined that union members were unlikely to succeed on the merits of their claim that the union's president lacked authority to enter into a temporary labor agreement. Thus, the district court's denial of a temporary injunction against implementation of the agreement was affirmed.

Case Name	Citation	Year	Role	Subject	*Holding*
United States v. Dozier	162 F.3d 120	1998	Authored Majority	Criminal law/procedure	*Affirmed:* Among other things, the court held that the underlying reasons for denying a downward adjustment in the defendant's sentence were permissible and readily discernible from the record.
United States v. Perkins	161 F.3d 66	1998	Authored Majority	Criminal law/procedure	*Affirmed:* Applying the standard of review most favorable to the defendant, the court found that the criminal defendant suffered no prejudice.
Evans Fin. Corp. v. Director, Office of Workers' Compensation Programs	161 F.3d 30	1998	Authored Majority	Labor law	*Petition for review Granted; Vacated and Remanded:* Evidence did not support decision of the Department of Labor's Benefits Review Board that employer waived its right to a credit against liability for injured employee's medical expenses.
Nat'l Ass'n of Mfrs. v. U.S. Dep't of Labor	159 F.3d 597	1998	Authored Majority	Federal courts	*Affirmed and Remanded:* D.C. Circuit declined to adopt a per se rule regarding eligibility of a group and its members to receive attorney's fees under the Equal Access to Justice Act, but allowed the fees under the facts of this case.
Serono Labs., Inc. v. Shalala	158 F.3d 1313	1998	Authored Majority	Administrative law	*Injunction Vacated; Remanded:* Record did not support preliminary injunction ordered by district court to enjoin FDA approval of a generic drug.

Table 1. (Continued)

Case Name	Citation	Year	Role	Subject	*Holding*
Cassell v. FCC	154 F.3d 478	1998	Authored Majority	Administrative law	*Denied petitions for review:* FCC's decision to deny requests for "finder's preferences" was reasonable.
United States v. Glover	153 F.3d 749	1998	Authored Majority	Criminal law/procedure	*Affirmed:* The district court correctly refused to give the jury an entrapment instruction. There was sufficient evidence for conviction and no constitutional violations.
In re Sealed Case 96-3167	153 F.3d 759	1998	Authored Majority	Criminal law/procedure	*Affirmed:* Warrantless entry and search were proper, and there was sufficient evidence to sustain weapons plea.
Grand Canyon Air Tour Coal. v. Fed. Aviation Admin.	154 F.3d 455	1998	Authored Majority	Administrative law, Federal courts& Transportation	*Denied petition for review:* FAA's rule intended to reduce aircraft noise from sightseeing tours was reasonable. Some of petitioners' claims were not yet ripe for review.
United States ex rel. Yesudian v. Howard Univ.	153 F.3d 731	1998	Authored Majority	D.C. local government & Labor law	*Reversed in part and Affirmed in part:* The court found sufficient evidence to support a jury's verdict that the employee satisfied the elements of a retaliation claim under the False Claim Act. An employee manual supported the employee's breach of contract claim under D.C. law.

Case Name	Citation	Year	Role	Subject	*Holding*
					Dissenting in part (Henderson, J.): The district court's ruling granting the employer's motion for judgment as a matter of law on the employee's retaliation claim should be affirmed because Yesudian failed to introduce evidence that the employer was aware of protected activity.
LaRouche v. Fowler	152 F.3d 974	1998	Authored Majority	Election law&Federal courts	*Affirmed in part and Remanded in part:* Challenges to political party's change in rules for selection of delegates at its nominating convention were not moot or non-justiciable political questions. The court lacked jurisdiction to hear Voting Rights Act claims, and it affirmed the dismissal of appellants' constitutional claims, in part because the political party's rules advanced its legitimate interest in winning elections.
United States v. Gartmon	146 F.3d 1015	1998	Authored Majority	Criminal law/procedure	*Affirmed and Remanded for re-sentencing:* Evidence was properly admitted and the prosecutor's misstatement did not constitute plain error. The court remanded the case because part of the sentence exceeded the statutory limit.

Table 1. (Continued)

Case Name	Citation	Year	Role	Subject	*Holding*
United States v. Andrews	146 F.3d 933	1998	Authored Majority	Criminal law/procedure	*Affirmed:* The Double Jeopardy Clause of the Fifth Amendment did not bar prosecution of a corporation's president, because he was not a party to a prior SEC civil lawsuit or the company's CEO, because no punishment had yet been imposed or attempted against him.
La. Energy & Power Auth. v. FERC	141 F.3d 364	1998	Authored Majority	Administrative law, Energy& Federal courts	*Denied petition for review:* FERC's approval of market-based tariff and its decision not to hold evidentiary hearing were not arbitrary or capricious.
Hunter-Boykin v. George Wash. Univ.	132 F.3d 77	1998	Authored Majority	Federal courts& Civil rights	*Reversed:* Racial discrimination claim was timely filed because D.C. law allowed private parties to agree to suspend the statute of limitations and a reasonable juror could interpret the agreement in the manner suggested by the plaintiff. *Concurring in reasoning and judgment(Edwards, C.J.):* The disputed tolling agreement has only one

Case Name	Citation	Year	Role	Subject	Holding
					reasonable interpretation, and therefore it appeared the plaintiff would prevail as a matter of law if she moved for summary judgment on remand.
United States v. Davis	127 F.3d 68	1997	Authored Majority	Criminal law/procedure	*Affirmed:* The district court did not commit error when conducting an out-of-court demonstration that was not exactly like the actual event; in limiting cross-examination of a police officer; or in admitting witness testimony.
United States v. Turner	119 F.3d 18	1997	Authored Majority	Criminal law/procedure	*Affirmed:* Warrantless search of vehicle, including trunk, was permissible because the police officer had probable cause.

Source: Congressional Research Service, based upon an examination of court decisions compiled through a search of the Lexis database.

Table 2. Concurring and Dissenting Opinions Authored by Judge Garland

Case Name	Citation	Year	Role	Subject	Holding
In re Aiken Cty.	725 F.3d 255	2013	Authored Dissent	Administrative law& Separation of powers	*Majority (Kavanaugh, J),Granted writ of mandamus:* NRC must comply with law governing the Yucca Mountain licensing process. *Dissenting:* In light of the court's discretion to refrain from ordering the doing of a useless act, the writ should not have been granted because the agency had insufficient funds to comply.
AKM LLC v. Sec'y of Labor	675 F.3d 752	2012	Authored Concurrence	Administrative law&Labor law	*Majority (Brown, J.), Granted petition for review and Vacated citations:* Citations issued by OSHA were not timely under the statute or regulations, and the continuing violations doctrine did not apply. *Concurring in the judgment:* Citations were untimely under the regulations, but this does not mean the statute could never permit a continuing violation theory under different circumstances.
Sottera, Inc. v. FDA	627 F.3d 891	2010	Authored Concurrence	Administrative law& Health care	*Majority(Williams, J.),Affirmed preliminary injunction:* Under Supreme Court precedent and the Family Smoking Prevention and Tobacco Control Act of 2009 (Tobacco Act), the FDA can only regulate customarily marketed tobacco products (including e-cigarettes) under the Tobacco Act, and not the Federal Food, Drug, and Cosmetic Act.

Case Name	Citation	Year	Role	Subject	Holding
					Concurring in the judgment: Supreme Court precedent did not address the issue; rather, in the absence of contrary agency interpretation entitled to *Chevron* deference, the FDA generally could regulate e-cigarettes only under the Tobacco Act.
Bennett v. Islamic Republic of Iran	618 F.3d 19	2010	Authored Concurrence	National security	*Majority (Griffith, J.), Affirmed:* Terrorism Risk Insurance Act precluded writs of attachment against Iran's former diplomatic properties. *Concurring in the judgment:* Under the act, property was immune from attachment when leased to a foreign mission because it was "used exclusively" for diplomatic purposes. However, property leased to private parties did not meet this criteria.
Saleh v. Titan Corp	580 F.3d 1	2009	Authored Dissent	Civil liability	*Majority (Silberman, J.),Affirmed in part and Reversed in part:* Federal law preempted state tort claims brought against private military contractors by Iraqi nationals detained at the Abu Ghraib facility; alleged actions did not give rise to cause of action under Alien Tort Statue. *Dissenting*: No federal law preempted claims.
FedEx Home Delivery v. NLRB	563 F.3d 492	2009	Authored Dissent	Administrative law& Labor law	*Majority (Brown, J.), Vacated order:* NLRB's determination of employment status was legally erroneous. *Dissenting in part:* Judge Garland disagreed with how the majority applied the common-law test for employment status but wrote that the court should have remanded the case due to the NLRB's unexplained refusal to allow the company to introduce certain evidence.

Table 2. (Continued)

Case Name	Citation	Year	Role	Subject	Holding
Ne. Beverage Corp. v. NLRB	554 F.3d 133	2009	Authored Dissent	Administrative law& Labor law	*Majority (Ginsburg, J.),Granted petition for review in part and Denied in part:* The court upheld part of the NLRB's order because it was based on substantial evidence; however, the court vacated a separate part of the NLRB's order because the agency erred in applying Supreme Court precedent to the facts of the case. *Dissenting in part:* Judge Garland was unable to conclude that the NLRB's determination was unreasonable.
Bismullah v. Gates	514 F.3d 1291	2008	Authored Concurrence	National security	*Majority (per curiam), Rejected petition for rehearing en banc.* *Concurring:* Rehearing the case would delay the Supreme Court's disposition of *Boumediene v. Bush,* 553 U.S. 723 (2008), which was contrary to the parties' and public's interest; Judge Garland thus concurred in the denial without reaching the merits.
Citizens for Responsibility & Ethics in Wash. v. FEC	475 F.3d 337	2007	Authored Concurrence	Election law& Federal courts	*Majority (Randolph, J.), Affirmed:* Group did not have standing to challenge FEC's order dismissing a complaint. *Concurring in the judgment:* Group lacked standing because there was no meaningful distinction between this case and the earlier case of *Common Cause v. FEC*, 108 F.3d 413 (D.C. Cir. 1997).

Case Name	Citation	Year	Role	Subject	Holding
Fin. Planning Ass'n v. SEC	482 F.3d 481	2007	Authored Dissent	Administrative law	*Majority (Rogers, J.), Vacated rule:* SEC rule exempting brokers and dealers from the Investment Advisers Act in certain circumstances was inconsistent with the act. *Dissenting:* SEC's interpretation of the statute was reasonable.
Valdes v. United States	475 F.3d 1319	2007	Authored Dissent	Criminal law/procedure	*Majority (Williams, J.), Reversed judgment of conviction:* The en banc court ruled that evidence was insufficient to convict the defendant of receipt of an illegal gratuity. *Dissenting:* Judge Garland disagreed with the majority's interpretation of the statute as applied to the facts of the case.
Lee v. DOJ	428 F.3d 299	2005	Authored Dissent	First Amendment	*Majority (per curiam), Denied petitions for rehearing en banc.* *Dissenting:* Rehearing was appropriate because the court failed to weigh the public interest in protecting a reporter's sources against the private interest in compelling disclosure when deciding whether the reporter's privilege could be invoked in a Privacy Act case. [Tatel, J., issued a dissent that Judge Garland also joined.]
United States ex rel. Totten v. Bombardier Corp.	380 F.3d 488	2004	Authored Dissent	Civil liability	*Majority (Roberts, J.), Affirmed:* False Claims Act liability required submission of a false or fraudulent claim for payment to be presented to the U.S.

Table 2. (Continued)

Case Name	Citation	Year	Role	Subject	Holding
					government and, since Amtrak was not the U.S. government, suit was properly dismissed. *Dissenting:* Majority's interpretation of the statute was inconsistent with its text and legislative history.
McDonnell Douglas Corp. v. U.S. Dep't of the Air Force	375 F.3d 1182	2004	Authored opinion concurring in part & dissenting in part	Administrative law& Government information	*Majority (Ginsburg, C.J.): Affirmed in part and Reversed in part:* Agency's decision to release some of a contractor's pricing information pursuant to a FOIA request was arbitrary and capricious. *Concurring in part and Dissenting in part:* Deferral to the agency's decision to release the information was appropriate because contractor failed to prove that disclosure would likely cause substantial harm to its competitive position. The majority's opinion came perilously close to a per se rule that some pricing information may never be revealed under FOIA.
United States v. Linares	367 F.3d 941	2004	Authored Concurrence	Criminal law/procedure	*Majority (Tatel, J.), Affirmed:* District court's erroneous admission of evidence relating to defendant's prior acts was harmless. *Concurring in part:* Error, if it occurred, was harmless, and it was not necessary to decide whether the evidence was actually inadmissible.

Case Name	Citation	Year	Role	Subject	Holding
Akinseye v. District of Columbia	339 F.3d 970	2003	Authored Dissent	Federal courts	*Majority (Henderson, J.), Reversed and Remanded:* District court lacked subject matter jurisdiction to hear a case seeking interest on late-paid attorneys' fees. *Dissenting:* Validity of plaintiffs' claim to interest went to the dispute's merits and, because the issue of subject matter jurisdiction was not briefed before the court, Judge Garland would not have disposed of the appeal on a ground not raised in the parties' briefs.
Am. Corn Growers Ass'n v. EPA	291 F.3d 1	2002	Authored opinion concurring in part & dissenting in part	Administrative law& Environmental law	*Majority (per curiam), Vacated rule in part, Sustained in part, and Remanded:* Part of EPA's haze rule was contrary to the act's text, structure and history, while other parts were consistent with the statute and reasonable. *Concurring in part and Dissenting in part:* Entire rule reflected agency's reasonable interpretation of the statute.
Wertheimer v. FEC	268 F.3d 1070	2001	Authored Concurrence	Election law& Federal courts	*Majority (Silberman, J.), Affirmed:* Plaintiffs lacked standing to challenge FEC's failure to act because they did not establish how a judicial ruling would result in anything more than a legal characterization or reporting of information that was already disclosed under existing law. *Concurring in the judgment:* Plaintiffs failed to establish standing because they did not articulate how a judicial ruling would provide them with information beyond what was already disclosed.

Table 2. (Continued)

Case Name	Citation	Year	Role	Subject	Holding
United States v. Wilson	240 F.3d 39	2001	Authored opinion concurring in part & dissenting in part	Criminal law/procedure	*Majority (Williams, J.), Vacated sentence; Remanded ineffective counsel claim; otherwise Affirmed convictions:* Evidence did not support an enhanced sentence under the U.S. Sentencing Guidelines. *Concurring in part and Dissenting in part:* Majority's interpretation of enhanced sentencing provision was too narrow; instead, Judge Garland would have used a totality of the circumstances test adopted by the majority of other circuits and affirmed the sentence.
Ross Stores v. NLRB	235 F.3d 669	2001	Authored opinion concurring in part & dissenting in part	Administrative law& Labor law	*Majority (Henderson, J.),Petition for review Granted in part and Denied in part:* The court upheld one of the NLRB's findings against an employer because it was supported by substantial evidence; however, the court set aside another finding because the underlying allegation was statutorily time-barred and not closely related to a timely filed allegation. *Concurring in part and dissenting in part:* Based on the facts of the case, the majority should have upheld that second finding. The underlying allegation was not time-barred because it was closely related to a timely filed allegation.

Case Name	Citation	Year	Role	Subject	Holding
Pub. Citizen Health Research Grp. v. FDA	185 F.3d 898	1999	Authored Concurrence	Government information	*Majority (Ginsburg, J.), Affirmed in part, Reversed in part, and Remanded:* FOIA release of confidential information in four drug applications would cause substantial harm to intervenor's competitive position; information in fifth application must be disclosed. *Concurring in the result:* The majority should not have addressed the meaning of a FOIA exemption because it was not necessary to the ruling and the issue had not been fully briefed and argued.
Hutchins v. District of Columbia	188 F.3d 531	1999	Co-authored Concurrence	D.C. local government	*Plurality (Silberman, J.), Reversed and Remanded:* Juvenile curfew law did not implicate Fifth Amendment rights of minors and parents, and, even if it did, the law survived heightened scrutiny; also, the law did not violate the First or Fourth Amendments. *Concurring in part and Concurring in the result (authored jointly with Wald, J.):* Curfew implicated Fifth Amendment rights, and the correct standard of review was intermediate (rather than heightened) scrutiny, which curfew survived. [Judge Garland also joined, in part, separate opinions authored by Edwards, C.J., and Rogers, J.]

Table 2. (Continued)

Case Name	Citation	Year	Role	Subject	Holding
Berger v. Iron Workers Reinforced Rodmen, Local 201	170 F.3d 1111	1999	Authored opinion concurring in part & dissenting in part	Civil rights	*Majority (per curiam), Affirmed in part and Reversed and Remanded in part:* District court and special master made several errors in fashioning remedy for racial discrimination, including errors in benchmark determination and explanation of some damage awards. *Concurring in part and Dissenting in part:* Plaintiffs failed to show the benchmark determination was clearly erroneous.
United States v. Watson	171 F.3d 695	1999	Authored Dissent	Criminal law/procedure	*Majority (Rogers, J.)Reversed and Remanded:* Prosecutor's misstatement about witness testimony during closing arguments substantially prejudiced the defendant's right to a fair trial. *Dissenting:* Judge Garland was unable to conclude that the defendant suffered substantial prejudice due to the error.

Case Name	Citation	Year	Role	Subject	Holding
United States v. Spinner	152 F.3d 950	1998	Authored Dissent	Criminal law/procedure	*Majority (Sentelle, J.),Reversed in part and Remanded in part:* Assault weapon conviction was a manifest miscarriage of justice due to insufficient evidence; narcotics conviction was reversed because the district court erred when it allowed the government to question a defense witness about a letter she wrote to the defendant. *Dissenting in part:* Evidence was sufficient to sustain the weapons charge, and the cross-examination was not prejudicial.

Source: Congressional Research Service, based upon an examination of court decisions compiled through a search of the Lexis database.

End Notes

[1] *See* U.S. COURT OF APPEALS FOR THE D.C. CIRCUIT, HANDBOOK OF PRACTICE AND INTERNAL PROCEDURES, UNITED STATES COURT FOR THE DISTRICT OF COLUMBIA CIRCUIT, AS AMENDED THROUGH MARCH 1, 2016, 2, https://www.cadc.uscourts.gov/internet/home.nsf/Content/VL%20-%20RPP%20-%20Handbook%202006%20Rev%202007/$FILE/HandbookMarch2016Final.pdf (last visited April 20, 2016).

[2] The D.C. Circuit often considers many hundreds of cases a year, though only a minority of such cases may have a written opinion. *See* Hon. Douglas H. Ginsburg, *Remarks Upon Receiving the Lifetime Service Award of the Georgetown Federalist Society Chapter Georgetown University Law Center*, April 26, 2011, 10 GEO. J.L. & PUB. POL'Y 1, 7 (2012) (noting that in 2010, panels of the D.C. Circuit, then composed of nine active and four senior judges, "disposed of 873 cases, 191 of them with published opinions"). Over his 19-year tenure on the D.C. Circuit, Judge Garland would have participated in a significant number of cases, either as part of a three-judge circuit panel or through considering or participating in the en banc rehearing of a case. An attempted search of the Lexis database for cases in the D.C. Circuit between April 1997 and April 2016, in which Lexis editors identified Judge Garland as one of the judges of the circuit panel presiding over the case, proved unsuccessful, as Lexis does not complete searches that are likely to return more than 3,000 results. Incremental searches of D.C. Circuit cases where Judge Garland is listed as a panel judge by Lexis editors, and which excluded cases where "Garland" is written in the opinion text within 10 words of "took no part" or "did not participate," yielded more than 5,000 combined results, but did not capture instances where, for example, an indication that Judge Garland took no part in the case was stated in a place other than the opinion. A separate search of the Westlaw database for instances in which the Westlaw editors identified Judge Garland as a panelist on a D.C. Circuit case, between April 1997 and April 2016, and which excluded instances where "Garland" appeared in the text of the opinion within 10 words of the phrase "took no part" or "did not participate," yielded more than 2,700 results. In any event, it should be noted that circuit panels may make rulings on numerous procedural issues within the course of litigation which are not captured by searches of Lexis or Westlaw.

[3] *See* 28 U.S.C. §2284 (providing for three-judge district court panels to be convened with respect to certain actions, including challenges to the constitutionality of the apportionment of congressional districts or state legislative bodies, and that at least one judge on the panel be a circuit judge).

[4] *See* Hon. Ruth Bader Ginsburg, as quoted in Irin Carmon, *Opinion, Justice Ginsburg's Cautious Radicalism*, N.Y. TIMES (October 24, 2015), http://www.nytimes.com/ 2015/10/25/ opinion/sunday/justice-ginsburgs-cautiousradicalism.html (noting that "an opinion of the court very often reflects views that are not 100 percent what the opinion author would do, were she writing for herself"); Steven D. Smith, *Lessons from Lincoln: A Comment on Levinson,* 38 PEPP. L. REV. 915, 924 (2011) ("[T]he fact that a judge joins in a majority opinion may not be taken as indicating complete agreement. Rather, silent acquiescence may be understood to mean something more like 'I accept the outcome in this case, and I accept that the reasoning in the majority opinion reflects what a majority of my colleagues has agreed on.'").

[5] For a listing of D.C. Circuit decisions subsequently reviewed by the Supreme Court in which Judge Garland had been a member of the reviewing circuit court panel, see CRS Report

R44479, *Judge Merrick Garland: His Jurisprudence and Potential Impact on the Supreme Court*, coordinated by Andrew Nolan, Kate M. Manuel, and Brandon J. Murrill, at "Table 1. Judge Garland and the Supreme Court."

[6] The "OpinionBy" segment restricts searches to the names of the judge(s) writing the majority opinion, as identified by Lexis editors.

[7] The "ConcurBy" segment restricts searches to the names of the judge(s) writing a concurring opinion, including opinions concurring in part and opinions concurring in part and dissenting in part, as identified by Lexis editors.

[8] The "DissentBy" segment restricts searches to the names of the judge(s) writing a dissenting opinion, an opinion dissenting in part, or an opinion concurring in part and dissenting in part, as identified by Lexis editors.

[9] The "OpinionBy" segment restricts searches to the names of the judge(s) writing majority, dissenting, or concurring opinions, as identified by Lexis editors.

[10] The "Judges" segment restricts searches to the names of the judges of the court hearing the case, as identified by Lexis editors.

[11] The use of this methodology to identify federal district court cases that Judge Garland was involved in generated six results in a Lexis search done on April 28, 2016, including a single case, *Little v. King*, 768 F. Supp.2d 56 (D.D.C. 2011), in which Judge Garland was credited as an author of an opinion. In contrast, a search done on April 28, 2016, of the District of Columbia Circuit—U.S. Court of Appeals database on Lexis for "OpinionBy(Garland)" yielded only two results, Adams v. Clinton, 90 F. Supp. 2d 35 (D.D.C. 2000), and Adams v. Clinton, 40 F. Supp. 2d 1 (D.D.C. 1999). In both cases, a per curiam opinion, which Judge Garland joined, was issued by the district court.

[12] *See, e.g.*, United States v. Goree, No. 02-3094, 2004 U.S. App. LEXIS 17297 (petition for panel rehearing denied); United States v. Goree, No. 02-3094, 2004 U.S. App. LEXIS 17298 (petition for en banc rehearing denied); In re Miller, No. 04-7117, 2004 U.S. App. LEXIS 17303 (motion for temporary restraining order and permanent injunction denied); Gray v. Poole, 2001 U.S. App. LEXIS 7238 (order issued without published opinion).

Related Nova Publications

Appointment Process of Supreme Court Nominees: Elements and Considerations

Rosa S. Gonzales

ISBN: 978-1-63485-345-3 Publication Date: 2016

The appointment of a Supreme Court Justice is an event of major significance in American politics. Each appointment is of consequence because of the enormous judicial power the Supreme Court exercises as the highest appellate court in the federal judiciary. Appointments are usually infrequent, as a vacancy on the nine-member Court may occur only once or twice, or never at all, during a particular President's years in office. Under the Constitution, Justices on the Supreme Court receive what can amount to lifetime appointments which, by constitutional design, helps ensure the Court's independence from the President and Congress. This book reviews the appointment process of Supreme Court nominees.

Elena Kagan: From Nominee to Supreme Court Justice

Samuel B. Earnst

ISBN: 978-1-61761-977-9 Publication Date: 2011

On May 10, 2010, President Obama nominated Solicitor General Elena Kagan to replace retiring Justice John Paul Stevens. If confirmed, Elena Kagan would be the first Solicitor General to be appointed to the Court since the elevation of Thurgood Marshall in 1967. Given that Solicitor General Kagan has made few public statements on important legal and policy issues, some have looked to her record as Solicitor General for some indication of her views. Understanding the role and responsibilities of the Solicitor General can provide a useful backdrop against which to evaluate Elena Kagan's statements and official actions and assess her professional qualifications. This book examines the office of Solicitor General and its successes before the Court, and examines the career of Elena Kagan and her nomination to Supreme Court Justice.

JURISPRUDENCE OF SUPREME COURT JUSTICE STEVENS

Harvey B. Lymont

ISBN: 978-1-61761-282-4 Publication Date: 2011

This book examines the decisions of retiring Justice John Paul Stevens with regard to: select federalism issues; the constitutionality of congressional term limits and the presidential line item veto; select opinions on intellectual property law; decisions on wartime detentions; death penalty jurisprudence; the jury's role in criminal sentencing; the Chevron doctrine; and the Free Speech Clause of the First Amendment.

Judge Sonia Sotomayor: Selected Opinions

Patrick K. Reed

ISBN: 978-1-60876-759-5 Publication Date: 2010

Judge Sonia Sotomayor was nominated by President Obama to the U.S. Supreme Court on May 26, 2009. This book explores and examines selected opinions written by Judge Sotomayor relating to the civil rights of individuals with disabilities and includes a discussion of cases relating to the Americans with Disabilities Act (ADA), and also reviews her opinions involving abortion and family planning practices. This book considers also Judge Sotomayor's extensive record, compiled from years as a lawyer, prosecutor, district court judge, and appellate court judge, to better understand her legal approaches and judicial philosophy. This book consists of public documents which have been located, gathered, combined, reformatted, and enhanced with a subject index, selectively edited and bound to provide easy access.

INDEX

C

D

G

H

I

J

K

L

M

N

O

P

Q

R

S

T

U

V

W